Against Racial Capitalism

'Whether the topic is education, race, housing, employment, displacement, violence, Neville Alexander's beautiful writing patiently connects theory and method with purpose. Conceived in the volatile conjunctures of South Africa's long struggle for self-determination, *Against Racial Capitalism* is absolutely necessary for all who struggle to understand and change twenty-first-century conditions.'
—Ruth Wilson Gilmore, author of *Abolition Geography: Essays Towards Liberation*

'Amidst all this talk of racial capitalism and abolition, there is one thinker we should all be reading: Neville Alexander. He is a revolutionary intellectual for our times and for our planet. For anyone committed to abolishing, not just studying, racial capitalism, this is the book to read.'
—Robin D. G. Kelley, author of *Freedom Dreams:*
The Black Radical Imagination

'Both profound and provocative. Grounded in history, engaged with revolutionary theory, and informed by a lifetime of practice, Neville's intellectual acuity and passion for freedom shine through in every page. Read, learn, and join the growing global struggle against racial capitalism, and for the just future that Alexander dreamed of and fought for.'
—Barbara Ransby, historian, writer, activist,
author of *Making All Black Lives Matter*

'Understanding and dismantling racial capitalism is one of the foremost challenges of our time. Not too often seen by international audiences is the brilliant work of South African revolutionary, anti-Apartheid activist, intellectual, and ten-year political prisoner, Neville Alexander. This amazing collection remedies that.'
—Steven J. Klees, Professor of International Education Policy,
University of Maryland

'A treasure chest for all opponents of racism and capitalism, introducing key writings of the late South African revolutionary Neville Alexander on the workings of racial capitalism in his country. More than that, it shows us Alexander the grassroots organiser for liberation. Throughout these pages, we encounter a great radical thinker profoundly committed to changing the world. This is a vital resource in the struggle for global justice.'
—David McNally, Director of the Project on Race and Capitalism,
University of Houston

'Much of the contemporary debate around racial capitalism owes an acknowledged debt to Neville Alexander's path-breaking interventions in the midst of the South African anti-apartheid struggle. This new collection of writings, superbly curated by Salim Vally and Enver Motala, reveals the extraordinary relevance of Neville's thought for activists and scholars today.'
—Adam Hanieh, Professor of Political Economy and Global Development,
University of Exeter

'By reading writings like these, we Palestinians can learn from the South African condition in recognising apartheid as both a system of institutionalised racial discrimination and a system of racial capitalism. A must-read for all those believing in a future vision of a secular-democratic state in Palestine that is based on a critical understanding of the limits and pitfalls of transformation in post-apartheid South Africa.'
—Professor Haidar Eid, al-Aqsa University, Gaza, Occupied Palestine

'Thoughtfully honours the writing and legacy of Neville Alexander and, in doing so, powerfully offers us coordinates for making a just society. In compiling this book, Salim Vally and Enver Motala inspire us all to continue Alexander's profound work for racial justice.'
—Arathi Sriprakash, author of *Learning Whiteness: Education and the Settler Colonial State*

'Thanks to the tireless work of his comrades Salim Vally and Enver Motala, Neville Alexander's moment is upon us. These careful selections from a half century of speeches and writings, many available here for the first time, are a crucial resource for activists mobilising against racial capitalism today. This volume is destined to become a classic.'
—Professor Zachary Levenson, University of Texas at Austin, author of *Delivery as Dispossession: Land Occupation and Eviction in the Postapartheid City*

'In our times of rising global fascism and predatory capitalism, Neville Alexander's writings provide us with insightful ways of thinking through and beyond the present, and a must-read for all of us who share his commitment to "non-dogmatic Marxism and internationalism".'
—Mario Novelli, Professor in the Political Economy of Education, University of Sussex

'Powerfully reignites the contributions of Neville Alexander and left organisations including the Black consciousness movement in South Africa, at precisely the moment when we most need its inspiration. Scholars, students, and activists committed to liberation struggles have much to learn from the writings of one of the most significant revolutionary intellectuals of the last century.'
—Antonia Darder, Professor Emerita, Loyola Marymount University

'This must-read, expertly curated by Salim Vally and Enver Motala, offers a genealogy of Alexander's political thought, insightful scholarship, and engaged praxis vis-à-vis issues of racial capitalism, multilingualism, education and more. Timely and relevant for scholars and activists concerned with advancing justice around the globe.'
—Monisha Bajaj, Professor of International & Multicultural Education, University of San Francisco

'Situates Neville Alexander where he belongs, among the great revolutionaries of the twentieth century. In Alexander's political teachings, we discover strategies for the necessary work of challenging the oppressive racial capitalist order and, through his life of struggle, we inherit a model of radical intellectualism, which refuses the false boundaries between theory and praxis. An essential guide for all who are struggling toward liberated futures.'
—Krystal Strong, Assistant Professor of Black Studies, Rutgers University

Against Racial Capitalism

Selected Writings

Neville Alexander

Edited by Salim Vally and Enver Motala
Foreword by John Samuel and Karen Press

First published 2023 by Pluto Press
New Wing, Somerset House, Strand, London WC2R 1LA
and Pluto Press, Inc.
1930 Village Center Circle, 3-834, Las Vegas, NV 89134

www.plutobooks.com

British Library Cataloguing in Publication Data
A catalogue record for this book is available from the British Library

ISBN 978 0 7453 4837 7 Paperback
ISBN 978 0 7453 4839 1 PDF
ISBN 978 0 7453 4838 4 EPUB

This book is printed on paper suitable for recycling and made from fully managed and sustained forest sources. Logging, pulping and manufacturing processes are expected to conform to the environmental standards of the country of origin.

Typeset by Stanford DTP Services, Northampton, England

Simultaneously printed in the United Kingdom and United States of America

Contents

PART IV
Post-1994 Essays, Talks, and Op-Eds

Foreword

Neville Alexander, a public intellectual and revolutionary, represented a powerful vision of a new society that created hope and kept alive the struggle for new possibilities. Grounded in a strong sense of social justice, this vision guided his work and thinking over the last six decades.

The sense of hope that he built through his ideas and practice was not some vague notion that everything will be fine, but a vision of hope, hammered out of the realities of South Africa. Central to Neville's vision of hope was the idea of constantly engaging and challenging the 'given', even in the most difficult of times.

This collection of Neville's writings, spanning over six decades, lovingly and thoughtfully edited by two of his long-time friends and comrades, Enver Motala and Salim Vally, not only provides us with the opportunity to engage with the ideas and practice of one of South Africa's outstanding public intellectuals, but it also gives us great inspiration to continue the struggle for a better South Africa.

Neville passionately believed that we could certainly build a more just and decent society in South Africa. Equally, he believed that this new society wouldn't just come about because we desired it. He knew from history and experience that keeping alive a vision of a just and decent society was of paramount importance – not just in the realm of ideas but also in actual day-to-day practice, from exploring new ideas about the liberation struggle to children's reading clubs; from critical insights into fundamental issues of national identity and 'race' to the educational struggles for a democratic South Africa; from urgent issues of language and power to compelling issues of decolonisation. Neville shaped a practice that integrated thought and action. Each area that he explored provided a glimpse of future possibilities and framed a language of hope.

At a time when the fault lines in our country grow wider and deeper, we need to find ways that will keep alive the vital idea that we can build a more decent society. In so many ways, Neville brought this alive in the work that he did.

The publishing of this selection of Neville's writings at this time gives us both the knowledge and inspiration to continue the struggle to build that decent society.

John Samuel and Karen Press

Acknowledgements

We are grateful to Neville Alexander's comrades, colleagues, and friends who suggested various texts and ideas for this collection. No less gratifying is the sense of community that has accompanied the process of assembling this book including inputs at the annual Alexander commemorative conferences where hundreds of participants each year discuss and link Alexander's ideas to ongoing struggles. There are numerous people to thank including many individuals who were active with Alexander over five decades of revolutionary struggles and a younger generation inspired by his praxis.

Some of the individuals requiring special mention include: Armien Abrahams, Britt Baatjes, Ivor Baatjes, Azeem Badroodien, June Bam, Koni Benson, Thabang Bhili, Sara Black, Eugene Cairncross, Lydia Cairncross, Sophia Kisting-Cairncross, Nompumelelo Cebekulu, Linda Chisholm, Andy Clarno, Roshan Dadoo, Eddy Dames, Antonia Darder, Charl Davids, Archie Dick, Na-iem Dollie, Mpikeleni Duma, Jane Duncan, Asher Gamedze, Kelly Gillespie, Xolisa Guzula, Rowayda Halim, Paul Hendricks, Elizabeth van der Heyden, Mondli Hlatshwayo, Thami Hukwe, Farrell Hunter, Na'eem Jeenah, Nadeema Jogee, Brian Ihirwe Kamanzi, Robin D.G. Kelley, Moemedi Kepadisa, Robert Krieger, Makoma Letlakalala, Zachary Levenson, Lybon Mabasa, Terri Maggott, Rasigan Maharajh, Siyabulela Mama, Itumeleng Mosala, Derrick Naidoo, Leigh-Ann Naidoo, Venetia Naidoo, Farieda Nazier, Mfanafuthi Prof Ndlovu, Trevor Ngwane, Noor Nieftagodien, Selby Nomnganga, Mario Novelli, Lungisile Ntsebeza, Yunus Omar, Omar Parker, Francesco Pontarelli, Lwazi Brian Ramadiro, Irna Senekal, William Shoki, Dinga Sikwebu, Amelia Simone, Luke Sinwell, Deena Soliar, Marcus Solomon, Crain Soudien, Shaun Whittaker, Lindia Trout, Hanif Vally, Ashley Visagie, and Andile Zulu.

A special debt of gratitude to Karen Press the literary executor of the Neville Alexander Estate who together with John Samuel encouraged us to pursue this initiative from the outset. We also thank Karen for permission to publish most of the articles in this collection, suggestions on the selection of the texts, and her comments on the introduction.

Much appreciation to the anonymous reviewers for their useful and critical suggestions and the immensely supportive and professional editorial and production team at Pluto Press particularly David Shulman, Anthony Bogues, Robert Webb, Martin Pettitt, Melanie Patrick, Bedour Alagraa, David Stanford, and Jonila Krasniqi.

Thanks to UKZN Press for permission to re-publish the chapters '"Race" and Class in South African Historiography: An Overview' and 'The Peculiarities of the Transition to Democracy in South Africa' from Alexander's book, *An Ordinary Country – Issues in the Transition from Apartheid to Democracy in South Africa* (UKZN Press, 2002); Sara Martinez Garcia from Springer Nature for allowing us to re-publish Alexander's chapter, 'An Illuminating Moment: Background to the Azanian Manifesto', originally published in the book, *Biko Lives!* (Palgrave Macmillan, 2008) and Megan Mance from Jacana Media for the chapter, 'The Elephant in the Room' originally titled 'Enough is as Good as a Feast' in Alexander's posthumously published book, *Thoughts on the New South Africa* (Braamfontein: Jacana Media, 2013).

It is our ardent hope that new generations of young people, dissatisfied with the state of South Africa and the world, will critically engage with Alexander's writing and practice in the spirit of advancing his praxis and will find inspiration for their own scholarship and activism.

Finally, we thank Carol Anne Spreen and Kulsum Motala for their companionship and support. All royalties from this book will be donated via the Neville Alexander Literary Estate to Alexander's family.

Abbreviations

ACM	African Common Market
ANC	African National Congress
ANCYL	African National Congress Youth League
APDUSA	African People's Democratic Union of Southern Africa
APLA	Azanian People's Liberation Army
APO	African People's Organisation
AWB	Afrikaner Weerstandbeweging
AZAPO	Azanian People's Organisation
BCM	Black Consciousness Movement
BPC	Black People's Convention
CAL	Cape Action League
CATA	Cape African Teachers Association
CODESA	Convention for a Democratic South Africa
COSATU	Congress of South African Trade Unions
CPSU	Cape Peninsula Students' Union
CAD	Coloured Affairs Department
COSAS	Congress of South African Students
COP	Commissioner of Prisons
CPC	Coloured People's Congress
CPSA	Communist Part of South Africa (prior to 1950)
DA	Democratic Alliance
DBAC	Disorderly Bill Action Committee
DEIC	Dutch East India Company
DoE	Department of Education
DP	Democratic Party
FOSATU	Federation of South African Trade Unions
FRELIMO	Liberation Front of Mozambique
GEAR	Growth, Employment and Redistribution
HEWSSA	Health, Education and Welfare Society of South Africa Trust
ICS	International Correspondence Schools
ICU	Industrial and Commercial Workers Union
IES	Income and Expenditure Survey
IFP	Inkatha Freedom Party

IMF	International Monetary Fund
IRC	International Red Cross
ISL	International Socialist League
Langtag	Language Plan Task Group
MK	Umkhonto we Sizwe
MPLA	People's Movement for the Liberation of Angola
NDR	National Democratic Revolution
NEPAD	New Partnership for Africa's Development
NEUM	Non-European Unity Movement
NF	National Forum
NIC	Natal Indian Congress
NICRO	National Institute for Crime Prevention
NLF	National Liberation Front
NLP	National Language Project
NNP	New National Party
NP	National Party
NUM	New Unity Movement
NUSAS	National Union of South African Students
OAU	Organisation of African Unity
OC	Officer Commanding
PAC	Pan-Africanist Congress
PanSALB	Pan South African Language Board
POLP	Primary Open Learning Pathway Trust
PRAESA	Project for the Study of Alternative Education in South Africa
PTSA	Parent, Teacher, Student Association
PUFLSA	People's United Front for the Liberation of South Africa
PPEN	Public Participation in Education Network
PPT	Permanent Peoples' Tribunal
RDP	Reconstruction and Development Programme
RENAMO	Mozambican National Resistance
RIP	Robben Island Prison
RSA	Republic of South Africa
SACP	South African Communist Party (post-1962)
SACHED	South African Committee for Higher Education
SACOS	South African Council On Sport
SADF	South African Defence Force
SAIC	South African Indian Congress
SAIRR	South African Institute of Race Relations

SASM	South African Students' Movement
SALP	South African Labour Party
SAP	Structural Adjustment Programmes
SAR	South African Republic (Transvaal)
SASO	South African Students' Organisation
SWAPO	South West African People's Organisation
SOYA	Society of Young Africa
UCT	University of Cape Town
UDF	United Democratic Front
UMSA	Unity Movement of South Africa
UNISA	University of South Africa
UNITA	National Union for the Total Independence of Angola
UNO	United Nations Organisation
US	United States
USSR	Union of Soviet Socialist Republics
WB	World Bank
WOSA	Workers Organisation for Socialist Action

The Life and Times of Neville Alexander

Key events in the life of Alexander	Year	Context of the times
	1910	The Union of South Africa created.[1]
	1912	The South African Native National Congress formed. Renamed the African National Congress in 1923.
	1913	The Natives Land Act becomes law restricting Black land ownership to 7 per cent and later 13 per cent through the 1936 Native Trust and Land Act.
	1922	White miners' strike develops into a general strike and an armed uprising called the Rand Revolt. The government of Jan Smuts uses artillery and aircraft to crush the Revolt.[2]
Neville Edward Alexander is born in Cradock in the Eastern Cape on 22 October 1936. His mother, Dimbiti Bisho Alexander, was a schoolteacher; his father, David James Alexander, was a stonemason and carpenter. Alexander had four sisters and one brother. Bisho Jarsa, Alexander's maternal grandmother, was one of a group of Ethiopian slaves freed by a British warship in 1888 and placed in the care of missionaries in Algoa Bay,[3] the Eastern Cape, South Africa. His schooling begins initially at Steytlerville near Gqeberha and later at the Holy Rosary Convent in Cradock, run by German nuns.	1936	
Alexander's father loses a leg while stationed in Egypt during World War II.	1939	World War II begins.
	1943	The Non-European Unity Movement (NEUM) is formed.

Key events in the life of Alexander	Year	Context of the times
	1948	The National Party (NP) is elected by the white population. The policy of apartheid begins. Laws passed include the Population Registration Act, which authorises racial classification, and the Group Areas Act, which segregates the population residentially. Other laws include the Prohibition of Mixed Marriages Act, the Immorality Act, and the Suppression of Communism Act, which banned anti-apartheid activities.
Alexander graduates from secondary school. Discussing his early political activity, he later mentioned, 'I had grown up at the feet of Rev. James Calata in Cradock'.[4] Calata was General Secretary of the ANC from 1936 to 1949.	1952	The ANC launches the Defiance Campaign against apartheid and the NEUM campaigns against various apartheid laws.
Alexander moves to Cape Town to read a degree in History and German at the University of Cape Town (UCT) and spends six years at UCT, obtaining a Bachelor of Arts, a Bachelor of Arts Honours, and a Master of Arts. He is politically influenced by Livingstone Mqotsi, Isaac B. Tabata, and Minnie Gool, all members of allied organisations of the NEUM, such as the Cape African Teachers Association (CATA) and the African People's Democratic Union of Southern Africa (APDUSA). Alexander joins the Teachers' League of South Africa as a 17-year-old student associate and the NEUM. He also helps form the Cape Peninsula Students' Union (CPSU) and joins the Society of Young Africa (SOYA).	1953	Bantu Education Act passed.
	1954	South Africa proclaims South-West Africa (now Namibia) as a province.
	1956	The Industrial Conciliation Act passed. The Act reserves the most skilled jobs for white people. The Tomlinson Commission recommends the formation of Bantustans or 'Homelands' in rural areas to further formalise and extend the migrant labour system and land dispossession.

Key events in the life of Alexander	Year	Context of the times
Alexander receives a scholarship awarded by the Alexander Humboldt-Stiftung to study at the University of Tübingen, Germany. He obtains a doctorate at the age of 26 on the work of the German dramatist, Gerhart Hauptmann.[5] His stay in Germany lasts from October 1958 to July 1961. He joins the Socialist Democratic Students' Union and is closely associated with Algerian and Cuban students involved in their liberation struggles. Alexander also becomes involved in the German metalworkers' union, supporting Italian migrant workers. Alexander addresses rallies and distributes leaflets aimed at workers 'at the gates of industrial establishments among them the Mercedes Benz factories around Stuttgart ...'[6]	1958	
	1959	Extension of the University Education Act authorises preventing Black students from attending 'white' universities and the Act establishes separate universities for Black students. Pan-Africanist Congress established.
	1960	The Sharpeville Massacre takes place on 21 March. Heeding a call by the PAC, 20,000 people gathered at the local police station. 69 people were killed by the police. The ANC, PAC, and the Communist Party banned; a State of Emergency is declared and thousands of people arrested.

Key events in the life of Alexander	Year	Context of the times
Alexander returns to South Africa in July 1961, begins teaching history at Livingston High School in Cape Town and joins APDUSA. Profoundly affected by the Sharpeville Massacre, he begins focussing on the feasibility of guerrilla warfare by clandestinely forming the Yu Chi Chan Club and subsequently with Namibian and South African activists, forms the National Liberation Front (NLF). Some of the initial members became leaders of the South West Africa People's Organisation (SWAPO). Alexander and others expelled from APDUSA for advocating armed struggle. Members include the late Judge Fikile Bam and Dulcie September, who later became the ANC's representative in France. Dulcie is assassinated in Paris on 29 March 1988.	1961	The ANC establishes its military wing, Umkhonto we Sizwe (Spear of the Nation) and the PAC establishes its armed wing Poqo (later the Azanian People's Liberation Army). The National Liberation Front is formed. The African Peoples' Democratic Union of Southern Africa (APDUSA) under the leadership of Isaac Bangani Tabata is formed in 1961.
Alexander arrested with ten other NLF members (six men and four women[7]) and after a lengthy trial imprisoned on Robben Island for ten years from 1964 to 1974. Despite the privations and physical hardships in the early years on the island – documented in Alexander's (1994) book *Robben Island Dossier: 1964–1974*, prisoners turn the prison into the 'university of Robben Island', in which Alexander plays a key role in both non-formal education such as literacy and supporting the formal studies of fellow prisoners. He forms close relationships with all prisoners, despite their political differences, and is close to Sisulu, Mandela, Masemola, Mkalipi, and Kathrada. He also completes an honours degree in history through the University of South Africa (UNISA).[8]	1963	Franz Lee and Irmgard Bolle establish the first Alexander Defence Committee in West Germany in 1963 followed by Alexander Defence Committees established by Connie Kirkby in the UK and by Berta Green Langston and her husband Robert Langston in the US.[9] The committees raise support for the detainees and their families. Prominent personalities associated with the different Alexander Defence Committees include Northrop Frye, Ossie Davis, Stokely Carmichael, Benjamin Spock, James Forman, Stuart Hall, Bertrand Russell, Theodor Adorno, Isaac Deutscher, and C. L. R. James.[10]
	1964	Eight members of the ANC leadership including Nelson Mandela sentenced to life in prison after the Rivonia trial concludes. The Unity Movement of South Africa (UMSA) is established in exile.

Key events in the life of Alexander	Year	Context of the times
	1969	Steve Biko and others form the South African Students' Organisation (SASO).
	1972	Black People's Convention established to coordinate the Black Consciousness Movement.
	1973	Widespread worker strikes begin in the province of Natal and spread to the Eastern Cape.
	1975	Supported by the US, South Africa invades Angola in 1975.
	1976	An Uprising of high school pupils begins in Soweto and spreads rapidly throughout the country. An estimated 800 mainly young people are killed. Thousands of young people leave to study abroad and join liberation organisations.
	1976 to 1981	Nominal 'independence' of Bantustans or 'homelands': Transkei (1976), Bophuthatswana (1977), Venda (1979), and Ciskei (1981). More than 3 million people forcibly sent to barren 'homelands' in less than a decade.[11]
In 1977, Steve Biko attempts to meet clandestinely with Alexander in Cape Town to discuss arrangements for bringing together all liberation movements, including their armed formations. Alexander, because of the restrictions of 'house arrest' and for other reasons is not able to meet Biko. Biko is arrested on his way back to the Eastern Cape and killed in prison. Alexander later regarded this as 'one of the most tragic moments in [his] life'.[12]	1977	Black Consciousness leader Steve Biko is killed in detention and Black Consciousness organisations are banned.

Key events in the life of Alexander	Year	Context of the times
Restrictions against Alexander lifted. He begins teaching part-time at UCT and becomes involved in student, worker, and community struggles. He establishes organisations such as the Disorderly Bills Action Committee (campaigning against the forced removal of Black people from residential areas declared as 'whites-only'), various civic organisations and the Cape Action League (CAL).	1979	The apartheid state lifts the prohibition of trade unions for Black workers. The independent trade union association the Federation of South African Trade Unions (FOSATU) is formed in April 1979. It was politically non-sectarian and committed to workers' control and socialist policies.
Together with others, Alexander plays an important role in the transformation of the South African Council for Higher Education Trust (SACHED) into one of the most important and vibrant organisations in the country establishing it as a home for radical and alternative educational practices. Alexander is appointed SACHED's Cape Town director in 1981. Alexander assists Samuel in founding Khanya College, a preparatory and bridging institution for student activists to enter universities in the mid and late 1980s.	1980	SA invades Angola again in June 1980 attacking SWAPO's operational command headquarters and intervenes on the side of UNITA against the MPLA until 1988. SA together with the US and Israel also support RENAMO against FRELIMO in the Mozambican civil war in the 1980s. According to some estimates close to two million Mozambicans and Angolans died in these wars.
With other members of the National Forum Committee,[13] Alexander convened the National Forum on 11 and 12 June 1983 attended by 600 delegates from 200 organisations. The Forum based on various resolutions and commissions adopts a socialist guiding document called the 'Azanian Manifesto' and draws up plans to oppose the apartheid regime's new constitutional proposals and plans campaigns for the boycott of the 'Tri-Cameral Parliament'.	1983	Formation of the National Forum and the United Democratic Front (UDF).
	1984	Elections under the new Tricameral Constitution widely boycotted by those classified as 'Indian' and 'Coloured'.[14]

Key events in the life of Alexander	Year	Context of the times
Alexander supports and helps to build various community organisations, trade unions and student groups. In 1986, he forms the National Language Project (NLP). Other organisations he inspires include the Vumani Pre-School Project, Primary Open Learning Pathway Trust (POLP), and the Health, Education and Welfare Society of South Africa (HEWS-SA) Trust.	1984 to 1986	Widespread resistance. States of Emergency declared, and troops move into townships.
	1985	Congress of South African Trade Unions (COSATU) established. International sanctions intensify. The New Unity Movement is formed in April.
	1986	Repeal of pass laws.
	1989	Fall of the Berlin Wall and the beginning of the dissolution of the Soviet Union encourages negotiations between the apartheid regime, representatives of capital and the ANC.
In April 1990, Alexander elected head of a new political formation, the Workers Organisation for Socialist Action (WOSA), committed to promoting working-class interests.	1990	The ANC, PAC, and the Communist Party are unbanned. Nelson Mandela is released from prison after 27 years. Namibia obtains independence.
Alexander appointed director of the Project for the Study of Alternative Education in South Africa (PRAESA), the Faculty of Education, UCT.	1991	Repeal of Group Areas, Land, and Population Registration Acts. Convention for a Democratic South Africa (CODESA) formed to negotiate a constitution.
WOSA together with other organisations form a platform called the Workers List Party for the election campaign.	1994	Election by universal franchise elects the Government of National Unity with an ANC majority. Mandela inaugurated as State President. Interim Constitution implemented for a five-year transition period.
	1995	Archbishop Desmond Tutu named chair of the Truth and Reconciliation Commission.
Alexander serves as deputy chairperson of the Pan South African Language Board (PanSALB), and as chairperson of the Language Plan Task Group (Langtag) under the then Minister of Arts, Culture, Science, and Technology, Ben Ngubane.	1996	The Cabinet approves the Growth, Employment, and Redistribution (GEAR) programme – a neoliberal macroeconomic strategy.

Key events in the life of Alexander	Year	Context of the times
Alexander is appointed by the Minister of Education, Kader Asmal, as the convenor of a panel – between 2000 and 2002 – to explore and make recommendations on language for higher education in the country. Alexander serves as a member of the Western Cape Language Committee until 2005.	2000 to 2002	
	2005	The second democratically elected president Thabo Mbeki sacks his deputy, Jacob Zuma, in the aftermath of a corruption case. Around 100,000 gold miners strike over pay, bringing the industry to a standstill.
	2007	Hundreds of thousands of public-sector workers take part in the biggest strike since the end of apartheid. The strike lasts for four weeks.
Alexander pioneers proposals for a multilingual society for the better part of 25 years and in 2008 is awarded the prestigious Linguapax Prize for his work on linguistic diversity and multilingualism. Together with Alexander, radical educationists launch the Public Participation in Education Network (PPEN). PPEN campaigns for a quality public education for all and against a multi-tier education system.	2008	Wave of xenophobic violence occurs in townships across the country. Dozens of people die, and thousands of Zimbabweans, Malawians, and Mozambicans leave South Africa.
	2009	Parliament elects Jacob Zuma as President.
With activists around the country Alexander launches the Truth Conference (later the Truth Movement) to discuss the realities of post-1994 South Africa.	2010	
Alexander diagnosed with cancer shortly before his passing on 27 August 2012. His last book *Thoughts on the New South Africa* is published posthumously in 2013[15]	2012	Police open fire on striking workers at a platinum mine in Marikana, killing 34 people.

Introduction

On 27 August 2012, Neville Alexander, a revolutionary scholar, educator, and former Robben Island political prisoner, who seamlessly combined rigorous scholarship with activism, died at the age of 75. He was arguably South Africa's foremost public intellectual to emerge from the turmoil and ferment of the struggle for liberation and a reference point for understanding some of the most important debates in our country over the past half-century.

Some of these debates included the strategy and tactics of national liberation after the Sharpeville Massacre; the unresolved national question in South Africa and the relationship between 'race' and class; the continuities of racial capitalism in post-apartheid South Africa; the role and purpose of schooling and higher education and the importance of nation-building and multilingualism.

Alexander's scholarship was not detached from, but deeply engaged with, the practical world around him. His life was a critique of the pretence of impartiality and the aloofness of the 'disinterested' scholar, and he was constantly promoting anti-capitalist alternatives in the present in opposition to the neoliberal trajectory embarked upon by the post-apartheid establishment. Such alternatives provided demonstrable and concrete possibilities for what could be achieved on a larger scale. Alexander's approach went beyond social critique and academic analyses. For him, the boundaries constructed by the requirements of conventional scholarship were artificial since societal engagement was inseparable from serious scholarly activity. He insisted that there should be no 'Chinese Wall' between scholarship and activism. Alexander's ideas were an orientation to activism in and outside the state, in the struggles of the poor and the marginalised, wherever injustice was found.

Alexander had a long view of history that fuelled his consistent optimism. He was convinced that in the contradictory social spaces that characterised unequal relations and the struggles against it by the poor and workers, there were possibilities for a genuine democratic future. Alexander was appalled by the 'looting of state resources' and profligacy in post-apartheid society. He appealed to us using Amílcar Cabral's words to 'return to the source'[1] to return to the modesty and generosity of spirit which inspired many of us in earlier times. Alexander was always reflective and humble and never wavered from his own self-description: a non-dogmatic Marxist, pan-Africanist, and internationalist. One of the most endearing characteristics of Alexander was his attentiveness to others, his self-effacing sacrifice, and tireless commitment to a radical humanism which made him such an outstanding revolutionary scholar.

We mourn him deeply, but his praxis has enriched our lives and provided future generations with a compass to direct us to the decent society Alexander firmly believed it was possible to reach.

Over the years this remarkable thinker and political being, through his praxis, developed a body of writings which would span not only issues in political and social philosophy, education and culture, history, ethical life, and contemporary reality, but they are also important for realising radical social change. In his writings, Alexander avoided both class-reductionist interpretations of social change and the essentialism of racist categorisation.

His was an outstanding voice in the definition of the struggle for social justice and a decent life, and for this, he engaged with many other leaders of the diverse strands of the liberation movement in South Africa about the nature of state and society. Alexander's arguments, conceptualisations, and clarifications were always aimed at strengthening the struggle against the racist, oppressive and exploitative racial capitalist regime. His writings have been widely read and recognised for their perspicacity and their prescience, but also for their importance in provoking national debates about the theory and practice of the struggles against racial capitalism. As early as 1985, in his book *Sow the Wind*, this is how Alexander viewed his contribution to the struggle for national liberation:

> The abiding focus of my own contribution is on subjects such as the link between racism and capitalism; the need for and the inevitability of socialist solutions to our problems hence the crucial need to ensure working-class leadership of our struggle; the importance of nation-building in order to eliminate ethnic and racial prejudice; the link between women's liberation, national liberation and class emancipation; the vital need to initiate and to sustain educational and cultural practices today that will systematically and inexorably undermine and counter the divisive and exploitative practices that derive from the pursuit of the interests of the dominating classes in an apartheid society.[2]

Predictably, his political practice and his writings were also the subject of contestation since his thinking represented a strongly socialist perspective that was both irreconcilable and in conflict with the ideas and practices of strands in the liberation movement that favoured a combination of liberal and nationalist perspectives on the liberation struggle.[3] It goes without saying that he was a deadly enemy of the apartheid regime and suffered the consequences of his opposition to it by being jailed for ten years and subsequently prohibited under 'house arrest' rules for five years, even though this was hardly a barrier to his continued role in the struggle for liberation.[4]

AN ENGAGED THINKER, POLEMICIST, SCHOLAR, AND ORGANISER

At barely 22 years of age, Alexander was already formulating his philosophical disposition towards important social, political, cultural, and organisational questions. In the May 1958 edition of *The Student* – the journal of the Cape Peninsula Students' Union of which he was the founding editor – he published an article titled 'The Universities'. In this article, he framed an incisive critique of what was soon to be promulgated as the Extension of University Education Act (No. 45 of 1959), in terms of which racially defined universities were to be established in South Africa.[5] In an article in the November 1958 edition of *The Student*, 'Education in a Modern World', he argued that although some important discussions related to 'matters of a purely educational import', he was concerned to provide an analysis of

> education as a social phenomenon. In other words, we are going to analyse certain philosophies of education with the intention of pointing out the broad and general philosophical and political directions which are implicit in the manner in which we express ourselves today. This involves centrally a discussion on what we mean by 'a Democratic System of Education in a Democratic South Africa' as well as on the social and historical reasons for this particular formulation.[6]

The article goes on to examine the origins of Western education and its contradictions, the differences between idealist and realist orientations to it, its roots in the Greek city-states of the pre- and post-Christian era and the impact of religion on education from the fourth century CE. In his article Alexander also discusses issues he would be seized with for the rest of his life, including the dominance of racist ideas and conventions as these applied to the South African education system and those elsewhere, and the relationship between a democratic education system and political democracy and its implications for theory and practice.

Even towards the end of his life, he was determined to engage publicly about his perspectives on both historical and quotidian issues in a conscious attempt to bring the most pressing questions facing society into the public arena. This was especially so in the context of the egregious failures he saw in the post-apartheid system. Writing about this very issue in his *Thoughts on the New South Africa* (which was published posthumously), he lamented the looting of public resources and

> the palpable signs of social breakdown all around us: the ever more blatant examples of greed and corruption involving public figures, who are expected to be the role models for our youth; the unspeakable abuse of children, of the aged and of women; the smug dishonesty, indiscipline and slothfulness of those who are paid to render public services; the lack of respect for life-preserving rules, such as those of the road; the unthinkable violence in so many communities, unknown even in conditions of conventional warfare; the boundary-crossing abuse of all manner of drugs in all layers of society; ... the trashing of the public health system; in short, the general mayhem and apparently suicidal chaos that ordinary people experience in their daily lives. These things are our everyday reality.[7]

Earlier, speaking in honour of the late Sipho Maseko, whom Alexander felt exemplified 'one of those young people of the 1980s, who were totally committed to the total liberation of South Africa and the continent as a whole', he lamented that the values which drove Maseko and others of his generation had 'been systematically eroded by the irruption of the narcissistic, dog-eat-dog virus that is spreading across the globe in the current era of the hegemony of neoliberal capitalism'. In that address he posed what he considered to be a key question:

> How is it possible in the era of neo-liberal barbarism to implant a different set of values among especially the younger people in South Africa and elsewhere, in spite of the many structural constraints that determine their individual existential projects and the massive bombardment of negative and self-destructive ethical messages emanating from the media and other ideological state and non-state apparatuses?[8]

He understood that post-apartheid South Africa created an atmosphere and conditions that were antithetical to such an ethical stance. In *Thoughts on the New South Africa*, he urges the reader to 'take a step back and try to get a perspective on what has actually been happening since 1990, when the new South Africa began'.[9] He hopes to 'inspire the reader to want to find a point of engagement with a view to initiating or becoming part of trajectories that can lead to that other country most of us had in mind during the years of *Sturm und Drang*, especially during the 1980s'.[10] And arguing from the perspective of a participant in the transition to a post-apartheid South Africa, and conscious of his own historical role in it, he writes:

> My thoughts about developments at the time they actually happened, as well as the intentions of my intellectual, scholarly or journalistic interventions, are worth recording and worth revisiting, in order to act as a possible launching pad (one among many) for a national rethink and dialogue about where we are heading as a society and where we think we ought to be heading.[11]

Alexander had a long view of history, constantly referring to the Gramscian notion of the 'war of position'[12] which fuelled his consistent optimism. He was hugely committed to public engagement on the most critical issues confronting society and was, for that reason, perennially engaged in discursive, polemical, and scholarly activities which exemplified his devotion to both the realm of ideas and the practices to which they related. He understood fully the polemical nature of many of his writings, precisely because through them he was able to stimulate the engagements which he considered to be essential to political development. As he said in the 'Foreword' to *Sow the Wind*, 'my entire intellectual formation was of a polemical nature, so that it is impossible for me to think "disinterestedly" or to study for the sake of studying. Usually, I have to engage in a dialogue; be dialectical, to arrive at some intellectual stimulation'.[13]

Alexander was equally conscious of the influence on him of those he engaged with in his intellectual development and referred to this issue on several occasions, sometimes, in ways which were self-effacing, claiming that he was no more than a 'conduit for views that reach back deeply into the history of our struggle and that have been shaped by the masses in struggle as well as by the leadership and by intellectuals who have tried to interpret the significance and the direction of that struggle'.[14] His polemical and scholarly writings, speeches, and organisational activities were wide-ranging and provocative, because they often represented an alternative to the politically and socially dominant ideas both in the liberation movement and in the general intellectual climate of his times.

A SEMINAL CONTRIBUTION TO THE 'NATIONAL QUESTION'

Alexander's major intellectual contributions centred on the 'national question', language, education, and culture, as well as on his thoughts about and direct participation in organisational questions in the struggle against racial capitalism in South Africa. He was both a critical social analyst and an 'argumentative' intellectual with a didactic commitment to organising the premises and practices he hoped to engender for socialist outcomes. He refers to this very issue in his seminal contribution to an analysis of state, society, and struggle in *One Azania, One Nation: The National Question in South Africa*, which he published in 1979 under the *nom de guerre* No Sizwe,[15] and which could be regarded as perhaps his foundational thesis for all his subsequent writing and actions. As we now know, Alexander clandestinely began drafting this book on Robben Island and completed it during his period of house arrest in Cape Town from 1974 to 1979. He was motivated to start writing the book after a celebrated debate with Nelson Mandela in Robben Island Prison. In his own words:

> I wrote [the book] really because of the debates I had with Mandela on the Island about post-apartheid South Africa, the new nation, nation-building, what it all means in terms of racial prejudice, racial attitudes, racial categories, class, gender and so on … The discussion took almost two years; we used to meet once a week and discuss whether there is a nation and how we would build a nation. Our position was that there is no nation, and we have to build a nation, and that this implied a whole lot of things about education, structural change and identity politics and so on … [16]

Reflecting on his aim in authoring the book, he says:

> it should be stressed that my approach has been motivated throughout by the desire to facilitate the unification of the National Liberation Movement by fomenting a discussion on the *basis* of national unity and

on the political-strategic implications of ideas about who constitutes the South African nation.[17]

In other words, he was motivated not only by the need to clarify the abiding confusion about the national question but also by the deliberate and constructive purpose of producing unity among the contending political organisations in the liberation movement. Although this might seem quixotic, that would be too facile a view of his intellectual and political orientation which, despite the attitude of some of his detractors, reinforced in him the necessity of seeking alliances with those forces that he considered to be potential participants in the realisation of a new society. It was this that made him argue for and seek non-sectarian coalitions and principled forms of unity, especially against what he perceived to be the pervasive 'reactionary nationalisms' in the ideas of both the apartheid regime and elements of the liberation movement itself. He refuted the 'propagation of bogus nationalisms, the main purpose of which is to dissipate the force of the class struggle by deflecting it into channels that will nurture the dominant classes'.[18] He explained that because social relations were mystified as 'race relations', there was a need to 'illuminate the character of the *real* (socio-economic) basis of inequality and the *real* (ideological) forms in which it is expressed', in the pursuit of liberation and the demise of apartheid.[19]

The necessity of demystifying ideas about 'race'[20] so dominant in South African society led him to set out a radical 'non-racial' alternative that enjoined those opposed to racism to engage in anti-racist practices. These actions were intended to demonstrate the possibilities for developing forms of consciousness which counteracted the pernicious influence of racist ideas, and simultaneously to build the political and social movement for an anti-racist society. Although he spoke about this in terms of 'non-racialism', his conception cannot be interpreted to suggest a liberal or declassed orientation to the politics of 'race', since conceptions of 'race' were for him inseparable from the exploitative nature of capitalist relations. For Alexander, the idea of 'non-racialism' was simultaneously about the political and organisational forms of resistance to racial capitalism.

Although it could be said that his non-racialism represented a radical ontology and was deeply humanistic, these objectives were directly related to social mobilisation and consciousness against a political regime and were not simply about the clarification of a concept. While it was important to lay bare the 'nonsense of race', for Alexander that was not an end in itself, since the purpose of clarification was as much about how the political struggle was to be prosecuted as it was about the socio-political and systemic implications of the deconstruction of racist ideas. This was inseparable from the forms of political and social mobilisation needed to achieve these ends, as his trenchant argument in *No Sizwe* about the entrenchment of a 'race realism' by the Congress Movement in particular was to show.

Alexander would show in that writing how the very forms of racial organisation predicated on the facticity of race were simply a capitulation to a social construct whose effects were pernicious and contradictory relative to any serious conception of nationhood or 'national consciousness'. Indeed, that the weaknesses evinced by ideologues who maintained the unassailability of 'race consciousness', and who thus favoured conceptions of 'multi-racialism' and even 'non-racialism', led inevitably to the forms of racialised political mobilisation whose consequences were likely to lead to the very socio-political morass which faces society today.

Alexander's prescient approach was intended to avoid the problem of making 'racial' difference a continuing political creed even in an ostensibly 'non-racial' society. His overarching purpose, which he refers to explicitly in *One Azania One Nation*, was to 'foment' a political discussion about nationhood and how it might be constructed against the long history of racist division and the entrenchment of its forms of consciousness.[21] This did not imply a negation of the existence of other forms of oppression since he perfectly understood the indivisibility of the multi-faceted nature of oppressive and exploitative regimes. The choice of 'race' as the primary metaphor for political division was self-evident, given its palpability and presence in the lives of oppressed and exploited communities. Yet it was simultaneously – in his writings about forms of oppression – not reducible to issues of 'race', because of his recognition that, 'almost everything from religion to politics to economic systems to what we refer to as values, has to be revisited, reconceptualised and rearticulated in a language that frees us from the clichés of the 19th and 20th centuries'.[22]

Alexander provides detailed definitions of the 'nation', necessary since general descriptions have limited value because of the many national forms prevalent in their development.[23] For Alexander, it is hopeless to try to fit Africa into a mode of European historical development, since Africa must be understood on its own terms based on its own modalities of development. Capitalist development is a spur to the development of nations whose boundaries are developed under specific conditions deter-mined by class struggle within societies and the national movements in them. For him,

> because the nation has to be constructed ideologically and politically on the basis of the developing, i.e. also changing, capitalist forces and relations of production, each of the antagonistic classes in the social formation, generally speaking, conceives of the nation differently in accordance with its class ideology.[24]

He uses Benedict Anderson's analysis, presented in his book *Imagined Communities*,[25] to examine this issue. In Western Europe, Anderson explains, print languages and the rise of capitalism replaced Latin, the sacred language, with local languages, giving rise to 'imagined commu-nities'. These distinguished themselves from religious and dynastically constituted communities, giving rise to 'modern national consciousness'.[26] In other words, the development of print languages is the connection between capitalist development and such consciousness. Anderson, however, critiques the idea that 'language is the badge of nationality', since 'nations can now be imagined without linguistic communality'.[27] This means that nations are a political and ideological construct; they are imagined because 'members of even the smallest nations will never know most of their fellow members'.[28] Alexander explains that although this is somewhat idealistic as a definition, Anderson's approach enables us to accept the idea of an imagined community as a social reality 'embedded' in the concrete conditions of capitalist or socialist relations of production in a defined territory. Anderson's precepts with reference to 'imagined' and 'language' suggest, for Alexander, that nations are historical con-structs that express political and ideological processes consistent with the development of struggles around relations of production and are constructed regardless of the diversity of languages or the geographic ter-ritory that contains the nation.

A CONTRIBUTION TO THE THEORY OF RACIAL CAPITALISM

Alexander had long grappled with questions of 'race', class, ethnicity, and nation in South Africa, and his ideas about racial capitalism devel-oped out of this engagement. His enduring contribution to the theory of racial capitalism comes from 'Nation and Ethnicity in South Africa', his address to the 1983 National Forum meeting in Hammanskraal, a town near Pretoria. Spurred by a call from Black Consciousness activists, the National Forum brought together some 200 organisations and 600 delegates, most of whom were to the left of the African National Congress (ANC) and saw the ANC's 'Freedom Charter' as a compromised, liberal document. At the end of the conference, delegates unanimously adopted the 'Manifesto of the Azanian People'; its opening sentences are drawn from Alexander's talk.[29] 'The immediate goal of the national liberation struggle now being waged in South Africa is the destruction of the system of racial capitalism', Alexander writes, 'Apartheid is simply a particular socio-political expression of this system. Our opposition to apartheid is therefore only a starting point for our struggle against the structures and interests which are the real basis of apartheid'.

Alexander returns to this issue a few years later as follows:

It is simply a fallacy to claim that Black workers are faced with two autonomous but intersecting systems of domination, *viz.* a system of 'racial domination' and a system of 'class domination'. However valid it might be for specific analytical purposes to distinguish between the 'racial' and the 'class' elements that constitute the system of racial capitalism, it is impossible to transfer such a dichotomy on to the social reality in political and ideological practice, except in terms of, or for the purposes of, ruling class mystification of that reality.[30]

In effect, Alexander's analysis of racial capitalism in South Africa focused on three interrelated dynamics:[31] *racialised dispossession, racial exploitation*, and *racialised job reservations*.[32] Racialised dispossession refers to the conquest of land by white settlers, the forced displacement of 'Africans' and ongoing state laws that prevented 'Africans' from owning or buying land in 87 per cent of South Africa. Alexander insisted that accumulation by racialised dispossession was not limited to the pre-capitalist era but was an ongoing, structural feature of racial capitalism in South Africa due to laws that 'sanctified the original conquest' and facilitated further displacement and dispossession.[33]

For Alexander, racism and capitalism were not merely theoretical constructs requiring reconciliation but represented the very basis of material life for all society and expressed itself not only in the political economy of colonial and apartheid rule but also in the forms of social consciousness and organisational strategies adopted within the liberation movement. Recent debates about the provenance of the usage of the concept of *racial capitalism* are, in some senses, somewhat academic and unhelpful[34] because while Alexander directly used the concept from the early 1980s at least, his critical views even before this period were a direct consequence of his understanding not only of the political economy of racist capitalism but also on its wider influence on the formation of socio-linguistic, cultural, religio-ethical, educational, gendered, and other ideas.

WRITINGS ON EDUCATION

The opening chapter of Alexander's book *Education and the Struggle for National Liberation in South Africa* is titled, 'What is happening in our schools and what can we do about it?'[35] He provides a general exposition of the state of the country to foreground the discussion of education. In reading any of Alexander's writings it soon becomes apparent that it is virtually impossible to separate his conception of education from his other theoretical and practical ideas, and in particular from his conceptions of language and culture, as all of these issues are fundamentally related to his approach to nationhood. In some senses, this is not surprising, because Alexander's intellectual orientation insisted on socio-economic, political, cultural, linguistic, and other relations as critical to social analysis.

As John Samuel observes in the 'Foreword' to *Sow the Wind*,

the single thrust that runs through much of Neville Alexander's writings is the dynamic relationship he perceives between the national struggle for liberation in South Africa and the future political vision. Central to this vision are such issues as the relationship between racism and capitalism, the role of the working class in the liberation struggle, the process of nation building and the role of education in social change.[36]

The opening chapter of *Education and the Struggle for National Liberation in South Africa* begins with a summary of the most important contextual issues that affected any attempt at an analysis of the education and social system in South Africa at that time – circa 1990. The most obvious of these was the economic crisis faced by the ruling class – no less a crisis of the 'world capitalist system'. In South Africa, its most obvious manifestations were the disinvestment campaign against the regime and the accompanying decline in profits, the consequential alarming growth in unemployment, increasing inflation and its effects on incomes. Alexander wrote that 'the present system will not be able to employ all our employable people, pay them a living wage, make it possible for them to live in decent adequate houses at prices they can afford, give their children free and compulsory education up to the age of 16 or matric'.[37]

This crisis was simultaneously a 'political crisis of the ruling class'. The events of the workers' strike in 1973 and the student uprising in 1976 had exacerbated the crisis of the apartheid state. For Alexander, the new constitutional dispensation of the 1980s was an attempt to win support from an emerging Black middle class in the face of the increasing proletarianisation of Black workers. The 'racist monstrosity' of the tricameral system, which attempted to seduce the middle classes into a form of representation, had inevitably failed, since even this 'crude attempt at political "reform" was still tainted by the legacy of Verwoerdian fascist and *Herrenvolk* thinking'.[38] These failed attempts at 'reform' were taking place even while the working class was increasingly radicalised and would not accept the 'reforms', seeking instead to overthrow the regime as expressed in the violent opposition to the imposition of collaborationist political and administrative structures on working-class and rural communities.

Education was implicated in these developments since most schools were in working-class townships and rural areas and had been directly affected by the events of the 1970s. The political and economic crisis manifested itself in schooling as much as in other aspects of life, and the apartheid state's bureaucratic organisation and policies had hardly changed throughout this time, especially regarding the levels of public expenditure, pupil–teacher ratios, fees, books, uniforms and other aspects of public expenditure. In effect, the material and 'ideological' conditions characteristic of apartheid continued to prevail. The De Lange Commission of 1980–1981 attempted to change elements of the apartheid education system, but even that was rejected by the oppressed. Subsequent attempts at introducing changes in the education system (including in the areas of curriculum, skills development, and so on) were also ineffective since the oppressed were unwilling to participate in these schemes.

While pointing to the growing power of the national liberation movements in the urban and rural areas of the country, profoundly strengthened by the flood of activists willing to take the struggle forward, Alexander refers to the many 'grave problems' which persisted in the ranks of the oppressed. He argues that while the struggles of students, their parents and teachers are not synonymous and are even sometimes contradictory, there is every reason to find synergies in prosecuting the national liberation struggle against the isolationist tendencies evident in many places. Moreover, some students had become 'victims of the romantic illusion that the students are the vanguard of the national liberation struggle and that they can make decisions without any reference to the workers movement'[39] which Alexander regarded as a 'dangerous delusion' since he held the view that

all other struggles, no matter in which arena they start, whether it is a struggle begun by women, youth, the churches, students or by other groups, have got to link up with the struggle of the organised working class if they are not to be defeated or to be deflected into reformist and even collaborationist paths.[40]

He points to the range of opportunities for democratic mobilisation within the education system and deals with the possibilities for 'alternative education' emerging from the crisis of schooling, based on a 'spectrum of practices some of which can be implemented in the government schools, colleges and universities while others, for the present, have to be implemented extramurally'[41] and for which some available precedents exist that can be built on.

The texts we have examined exemplify much of Alexander's approach to education as inextricably linked to the wider socio-economic, political, organisational, and cultural issues facing society. Towards the end of 2008, Alexander and other radical educationists launched the Public Participation in Education Network (PPEN). In its 'Call to Action', PPEN declared that the failures evident in the education system had induced cynicism among various communities and even among educators, school managers, and other public officials. It warned that these sentiments would further entrench the sense of powerlessness and a loss of hope about the possibility of meaningful outcomes for society as a whole. Alexander expanded on the nature of the crisis identified by PPEN, but also discussed ways of reversing this trend. In an article originally titled 'The Truth about Education in the New South Africa', published as 'Schooling in and for the New South Africa' Alexander[42] lamented that

fundamental mistakes of a conceptual, strategic and political-pedagogical character [policies such as Outcomes-Based Education, teacher redeployment and others critiqued by Alexander at the time] were made in the process of transition from apartheid to post-apartheid education during the period 1993–1998 approximately. Not everything was wrong, of course, but many of the beacons that should have facilitated a soft landing for the new system were placed wrongly.

He continued this metaphor by explaining how subsequent attempts to correct the deficiencies 'were doomed to fail, precisely because they did not replace these beacons and, instead, themselves became no more than decoy beacons that had to end up in numerous but related crash landings'.[43]

Alexander identified and discussed a few key omissions and mistakes, including the failure to move away from the spatial apartheid location of schools which perpetuates racial and class divisions and the unequal allocation of resources, the inadequate professional development of teachers, and the blind spot of language policy in schools. He spent many years promoting early childhood development, reading and multilingualism in communities and schools, and explaining its importance for cognitive development, overcoming divisions and building national unity but also the promotion of African languages to address the skewed and unequal power relations in our country.

THE LANGUAGE QUESTION, CULTURE, AND IDENTITY

The language question was one of Alexander's central political and analytical preoccupations, especially given its relationship to education, culture, and consciousness. Alexander's thinking about nationhood, in turn, was inseparable from his orientation to culture, making education inseparable from the social and human questions that concerned him and the relationship of knowledge to these. There is a raft of commentaries which reflect on his orientation to education, and many of these were captured at one of the memorial conferences on Alexander's life, held at Nelson Mandela University in 2013.[44] For example, Porteus's view of his orientation was that

Alexander's approach [to] and interest in education are difficult to separate from his larger social quest – a quest for a different kind of society. He was deeply aware of the brutal history of racialized capitalism from which we emerge. He was deeply aware of the brutalizing future implicit in our current social trajectory of capitalist accumulation within a racialized consciousness. And he was committed to a different kind of future. He was an unapologetic socialist. He resisted the more conventional vocabulary, formulations and insistences inherited within the Left, preferring formulations that resonate with the life, times and evidence available to today's young people in particular. His view of education, therefore, was unremitting 'politically' infused with sociological, philosophical and ontological concerns. If education is ultimately about building the character of our social project in the future, he asks, what is the character of the historical community we want to build?[45]

Alexander was thus able to explicate his orientation to the wider canvas of socio-political, cultural, and socio-linguistic ideas as the lens for understanding educational issues. It meant, for instance, that how social identities were viewed was inherently about the national question, and in this education's role was indispensable for the construction of an identity that dealt with apartheid fragmentation and racism.

Brigitta Busch's introduction to the volume, *Interviews with Neville Alexander*[46] discusses his orientation to the language question – its formative role in his general thinking and interconnectedness with wider social issues in his reflections on 'the power relations inherent in language, of processes of inclusion and exclusion linked to ways of speaking'.[47] His 'language biography', set out in the series of interviews he had with Brigitta Busch, Lucijan Busch, and Karen Press, was not just about his personal experience but about its links to socio-political issues, and that personal experience was inseparable from historical processes. By the late 1980s language policy had come to the centre of his intellectual and activist work, but it was always clear that his interest in language was not an end in itself but rather the key element in his conceptualisation of the national liberation struggle and the abolition of social inequality.

Lwazi Brian Ramadiro echoes these sentiments when he suggests that Alexander's approach to the language question was informed 'by a fundamental thesis that in unequal societies, language is necessarily a class question'.[48] That is why Alexander insisted that the language question was simultaneously a question about the very nature of the society in which it was embedded, and therefore one that had to be examined closely. There were inevitably larger questions to do with power, politics and history implicated in the examination of language.

His interest in language grew from his earliest interactions with it as a child in both formal and informal settings, and while incarcerated in Robben Island Prison, and remained central to his philosophy and work throughout his adult life. He regarded the question of language – both language itself and language policy – as critically important for understanding the relations and identities engendered in social systems, together with its 'appealing and expressive functions', in the struggles against apartheid and the quest for an egalitarian society. The importance of language is, as Busch et al suggest, not only based on the 'singularity of individual experience' but also about how 'personal experience is linked to the social and the political, how language ideologies impact on the ways in which experience is lived, how language attitudes are forged'.[49] Although Alexander did not think it adequate that a socially formed language biography should be an end in itself, since he regarded self-awareness as a 'precondition for necessary transformative action'.[50]

Alexander's work on multilingualism and on mother-tongue-based literacy is one of the distinguishing aspects of his critical legacy; given the many years he spent trying to persuade policy makers, schools, and academic institutions to recognise its importance for planning. He was insistent that it was necessary to make 'the multiple language resources that children brought with them visible' so that the 'multilingual habitus' of school routines which had taken hold among teachers could be re-examined for the realisation of 'aspirations, and desires of their students even beyond the canon of the language or languages of instruction'.[51]

As Ramadiro has argued, Alexander's work can be thought of as setting out important principles concerning the question of language as related to culture and consciousness.[52] For Alexander, language was inextricable from a study of society, as indeed social studies were unavoidably about language issues too. The implication of this was simply that questions about language could not be abstracted from a study of society because of its relevance to socio-political analysis. Concepts relating to 'language', 'culture', and 'identity' had to be understood historically and politically in 'socio-constructivist terms', since these concepts represent human interactions and relationships through which meaning is created by individuals acting within social institutions. Alexander argues that the concept of 'culture' has been 'reified' and regarded as static and differentiated, using approaches which were adopted in both the USA and the USSR. This requires a critical examination of what is given. Culture is inseparable from language, but that does not signify an uncomplicated correspondence between them since languages appropriate culture to the degree that it is necessary to do so for the purposes of communication, and other relationships. Through the latter process languages also influence each person's world view in the process. This is especially so in Africa, which is rarely characterised by a monolingual habitus or 'singularly dialectal lives'. And for that reason, language cannot be considered the sole determinant and defining attribute of ethnicity for most communities. Yet it is important to understand how ethnicity and culture are often mobilised for political purposes. Alexander shows how 'in divided and unequal societies like South Africa ... sub-national identities such as "race" and ethnicity are encouraged to divide and subjugate the oppressed'.[53] For Alexander:

> It is important to remember that even though they are constructed, social identities have a primordial dimension for most individuals, precisely because they are not aware of the historical, social and political ways in which their identities have been constructed. This is, ultimately, the psychological explanation for the tenacity of such identities.[54]

CONFRONTING RACISM

It was in this connection that he warned against the genocidal opportunism of demagogues using racist constructs of identity and culture for political and socio-economic ends.[55] For that reason, too, it was necessary to promote a 'national consciousness' that could counter the influence of ethnic, religious, and racialised social identities by advancing the goals of a broader African and internationalist consciousness. National consciousness was thus not an end in itself but part of a continuous project of forging wider human understanding. Alexander refers to the importance of understanding that the opposition to racist ideas is simultaneously about the quest for national unity, especially in the context of the divisive and racist practices of the apartheid regime.

His examination of the famous *Brown vs Board of Education* case in the USA is illustrative of the relationship between social identity and post-apartheid education's potential role in shaping it.[56] His argument in this paper is that social identities are not given but are constructed, and he warns about the danger of perpetuating apartheid-era racial identities in the pursuit of policies such as the affirmative action policies to which the post-apartheid government is committed. Thus, the paper avers that 'de-racialization should extend beyond formal desegregation to school integration, as exemplified in the non-racial ethos of the new curriculum. The eradication of racial thinking is identified as the next historic task facing the new South Africa'.[57]

His main arguments are that social identities are changeable and fluid, and that change can be facilitated by an approach that considers the material reality of the citizens of a society. The failure to do that could lead to genocidal conflict. He is critical of the established approach in the USA based on 'ethnic' identities and its effect on the continuity of racial prejudice, conceding that in practice different approaches could be adopted to the problem of eliminating racial prejudice in each country.

The *Brown vs Board of Education* case is useful for South Africa, Alexander argues, only if interpreted in ways that do not deepen approaches to identity, which heighten prejudice and social fragmentation. This is dependent on the role of the state. This role is important because 'race' discourse is the hegemonic discourse of those who wield power in society, even if its opposition mediates that power; the state is the final arbiter, by virtue of its monopoly on the use of force to shape identities historically. This was demonstrated by the architects of apartheid who organised the process of racial classification that became generalised, because it was rooted in the material reality of life. This made the state's designations consistent with people's lived experience of class and social status, and the result was the imprinting of the subjective experience of 'race' on the population, even in private spaces.

An approach to the elimination of racism – whose ideological basis was premised on the identification and enforced adoption of 'race' categories – could simultaneously silence any discussion of its persistence and fail to create the society it envisages. He argues, moreover, that social identities are inherently unstable and are therefore changeable through conscious planning, which is necessary and possible through open and democratic processes since racial identities form the backdrop to 'ontological commitments, racial and ethnic identities and their role in shaping the history of struggle'.[58] In his view, the majority of South Africans place a great deal of weight on their primary identity determined by 'race or ethnic group', which reflects the power of contemporary racial ideology. The state's approach to affirmative action is truncated by its inability to alter the relations of power shaped by racial capitalism – neither regarding the power of the armed state nor in terms of the forms of wealth associated with the financing of the racist apartheid state and their continuities in the 'non-racial' post-apartheid state.

Moreover, as a socialist internationalist Alexander remained open to the construction of a universal identity not constrained by national boundaries, while recognising the variety of social orientations and identities which human beings are given to, provided these do not infract against the claims of a common humanity.

For Alexander, language is deeply implicated in the constitution of historical subjects and understood properly, could play a useful role in interrogating *a priori* constructions of culture and identity. A combination of word and deed could counter the ideas of ethnic identities and consciousness while promoting national consciousness, considering the rich cultural diversity existing in South Africa. He was critical of the 'Rainbow Nation' metaphor that came into use after 1994 and achieved much favour in public discourse. He argues for a change of metaphor and the necessity of reshaping that discourse, by rethinking the relationship between 'nation' and 'culture'. He favours the idea of an evolving culture and suggests

> an hypothesis that under these circumstances what I call a core culture can evolve. It is based on the interaction, or perhaps influence of all the relevant currents. The precise definition of the core at any given moment depends on the changing social formation. The tributary cultures do not, and should not, disappear. Instead, they continue to swell the common pool and themselves change in certain respects and continue to be tolerable if they do not support the need and consequent desire for a degree of commonality.[59]

It is in this connection that he talks about the metaphor of the Gariep River, which is both redemptive and contextually useful since it signifies the idea of a river and all its tributaries.[60] This enables one to visualise and to signify a host of cultures in the process of identity formation, in place of the reified notions of existing and inherited identities, even though the 'tenacity' of such identities must not be under-estimated. In this conception, 'settler colonial societies such as South Africa have been constituted, culturally speaking, by the confluence of different tributaries'.[61] This metaphoric approach does not privilege any mainstream culture; it regards the flowing together of the tributaries as the mainstream, with a combination of African, European, Asian, and, more recently, modern

American cultures influencing each other in every domain of social life such as sport, religion, music, language, and so on.[62] These tributaries themselves eventually flow into the ocean of humanity.

How we understand culture is also critical to the discursive domain and must be disaggregated, especially with reference to the areas of practice in which culture is implicated. The corollary of this is the need to use fluid rather than static concepts of culture that depend on specific cultural practices, traditions and customs, thus recognising that language is not merely a reflection of social reality but is also constitutive of it and can be transformative. For Alexander, no culture 'taken as a whole' is superior to others and identities are fluid and are constructed within relations of power which reflect ideological and material proclivities.

CONCLUSION

Inevitably, in producing a selection of Alexander's writings to fit into a single volume, difficult choices have to be made, especially since these writings embody the life and work of a creative and non-dogmatic radical over many decades. In the preamble to each of the four sections of this collection – relating to the different periods of his political life – we have written a brief introductory note to contextualise and provide a brief background to the writings in that section and at times indicated writings that have been excluded. The texts we have chosen, represent, in our view, an intellectually coherent body of ideas inseparable from the radical political and social practices which characterised his life. Sharing Alexander's insights is not only about recognising the value of his political philosophy, supported by his life in struggle. It is that and much more since what can be drawn from him is a perspective on human dignity and the struggles necessary for its achievement.

Alexander's life is also instructive, because despite his extraordinary contribution, we are in many senses in an even more precarious world today, wracked by even greater global, regional and national conflicts than it was a decade or so ago. Pankaj Mishra's *Age Of Anger*[63] captures some elements of these times, especially since it points directly to the re-emergence of the blight of fascism globally. Alexander would have found the reason for that in the complex relationships between history, culture, language, ideology, and the material socio-economic and environmental conditions under which the great majority of humanity is forced to live. But he would have pointed to the inevitability of the struggles against these conditions, and the importance of finding both the analytical and organisational premises for resisting the many forms of exploitative oppression, patriarchy, racism, prejudice, and ecological catastrophes that shape people's lives today. We would be reminded that

> the world is changing rapidly, and we should not get stuck in the time warp of real capitalism as though there is no alternative. Another world *is* possible, indeed probable. The barbarism of real capitalism as we know it on the continent of Africa is not the only way.[64]

Alexander's life and work are important because exemplars of such highly developed consciousness are rare. His critical interventions are profoundly important for sustaining the life of struggle against rapacious and uncaring political and social systems, by providing an analytical framework that can be useful, at any time, for understanding and organising against the powerful global and national interests at the root of inhumanity. Alexander would urge critical reading of his own work since he himself abjured easy political or intellectual approaches based on simplistic characterisations. We urge that his writings be read in that spirit, since they represent a critical heuristic for continuous rethinking about the critical issues of our time.

PART I

Prison Writings: 'The University of Robben Island', 1964–1974

Introduction to Part I

Alexander began writing the *Robben Island Dossier: 1964–1974* and *One Azania, One Nation: The National Question in South Africa* while in Robben Island Prison and completed the manuscripts while he was serving five years of 'house arrest' after his release from prison.

We include excerpts from the *Robben Island Dossier* consisting of the treatment meted out to prisoners around physical violence, the warders' demeanour, and the conditions surrounding work, food, and education. Alexander had to initially conceal his authorship of the dossier, but many years later spoke about the brutality he personally experienced on the Island, especially in the early months of his incarceration including an instance when a beating by warders pierced his eardrum.[1] There was another reality to Robben Island which Alexander called 'the university of Robben Island'. Alexander's role in this undertaking is best expressed by a fellow prisoner in the isolation cells and one of the leaders of the ANC, Ahmed Kathrada:[2]

I was privileged to spend the better part of ten years with Neville. We were among about 25 inmates, completely isolated from the hundreds of other political prisoners on Robben Island. My relationship with him was primarily that of two friends, and of teacher and student … At the lime quarry, where we worked with picks and shovels, we spent quite a bit of time together, especially when he was not teaching.

Neville's passion for education was shown by his ever-readiness to assist all of us who were in need. He also helped to rope in other teachers to form RITA – Robben Island Teachers Association. There were three elderly inmates from the Transkei who were completely illiterate. Witnessing all of us busy with studies, they developed an acute hunger for education. During the brief period they spent with us, they managed to acquire some very basic education, and were able to converse in English. Then there was my neighbour, who never received a visit for the 15 years that he was with us. Both he and his family members were illiterate, thus letters between them were infrequent. But that also began to change when he and the three men I mentioned received tuition from RITA members and he too was able to communicate with his folks. In my *Memoirs*[3] I wrote: 'Thanks to Dr. Neville Alexander and his group of dedicated teachers, my neighbour left the Island literate'.

I personally owe a deep sense of gratitude to Neville. During my university studies on the Island he enthusiastically helped me with history – his forte. But he did much more. He was entirely responsible for my passing two additional subjects that had not been part of his own studies – sociology and library science. He studied my textbooks, and guides, mastered them, lectured to me, and ensured that I got through!

One Azania, One Nation is undoubtedly the seminal and original contribution to any discussion of the 'national question' in South Africa and the most comprehensive statement of Alexander's views on the subject. It provides a thoroughgoing examination of the various historical approaches to nationhood pointing to the wide range of perspectives representing those of political analysts, academics, and scholars and, most importantly, the ideologues of apartheid and the views held by the organisations of the oppressed. Alexander's coruscating critique subjected many of the prevailing conceptions on this issue to a searing scrutiny that was important not only for proper theorisation but also for the practical strategies of liberation organisations. These ideas continue to inspire strong debate amongst serious thinkers and practitioners engaged in the difficult questions of social 'transformation' both in South Africa and internationally. Excerpts from the introductory chapters are published in this collection. The entire book can be accessed here courtesy of the Estate of Neville Alexander: www.marxists.org/archive/alexander/one-azania-one-nation.pdf

The third publication written on Robben Island is the essay 'A Note on Beauty', which will be published separately. It exists only as a neatly handwritten text by Alexander in a school exercise book.[4] The essay was written, widely circulated, and discussed on the Island. Alexander always viewed the essay as a key expression of his thinking regarding questions of human dignity, racism, prejudice, and ideology. He writes, 'for a people desirous of constructing a really new society there are few topics which can be of such importance and interest'.

Robben Island Dossier: 1964–1974

This introduction to the *Robben Island Prison Dossier: 1964–1974*,[1] is written almost 20 years after the original text. In that text, there was a blank space under the heading 'Introduction'. Instead of the Introduction, a letter, or where this was deemed too dangerous, an oral message, had to serve the purpose. This clandestine mode relates directly to the genesis of the document.

It was an unspoken injunction understood by all prisoners who were released from the island that one of the most important contributions they could make to the well-being of those they left behind was to let in the light of public scrutiny on the goings-on in that prison. We knew that the 'vile deeds' of the prison authorities could not withstand the light of day. Any exposure, no matter how mild, would have the effect of (at least temporarily) reining them in and thus gaining metaphorically (and in some cases literally) a lease on life for the inmates. In our specific case, i.e. the four remaining male prisoners sentenced in 1964 with seven others (four females and three males) for alleged conspiracy to commit sabotage via the activities of the Yu Chi Chan Club and the National Liberation Front, there was an explicit agreement that we would explore all possible ways to bring to the attention of as many international organisations as possible, as well as to the relevant South African groups, what was really going on in Robben Island.

For various reasons, I chose to write a report based on information (dates, events, names of people, etc.) which I had collected during my ten-year period of incarceration and which I managed to conceal in various ways. Because of contact with people who had considerable leverage, my report, unlike those of some prisoners I heard of later, managed to reach individuals in international organisations who could use the information as a point of (necessarily unacknowledged) reference when they had to deal with any issue relating to the conditions of political prisoners in South Africa.

Because of the ever-present threat of prosecution under the draconian Prisons Act (no 8 of 1959), both my authorship and my role in proliferating the information contained in the dossier had to be concealed. A thin disguise in the form of the third person singular pronoun was supposed to assist in keeping my authorship secret in case the document did fall into the wrong hands. Consultations with prisoners who had been incarcerated in the 'general section' for most of the period in question provided me with information which, because I was for most of the period held in the 'isolation section', in some small way could also complicate the task of would-be sleuths. It was a very serious matter since I was not only flouting the Prisons Act but also transgressing my house arrest order in terms of which I was prohibited from 'publishing' anything. 'Publishing' included explicitly the kind of text I was sending into the world.

The intended readership to a very large extent co-determined the content and style of presentation of the report. Besides a genuine commitment to reporting strictly only that which I knew to be true, I realised, of course, that any material produced in anger and without due regard to accuracy and probability would not be treated seriously by the men and women I was attempting to reach. Consequently, a certain pedantic meticulousness is there for all to read even though, on occasion, my real emotions broke through the screen of academic precision. I wrote this piece to the end within four months of my release from prison in 1974, both because I wanted to use the period when things were still fresh in my memory and because of the timetables and agendas of certain international organisations, including the UN Special Committee and General Assembly as well as the International Commission of Jurists.

The dossier has to be seen against this background and in the context of the extreme repression of the mid-1970s. It is by no means an adequate sketch of what went on in Robben Island but I trust that it does capture in some ways the sociology and the social psychology of that very special prison. With the publication of this text 20 years after it was written, I put behind me in a formal sense that vitally important and formative period of my life that I shall always associate with Robben Island. My special thanks to Martin Hall and the UCT Press for encouraging me to believe that this document does have a certain historical value.

Neville Alexander, Cape Town, February 1993

PHYSICAL VIOLENCE

From 1962 to 1964 assaults, very often brutal and mass assaults, of political prisoners was a weekly, often a daily, occurrence. It should be remembered that non-political prisoners are subjected to this sadistic regime throughout their incarceration, and that no distinction was made in that period between political and non-political prisoners. In fact, political prisoners were treated much worse precisely because their cases received so much more adverse publicity than those of common-law prisoners. Because they were presented as challenging the hegemony and privileges of the White man, and because the government had decided to 'stamp out' the liberation movements, this policy of the department of prisons, in effect if not in intention, was to intimidate and ruthlessly break the morale of political prisoners.

It is no exaggeration to say that a man's life was totally and constantly at the mercy of the whims of crazed White males out to take revenge on behalf of an oppressing community on those who had the temerity to question the morality and the permanence of that structure of privilege and exploitation.

The causation of assaults was (and remains) various, but there is no doubt that the major basic cause is the combination of race prejudice and political revenge. The average White warder (99 per cent of the personnel of the department of prisons) has a master-race psychology. He considers his whole personality, his being, to be in jeopardy if any Black man questions any aspect of his presumed superiority. The authoritarian, *Herrenvolk* personality is an absolute; to shake any element thereof is to jeopardise the whole. Hence, the violent, irrational response to otherwise trivial friction.

Not only is the political prisoner a Black man, but he is a 'terrorist', a 'saboteur', a 'murderer', who wants to kill, rape, and otherwise threaten the sanctity of White women and children. The White male's sexual aggressiveness, his adequacy as a man, is considered to be in the balance. The consequence is insane, unlimited violence, a sadistic confirmation of the White man's potency, an atavistic destructiveness which wants to affirm the 'humanity' of the White by dehumanising the Black, by transforming his race enemy into an animal. The resulting savagery on both sides, is one of the most traumatic experiences a human being can have, one of the most demoralising phenomena a prisoner has to live through and to witness. The helplessness of sensitive people when confronted with naked brutality, the complete senselessness and absurdity of human existence in these conditions, drives many a man to desperation. There is no doubt that but for the antidote of firm political convictions and the anchorage of unshakeable philosophical optimism, many (genuine) suicides would have resulted. As it is, a few attempted suicides have tragically to be recorded.

This general exposition of the basic causation of physical pressure on political prisoners in South African gaols needs to be complemented by an enumeration of concrete instances. Examples, obviously, are legion. Only a few representative instances will be quoted here.

In March 1964, a mass assault on political prisoners took place. Since this incident is documented elsewhere, an outline of what occurred will be given here. It was alleged that the prisoners, who were working mainly in the stone quarry, were refusing work, or that they were on a go-slow strike. Naturally, this had no foundation whatever. The whole thing was a carefully planned plot (a 'bomb' in prison jargon) to intimidate the prisoners who had shown signs of restiveness under the intolerable pressure to which they were being subjected. A 'carry-on' was to put them in their place. This meant that prisoners were rounded up early from all work-stations and transported to the prison, where they were awaited by a gang of warders, all armed with pick-handles and batons. The moment they were inside the command was given and a pogrom began. The young White warders were given the opportunity to vent their frustration to the full.

A number of prisoners, including Andrew Masondo (a former lecturer in Mathematics at Fort Hare University College) and Dennis Brutus, were severely wounded.[2] Brutus, in fact, carried the scars of that day on his body until he left prison in 1965. Even more ironical was the fact that he had arrived on that day together with a group of prisoners from Leeukop Prison, who were being transferred to Robben Island Prison. Hence, even if the allegation of refusing to work had any substance in it, it is evident that this particular group of prisoners could not have been involved. Though attempts were made subsequently to take these assaults to court, none of them succeeded, for reasons which will become clear later. This particular mass assault is notorious in the annals of the Island, mainly because it involved just about every political prisoner then in custody.

In June 1964, a mass assault on 'gangsters' took place on the instructions and under the guidance of the Officer Commanding (hereafter OC) himself. Just previously the inhuman torture perpetrated in the *Landbouspan* (Agricultural Team) during 1963 has been exposed in the overseas press as well as locally. In typical fashion, the authorities placed the blame for these illegal acts on the 'gangsters' who abound in all South African prisons. It was alleged that the whole exercise was the work of the 'Big-Five' gang (whose members were in fact mere henchmen and minions of certain warders). So, in order to show the 'world' that the authorities were prepared to deal with the 'guilty parties', a 'carry-on' against all known members of gangs was staged. A subsidiary intention was to intimidate the political prisoners.

On the third Wednesday of that month, those unfortunate prisoners were loaded into trucks before work stopped. They were told to wait at the 'stripping line', i.e. the open square where all prisoners entering the gaol's precincts are stripped naked in order to be searched for unauthorised articles. As the rest of the prisoners came back from work, a few pimps went about pointing out those who were supposed to be gangsters. No political prisoner was involved in any of this. The prisoners were ordered to strip, then searched, while a double row of warders lined up from the stripping line to the entrance of the cell which had been set aside for these 'gangsters' for the night. All of them were armed with pick-handles and batons. The 'gangsters' were then forced to run the gauntlet. The rest need not be described. Suffice it to say that the bravery of most of these prisoners left an indelible impression on all who witnessed the savage punishment given to them. They were then locked up in the cell and again assaulted in the night. They were forced to admit their 'guilt' and to apologise for causing so much trouble and embarrassment to the *Oubaas* (Old Master, i.e. the OC). But the most sickening part was to take place on the next day.

In the evening the OC, Colonel Wessels, a drunk and a complete moron in spite of his university education, turned up in the cell where these poor men sat huddled together in one blanket each. They were naked, in order to be further humiliated and because most of them were so badly wounded that they could not wear clothing close to their bodies in any case. After a hypocritical address, in which he told them that he was *in loco parentis* to them and that a father has to beat his children when they were naughty, he offered them two ounces of tobacco per man and told them to forget the whole incident and to start on a clean slate.

He had obviously realised that he had committed an imbecile blunder by allowing political prisoners to observe this chastisement of their fellow prisoners. Needless to say, the matter was never heard of again and when certain prisoners tried to bring it to the attention of higher authorities, they were themselves threatened with the same treatment for 'making false allegations against members of the prison service'. Such incidents are only too common among non-political prisoners in all South African prisons.

A last example of a mass assault under slightly modified circumstances may be quoted. On 28 May 1971, a certain Head Warder Carstens,[3] who at the time was in charge of the single-cells section of the prison, arbitrarily deprived two young political prisoners from Namibia of their meals for the day. On the previous day, he had done the same thing to two other Namibians.

The 35 Namibians sentenced in the first 'Terrorist Trial' in South Africa in 1967 had been brought down to the single-cells section a few days previously but were not allowed to communicate with the other prisoners housed in that section.[4] As a result of his provocative action the prisoners (i.e. all the prisoners in the section) went on hunger-strike demanding that their two comrades should be properly charged. In retaliation, a gang of warders, led by Chief Warder Fourie, raided the single-cells that night from 1am until approximately 4 am. Each prisoner was forced to stand in his own cell, stark naked and with his hands up against the wall, while the warders ransacked his cell for alleged unauthorised articles. Needless to say, not a single such article was unearthed. But 28 prisoners were assaulted, some of them severely. Most of these were Namibians, including Toivo ja Toivo, who was alleged to have been the ring-leader and an agitator.[5]

Jafta Masemola was beaten unconscious, while Abel Chiloane was so severely injured that for days he urinated blood.[6] Attempts to get the assaults reported to lawyers were stymied, and the doctors were simply not available for three whole weeks, by which time visible injuries had healed up. Psychologically, this was a turning point for Robben Island Prison. The authorities came to realise that the prisoners had been so angered that if at any stage this type of thing were to be repeated there would be a shooting and a killing.

In addenda to this document, some assaults on individual prisoners are described. So many individual assaults took place that it would be pointless to try to cover all of them in a document such as this.

By late 1973 few, if any, assaults were taking place. It is not inconceivable that assaults may still take place in individual cases,[7] but there is no doubt that at present there is no express policy of violence decided at the top. Yet there is no guarantee whatever (despite the injunctions of the Act and of the Regulations) that a violent phase could not recur. Reference has already been made to the 'pendulum policy', and indeed whereas the period from late 1967 until late 1970 was relatively free of the most outrageous assaults on the defenceless prisoners, the years 1971 and 1972 were years during which the lives of the prisoners were as much in jeopardy as in 1962 to 1964. A way must be found to ensure that the law as it stands in regard to assaults on prisoners is carried out and not violated regularly as still happens in gaols other than the political prison on Robben Island.

Three other facets of this problem must be referred to:

(a) There is hardly any redress for the prisoner who has been assaulted. The authorities see to it that he does not get in touch with his legal advisers, either by preventing him from writing to them, or, if his relatives and friends get the attorneys to make inquiries, they do not allow the latter to come to Robben Island, usually on the grounds that they are themselves investigating the complaint and that they would prosecute if they found adequate grounds to do so. It appears that Mr Andrew Masondo, whose arm was broken as the result of an assault, has been the only prisoner to be granted damages after he succeeded in bringing his complaint to court. In earlier years, the authorities on occasion played ducks and drakes with the tarnished dignity of the South African judiciary by charging prisoners who complained of having been assaulted with assault on the warder concerned. Perhaps the most brazen case was that of Mr Louis Mtshizana, an attorney in ordinary life, who was so charged in 1969. Even that court could see that this transparent manoeuvre had no foundation whatsoever.[8]

(b) When a prisoner has been assaulted, it rarely happens that the medical officers and medical orderlies co-operate with the victim by, for instance, taking down a full statement of the context of their examination of the patient. Except possibly in extremely severe cases they simply ignore the aetiology of whatever wounds, injuries, etc., they are treating the prisoner for. The general attitude of, and in some cases the specific instructions of the authorities to, the medical personnel discourage any 'extra-professional' interest the doctors might have. Of course, some of them have been working in the prison service for years and have virtually become glorified first-aid men. Of course, the authorities, if they find the occasional doctor who will not play the game, or for other reasons, often set out deliberately to prevent the patient from seeing the doctor until the wounds have healed.

(c) The prisoners themselves have naturally constantly lodged complaints to senior officers or to other visitors regarding the general question and particular instances of assault. There can be no doubt that it was these representations and exposures that led to the change in policy from about 1967. Such action will doubtlessly continue but it should be remembered that this is a long drawn-out process, during which the prisoners continue to be harassed and assaulted. The utter defencelessness of the prisoners is pitiful to behold and apart from physical pain and injury there is the utter desolation of the mind which such maltreatment brings with it. The hatred and the tendency to reckless and even irresponsible behaviour which result have caused very serious problems for the prisoners themselves. On a number of occasions in all sections of the prison, serious confrontations were avoided by a hair's breadth usually through the timely action of one or other of the older inmates.

The apparent ending of the policy of violence should not mislead anyone to believe that the torturing and harassment of prisoners by officials has stopped, on the contrary, as will be seen, the theatre of war has been changed, but war is being carried on by other means.

WARDERS' DEMEANOUR

In the early years, almost all the warders behaved in a stereotyped manner, the stereotype being that of the rural, *backveldt* farmer with his slave-owner's mentality. Subsequently, as indicated above, a mask was assumed which superficially made it appear that things had changed radically for the better. Yet prisoners have to experience daily the same kinds of indignities and debasements of the earlier years, except that this does not happen so persistently throughout the day as during the early and middle 1960s. Elderly warders, not yet initiated into the peculiarities of Robben Island Prison, as well as some of the younger ones, newly arrived from the prison college, unfailingly behave just as most warders used to do in the earlier period.[9]

This behaviour implies, *inter alia*: (a) Shouting at prisoners in the most insulting and abusive manner whenever anything has to be communicated; the prisoners individually and collectively insisted on being addressed in a civil manner, and often refused to carry out an order which was conveyed in this abusive manner. Today there is much more civility, although there are also degrees of civility according to the section in which prisoners are housed or according to which individual prisoner is being addressed. Thus, to illustrate, the prisoners in the single-cells section are treated much more politely (albeit grudgingly so) than those in the general section, and these in turn are treated much better than those in the 'terrorist section', the inmates of which are even now often treated with the most offensive contempt imaginable. Moreover, even within sections there are often great variations of response. The very same warder who might have been swearing and cursing at one prisoner could the very next moment approach one of the more well-known or 'influential' prisoners in a completely different manner.

The task of educating and, in the proper sense, rehabilitating, new warders or old warders newly arrived on Robben Island is a tedious, burdensome duty imposed on all prisoners by the necessities of surviving with dignity. The patient, tactful, often hurtful, discussions occasioned by this need are one of the great human events on the Island, for here many of the (Black) prisoners and (White) warders for the first (and probably in most cases for the last) time are able to exchange ideas about the way of life of South Africa even if in various senses they are not speaking to one another from a position of equality. Very often this task is made difficult by the opposition of some prisoners who feel that such fraternisation is futile at best and servile at worst.

Though the fact that all warders, with a few laudable exceptions, by virtue of the social pressures on them, in the ultimate analysis always behave brutally when ordered or expected to do so, would seem to confirm the futility of this noble effort, yet it has a practical short-term importance which only the man at the receiving end can really appreciate. There is a great difference between being addressed as *bandiete*, *Kaffers*, *Hotnots*, *Koelies*, and so on through the whole startling range of the local caste vocabulary, and being called 'gentlemen' or even *Mense*, etc.[10]

The climate is so different, no matter how superficially the latter practice may be rooted, that any number of disappointments is rather risked than to have to exist in the horror of an openly racist hell, as had to be done during the period 1962–1967. The department itself has also done something by way of training its men in a more enlightened spirit.

(b) Having the prisoners call the warder *Baas*, *Inkosi*, etc. Just as a non-political prisoner's life would be worth nothing if he did not do this, so in 1962–1964 the political prisoners who refused to kowtow in this manner courted death in the most literal sense. Many assaults were caused by a refusal to say *Baas*. Virtually all prisoners used this searingly, brandingly debasing terminology until a stand was taken by certain prisoners and followed by the rest.

Today only the most dissolute turncoats still use this hateful phraseology. Warders have to be lectured by the prisoners on the decorum of being called *Meneer* rather than *Baas*.[11] Many warders, especially the older ones, believe sincerely that Black prisoners are animals (baboons usually). This is the cunning of the inferiority complex. Such warders always prey upon the semi-literate men of peasant origin who happen not to be proficient in English or in Afrikaans. This shameful opinion leads to the gravest indignities and insults and all that the abused prisoner can do is to 'grin and bear it' because complaining seldom leads to results other than retaliation.

The absolutely incredible depth of such warders' ignorance and hallucinatory situation can be gauged from a story such as the following: when a new medical orderly during 1968 first came to the single-cells with the medicine tray to dish out drugs and ointments he refused to do his duty unless the prisoners called him *Baas*. They refused, or course, and he marched away. The section officer had to speak to him at length before he agreed (rudely and reluctantly) to give the men their medicines. Prisoners spoke to him for months until he became one of the most understanding and sympathetic warders in the hospital. This is a minor incident which could be repeated in different variations *ad nauseam*. Many warders still resent the fact that they are not spoken to as members of a superordinate caste by lower-caste people who – to add insult to injury – have the opprobrious status of 'prisoner' and are thus really outcasts in their eyes.

(c) Expecting personal favours as a matter of course from prisoners. Prisoners are expected to carry their lunch baskets, polish their shoes, etc. Few prisoners are now prepared to do this as they know that there is no legal compulsion for them to do so. Indeed, the Regulations specifically forbid this. Of course, many prisoners realise that petty refusal to perform a trivial task which is in no way humiliating exacerbates the atmosphere and leads to retaliation which is disproportionate to the 'offence'. Yet it *is* irritating and provoking to see a youngster in uniform order one who could be his grandfather to shift a chair for him a few feet when he is totally free to do so himself.

(d) 'Playing' with prisoners in the most insulting way, i.e. throwing stones at them, knocking them about, well knowing that they may not hit back on pain of being severely assaulted. Political prisoners have seldom allowed this kind of familiarity to develop and in the few regrettable cases where it has happened there was usually a basic political flaw in the make-up of the prisoner concerned.

(e) Giving frivolous commands to prisoners. Nowadays political prisoners flatly refuse to carry out any illegal or unreasonable commands no matter what the consequences.

The elasticity of the warders is truly phenomenal. Few people can realise to what extent the National Party's indoctrination of South African Whites, especially of those in the civil service, has succeeded.[12] One sees this very clearly in the sedulous somersaults performed by warders and officers regarding their attitudes to and treatment of Black prisoners. These men are mere automata, will-less instruments of government policy; when some higher-up throws the switch, the rest follows almost mechanically, i.e. few, if any, warders refuse to carry out an instruction no matter what its nature.

One of the most bewildering and breath-taking metamorphoses was that of an officer who subsequently became the OC and now even appears to have become a kind of departmental spokesman on matters relating to Blacks. From having been a mere hooligan, commissioned for no apparent reason and in effect to torment and oppress unfortunate prisoners, he became a suave, 'polished' diplomat, ever ready to accede to reasonable requests and always seeking to draw out the prisoners in discussions on social, political, and cultural problems. Almost all warders lead this Jekyll and Hyde existence. By means of cross-reference, it has become possible to establish that the 'kindest' most civil warders in their own milieu are just as abusive and contemptuous as those who continue to display their hostility openly. This group schizophrenia, this living in two different worlds simultaneously, undoubtedly conceals profound philosophical problems but this is not the place to generalise and speculate about these.

WORK

All political prisoners are sentenced to 'hard labour', a very vague term, which is interpreted most whimsically, depending on policy, temperament, and atmosphere at the various levels of the prison bureaucracy.

Unlike common-law prisoners who, at least theoretically, have the possibility of receiving training in some skill or other, the political prisoners on Robben Island have none. In all the years only a tiny minority has received some semblance of training in trades such as stone-dressing, plumbing, tailoring, and shoemaking. Not only are they denied access to skills normally accessible to any prisoner who 'behaves' himself, but they are also deprived of the tiny gratuity which the prison authorities pay their skilled wards.

Not only have the authorities refused hitherto to adopt a general policy of training political prisoners in skilled work but they have also refused as a general rule to encourage those few prisoners who have acquired skills in crafts such as weaving, metalwork, cardboard-work, etc. by refusing to buy for them the materials that would enable them to practice their crafts. Since the creative urge will manifest itself no matter what the odds against it, such gifted people have often produced miraculous artefacts virtually from nothing, from odd bits of wood or stone, from the flotsam and jetsam which wash the shores of Robben Island so abundantly.

It is one of the most bitter comments on the *Herrenvolk* mentality of many warders to say that, far from standing in awe before such creativity, dexterity, and patience, they have taken a sadistic delight in either destroying or confiscating or frustrating the artefacts so produced. Some of the Namibians and others used to make beautiful woven belts from pieces of nylon thread washed up by the sea. These were regularly confiscated and burnt by some warders and as regularly replenished by the prisoners. The desire for colour and pattern, the artistic urge to create something meaningful, cannot be killed by the morony and barbarism of the custodians! The favourite legal 'cover' for this vandalism was the argument derived from the Regulations (which are observed more usually in the breach) that such articles were 'not authorised'. Yet it would be the easiest thing to legalise them!

The behaviour sketched above stems from the deliberate policy of making political prisoners do the most menial, most soul-destroying labour year after year with a view to crushing their morale and dulling their thinking powers. The vast majority of the prisoners have for all the years done one or other of the following jobs:

(a) quarrying stones in the stone quarry;
(b) quarrying lime in the lime quarry;
(c) chopping wood;
(d) crushing (knapping) stones in the yards or at the quarries;
(e) making or repairing roads with pick and shovel;
(f) dragging seaweed from the beaches and from the sea;
(g) general cleaning in the yards and cells;
(h) 'staff jobs' in the hospital, offices, kitchens.

It should be remembered that they have done so despite all attempts to get the authorities to change the quality of the work. The valid argument was often put to the authorities that not even the most hardened criminals are expected to work at this kind of labour for more than a couple of years, and that it was thus doubly onerous to let the political prisoners spend their entire term of imprisonment sweating it out in the quarries and elsewhere.

It was in this connection, incidentally, that Brigadier Aucamp told Nelson Mandela that prison policy regarding political prisoners is decided on in conjunction with the police, i.e. the security branch. It should also be recorded that in 1965 (February), soon after the single-cells prisoners had started working in the lime quarry (after a stint of the soul-destroying knap-line) the COP himself assured them that if they worked well they would soon be transferred to work of a more satisfying kind. Lest the mischievous inference be drawn that the proposition contained in the antecedent of this statement was not realised in practice, it should be stated that some of the most experienced warders – who had no special liking for the prisoners – admitted directly and indirectly that considering the age-composition and the prevalence of physical ailments in this group, their work in the first few years left little to be desired.

In this connection, also, the most blatant breach of faith has to be recorded. In 1968 the representatives of the International Red Cross (IRC) were told by the highest authorities that the prisoners were no longer working in the lime quarry.[13] Care was taken to ascertain that there had been no misunderstanding about this. Yet even while the authorities were telling this to Mr Senn and his colleagues the prisoners were continuing in the lime quarry. While the Red Cross representatives were on Robben Island in that year, and for a few days thereafter, the prisoners in the single-cells section were taken to work elsewhere but soon they were back in the quarry. This farce went on year after year until any temporary removal from the lime quarry could be infallibly interpreted as a sign that some important (usually foreign) visitor was expected. Red Cross representatives have been shocked, dismayed, and even disgusted every time they were informed that these prisoners were still at the same kind of work. The matter would be a cause for mere sadness if it did not have a nasty sequel to which reference will be made in a different context. This kind of blatant contempt for the prisoners – of which more examples will be quoted in due course – is perhaps the most important cause of the almost complete lack of confidence in the authorities on the part of most prisoners.

No good purpose would be served by a detailed account of the harassments and torments to which prisoners have been subjected in connection with work. Instead, a few representative instances and episodes will be cited.

It should be borne in mind that there were four distinct phases of treatment corresponding to the swinging of the 'pendulum', however *ex post facto* the pendulum argument actually is. From 1962 until early 1967 working conditions and the work climate were the worst imaginable, the periods 1962–1965 and August to November 1966 brought periods of real hell during which the savagery of the warders was given free rein and without any doubt officially encouraged. Then from 1967 until late 1970 there was a period of relative sanity with only occasional flare-ups of violence and open injustice, to be followed by the relapse of 1971–1972 which set back the progress made in the preceding period in a most lamentable manner since it shattered the illusions about the sense of fair-play of the authorities. The period since 1973 has seen a resumption of progress as far as the work climate is concerned.

It should also be remembered that in fact there is not much work to be done on Robben Island. Relatively little lime or stone is required for local use and there is no profit in transporting it to the mainland. Hence the pointlessness of the whole thing weighs heavily on the prisoners who are, of course, treated as automata, never being told what the ultimate practical goal of their work is. Often mountains of stone and lime, quarried by antediluvian methods and with the most primitive instruments have lain literally for years, blown away by the wind and washed away by the rain without any use being made of them.

In bad periods irresponsible and power-crazed wardens have often compelled prisoners to move these mountains from one spot to another only to instruct them a few days later to move them back to the original location. Such humiliations are the bitter bread of imprisonment, which had to be eaten daily in the early years. To add insult to injury, these warders would ridicule and laugh at prisoners whom they forced to do these things. Needless to say, refusal to carry out such frivolous orders was rewarded with dire punishments and triumphant pharisaical accusations of insubordination, insolence, etc.

To come to a few concrete instances: for years the 'knap-line' was one of the main points of friction and confrontation between the political prisoners and the authorities. Anyone who has seen what is involved will realise that this form of retributive punishment can drive the most phlegmatic man into a state of fury. Prisoners have to sit from 7:30 or so in the morning until 4 pm with only one hour break for lunch, crushing large stones with a five-pound hammer down to a fine gravel to be used on roads and in concrete mixtures, *inter alia*. To the novice, of course, it is a traumatic, nightmarish experience especially when he is faced with the threat of punishment for not crushing the prescribed quota (and the authorities continue to enforce piece-work even though their own courts have ruled that such enforcement is illegal in terms of the Act and the Regulations).

The work is maddening enough: the very knowledge that there are pneumatic machines which can produce in a few hours what a span of prisoners produce in one year is enough to drive one to desperation. To have to sit in the sun without moving and (for months at the beginning) without being allowed to speak to one's neighbour was hell on earth. But some officers went further: they would often punish the prisoners by seating them in the most disadvantageous places in the quarry, especially those corners where the cold north-westerly or the fierce south-easterly winds could buffet them throughout the day.

Any crisis in the prison would lead to an increase in the number of prisoners placed on the knap-line and in the inconvenience factor introduced by the authorities. Invariably, especially in the general section, a confrontation would ensue leading to dangerous and nasty situations. Whenever the majority or all of the prisoners fulfilled the quota, the latter would be increased and/or the size of the stones decreased. Such open harassment tried the patience of the prisoners to the utmost. Any failure to fulfil the quota was transformed into a charge of 'refusing to work' with the usual consequence of dietary punishment.

In 1968 the magistrate's court in a test case ruled that piece-work was illegal. Thereafter the method of exposing the prisoners to the elements was intensified until one of the most serious confrontations between prisoners and authorities occurred.[14] It should be noted that this petty persecution – which often had major consequences – went on over a period of many years and, indeed, continues in a disguised form to this very day. The whole should also be seen in the context of prisoners who are not given enough to eat and do not have adequate clothing to put on. Often prisoners have been forced to work in the rain without the protection of waterproof coverings. On the knap-line, where there is little movement of the body involved, this could be disastrous, especially at the time when prisoners had no change of clothing.

One of the worst incidents, extreme but revealing a pattern of behaviour, occurred in the period August–September 1966 until November

1966. It was at this stage that it became very obvious that the political prisoners were in some ways being treated as hostages who had to be made to pay for the activities of revolutionary organisations with which they were associated, and often of organisations and individuals entirely unrelated to them.

In August 1966 the first Namibians accused of 'terrorist' activities were arrested and on 6 September 1966 Dr Verwoerd was assassinated.[15] A few days later a regime of brutal violence was introduced especially in the single-cells section. A certain warder, Van Rensburg, apparently specially chosen for his heartlessness, and hooliganism, was brought to be in charge of the single-cells working span. He began to force prisoners to do superhuman work. They were expected to wield their picks and shovels continuously, without letting up until 12 noon when lunch was supposed to be given. Any interruption of work was immediately followed by the threat and often by the reality of being charged for 'refusing to work'. The hardest possible areas of the lime quarry were selected to be worked on and the many elderly and sickly people in this span experienced the roughest time of their whole prison career. As far as possible younger and healthier people tried to cover up for them. Moreover, all this calculated harassment was accompanied by a stream of the most vulgar abuse and race-baiting that a South African white of the worst description is capable of. All attempts to make Van Rensburg behave more sanely were non-starters and merely led to an intensification of the whole thing.

The position was reached where the prisoners simply refused to speak to this person under any circumstances. Had Mrs Suzman not come in February 1967 there is no saying what might have happened. It was the knowledge of her impending visit which forced the authorities to let up and the visit itself and the reporting of this particularly contemptible form of persecution to her were directly responsible for the eventual transfer of this person to another prison (Bellville), there to practice his pettiness and express his sadism to his heart's content on the defenceless 'criminals' held in that institution for 'safe' custody. Van Rensburg, incidentally, had a swastika tattooed on his middle finger and though this may have been connected with a Nazi tradition in his family (he maintained that his father had had this nefarious symbol tattooed on the son's finger before he was of an age to know what it meant) it is not unlikely that he was a member of the notorious 'Big-Five' gang of pimps, sodomists, and trouble-shooters, to which many of the more disreputable warders also belong, a fact which Van Rensburg obviously would not have been too keen to divulge to these prisoners! For some arcane reason the 'Big Fives' chose the Nazi trade mark as their badge.[16]

The situation in the lime quarry led to one of the worst events in the history of Robben Island on 4 January 1971. About the middle of 1970, the single-cells prisoners working in the lime quarry began to lose all hope of ever being taken from there. Most of them had already been working there for six full years with only very brief intervals when they chopped wood or made the road to the landing strip. Consequently, the prisoners were psychologically beaten; all ways of trying to make the work interesting failed, more especially after the authorities prohibited singing at work. One of the ways in which the prisoners tried to keep up discipline was by singing rhythmic communal songs and working to the beat. The prohibition derived from the allegation that the prisoners were singing 'freedom songs', whatever that might mean! Gradually prisoners began to work only when they were egged on to do so and even those who tried to maintain a voluntary discipline at last gave up, so that by the end of 1970 there was little work going on in the quarry.

Numerous discussions were held with the authorities during this period in an attempt to get an alteration of work, but all to no avail. Then, in December 1970, a new commanding officer, one Colonel Badenhorst, who was due for retirement in 1971/1972, and who turned out to be the crassest scoundrel ever put in charge of the prisoners on Robben Island, was appointed. Two weeks after his appointment, i.e. on 4 January 1971, he struck his first blow. Without warning, and without giving the prisoners an opportunity of defending themselves, he accused the 16 prisoners who happened to be in the quarry on that day of refusing to work, and summarily demoted all of them to the next lowest grade. Despite protests and subsequent attempts to have the injustice redressed, his decision stood and had drastic psychological and material consequences for many of the prisoners in that they lost their study privilege, *inter alia*, as the direct result of this act of his. This is but one single instance of how labour has been, and is, used to harass, torment, and generally to disadvantage prisoners.

One point remains to be made: Throughout the years all prisoners have constantly asked for better and more rewarding types of work. This is a request made on principle and also because it is a practical necessity. The IRC representatives have annually put forward very constructive proposals but few, if any, of these have hitherto been followed up by the authorities at RIP. There are many things which prisoners could do on the

Island that would be much more interesting. Apart from trades and crafts, there is the possibility of administering the whole prison, due allowance being made for security precautions deemed necessary by the authorities. Yet it must be realised that the tedium of the work, the loss of interest in all forms of prison work, and the antagonistic attitudes engendered by the callous abuse of power by hypocritical authorities, have brought about a situation, psychologically speaking, where in very many cases it might prove a difficult task to get prisoners to perform enthusiastically any work the authorities might give them. In any case, there is no doubt that for most, if not all, the prisoners' work, apart from general cleaning, ought to be optional, more especially for the older men. It is a fact after all that the majority of the prisoners have already completed eight years and a large percentage have finished ten years on Robben Island. Work cannot be used to 'rehabilitate' political prisoners, who have not been arrested because of being work-shy or anti-social in other ways. Hence compulsory labour is really a form of humiliation and punishment. Since warders are taught to view all prisoners as criminals, the consequences in times of crisis, whether such crises are genuine or simulated, have always been catastrophic for the prisoners.

FOOD

It is claimed by the prison authorities that the prisoners' diet is prescribed after testing by trained dieticians and medical specialists. There is no reason to dispute this. After all, men do no less for their pigs, poultry, and other slaughter stock in our day. What is not to be disputed also is the fact that for many years the authorities seemed to confuse prisoners and pigs, in that the fodder that was prepared for the men would normally be thrown to the pigs. Quite possibly, the calorie prescriptions were met but there is no prescribed manner of preparation. Besides the normal hazards of large institutional feeding, the factor of contempt and indifference to the comfort of their charges gave rise to meals that would have been inedible if it were not true that hunger is the best cook. As long as the provisions of the Regulations pertaining to diet appeared to be met, the authorities were satisfied. Lunch and supper, especially the supper of African prisoners, were sometimes so full of sand and miscellaneous kinds of dirt and insects that even the strong stomachs of the most hard-bitten would somersault, and it was an ineffable tragedy to see how hungry people would sometimes leave food uneaten.

Perennial representations were made for the better preparation of food, suggestions were given, but all this made little difference until in 1973/1974 some political prisoners, chosen by the inmates themselves, went to work in the kitchen. Since then the preparation of food is incomparably better and under the circumstances probably the best possible.

The diet scales of South African prisoners are now well-known. The major objection to them is, of course, the discrimination between Whites, Coloureds and Indians, and Africans.[17] The political demand for equality of treatment is raised on every possible occasion by the political prisoners.[18] Quite apart from the lack of scientific basis for discrimination, this practice – like discrimination in clothing but so much worse – represents the absolute limit of contempt for people. In a country where – at least for the urbanised majority – basic eating habits are the same for all, it is a most revealing fact that government classified its prisoners according to a scale of (material) values. Since all Black prisoners are incarcerated together, it is most disconcerting that there should be discrimination among them also. While in a politically conscious and enlightened community as on Robben Island, this can have no more than irritation value, it is a well-known fact that this irrational 'differentiation' contributes markedly to the reinforcement of racial prejudice among many non-political prisoners. Thus, for many African prisoners, it becomes a mark of elevated status to be given 'Coloured' food for whatever reasons (illness, pimping, good behaviour, promotion) while many Coloured and Indian prisoners consider themselves to be superior human beings because of the better food they are given by the *Herrenvolk* authorities. These frank statements are made despite knowledge of the 'sociological' and economic arguments used by government apologists to justify discrimination. The sociological fraud is perpetrated so easily that it becomes tedious rather than necessary to expose the dishonesty of such arguments There is no reason at all why all prisoners should not be given the same diet.

A glance at the changes in the diet scales will reveal that certain relative qualitative changes have taken place over the years. Generally speaking, these have been changes for the better. In particular, the tendency has been away from the over-starched diet which used to be the bane of prisoners, especially African prisoners. What has been called the 'policy of the full belly' is gradually giving way to a more civilised diet although at times this tends to become a 'policy of the empty belly'. Though food riots have never taken place on Robben Island, it is a fact that on occasion hunger strikes have been resorted to because of unsatisfactory food. In general, however, the attitude of the prisoners has been one of patiently repeating reasonable requests and making serious suggestions for improvements.

One of the most unjust aspects of the diet is the lack of fruit. For a place which is situated so near to some of the largest orchards in the country, RIP is suspiciously free of fruit. The only occasions on which fruit has been seen were those on which the IRC representatives were allowed to give money to the prison command for a few issues of fruit, oranges.

EDUCATION

This is a vast subject which it is impossible to discuss adequately in a document of this nature but because of its importance all the major relevant aspects are treated in some detail here.

The Prisons Act provides that every prisoner shall be encouraged to pursue an approved course of studies during his imprisonment. As far as Black prisoners in South Africa are concerned this noble injunction on the Prison authorities remained a dead letter for numerous reasons, the discussion of which belongs more properly to a political document. Until the influx of political prisoners serving long terms of imprisonment in the early 1960s, this was the position.

Suddenly, as from 1962, the authorities were confronted with hundreds of prisoners the vast majority of whom were eager to study and were also able to muster the resources privately in order to do so. The result was predictable, and it should be recorded that some of the political prisoners were fully aware of the problem, *viz.*, that the department of prisons was technically unprepared to meet such a situation. Hence, while a few individuals did manage to get registered right at the outset, the majority of the prisoners had to wait up to two and even three years before they could be registered. Since many of the prisoners were in a position to pursue undergraduate and even post-graduate studies, the department was acutely embarrassed as it simply did not have the personnel to administer such an operation.

There are very few graduates (relatively) on the staff of the department of prisons and such men are usually drafted to headquarters to man the central administration. The department could not, therefore, simply delegate the work of organising the education of political prisoners to an appropriately qualified person. Let it be stated therefore, that having regard to all the circumstances, and despite numerous and fundamental criticisms, it redounds to the credit of the department that many prisoners were able to complete their studies successfully. A solution to the problem was eventually found in a way which, though reasonably efficient, had many drawbacks since ultimate decisions on all important matters were taken by presumably qualified people in Pretoria while local decision-making was restricted as far as possible. What happened eventually should have been foreseen. Rules of thumb were made, for instance, in connection with questions such as censorship and the passing of books and other study materials. The local man, usually a matriculant, would in his own interest apply these rules strictly according to his lights. Again, the results are easily imagined; whimsical, arbitrary, fortuitous, these are the terms which describe the situation. A post-graduate prisoner's achievement in an assignment would depend on the temperament or the penetration of a junior warder who may or may not have passed his matriculation examination!

It should be stressed that once the department had survived the initial paroxysm of savagery (about mid-1965) it did not manifest any basic objection to prisoners studying even though most warders found it galling that the men they hated so should be officially permitted to improve themselves. This latter aspect is one of the many Frankensteins spawned by the colour bar to the detriment of the disfranchised oppressed people. For it follows that if the prison's department wanted to carry out the stated intention of the legislature regarding the education of prisoners it would have to take cognisance of the possible sense of inferiority of the majority of warders (who have just about passed the Junior Certificate) in a milieu of prisoners many of whom had either passed or were busy studying for their matriculation certificate.[19] In short, as long as it was a question of persuading reluctant 'criminals' to study (and in most cases to attain some level of literacy) the warders would not be affected adversely since many of them would even experience a childish delight in assisting (or ridiculing) the supposedly 'stupid' prisoner. But as soon as the 'stupid' prisoner happens to have or to obtain a higher formal educational standard than his custodian, the latter is apt to feel that someone in authority is trying to embarrass him, especially when the prisoner happens to be Black.

As far as Robben Island is concerned the facts are approximately as follows: more than 30 per cent of the prisoners at all times have had a better formal education than the average warder. Many have had better formal qualifications than any member of the prison administration. A small minority was completely illiterate, and a larger minority could not read or write English and Afrikaans but was literate in a Bantu language.

It is, of course, a well-known fact of perceptual psychology that indoctrination is a method of altering one's perception of the world, and it should surprise no one to learn that most warders originally could not see the political prisoners as anything other than animals and sub-humans. As long as they were interested and permitted only to torture, torment, and harass their charges this percept remained constant and probably the majority really believed themselves to be superior beings. Hatred and policy insulated them from contamination and feelings of inferiority. But obviously in such an environment the authorities could never allow hundreds of prisoners to study, and thus to behave as 'superior' beings among a set of White warders, for most of whom the zenith of social intercourse is represented by a loud-mouthed controversy in the local bar about the relative merits of this or that rugby team or some such inanity.

Not until the department had endeavoured to alter this perceptual squint by means of a crash programme of educating the warders could it really begin to allow many prisoners to study. Of course, many of the die-hard warders had to be removed physically before anything could be done. A transitional stage in warders' attitudes towards prisoners' studies (both in general and in individual cases) is represented by the habit of ridiculing or playing down the importance of the prisoners' student activities. By way of a heart-breaking example, consider the regularity with which one hears ordinary warders (also studying privately for matric) asking pathetically from the warder in charge of studies whether the prisoners writing matric write exactly the same papers as they themselves do! Many, even after being assured that this is unfortunately the position, continue to maintain that either the papers are not the same or that the examiners do not mark the papers written by Blacks as strictly as those written by Whites.

Only after many years did a large section of warders begin to respect some of the prisoners not only for their educational achievements but also for their courage in persevering under adverse conditions. Many warders maintain – no doubt with a measure of truth – that the prisoners have an advantage (!!) over the warders in that their enforced isolation leaves them no option but to study. From this last statement, another facet of this problem emerges, *viz.*, the fact that in recent years on the side of the warders a feeling of rivalry has been born. Many warders, it seems, actually study because they realise their limitations and disadvantages *vis-à-vis* the political prisoners and because better educational qualifications imply promotion and better wages. To write the same examination as a Black prisoner and to do worse at it would, of course, explode the private *Herrenvolk* myth. Hence all the subterfuges invented by the frantic minds of those who come face to face with the unpleasant reality of Blacks doing well when given the opportunity. Though the prisoners have always welcomed this rivalry – no matter how unhealthy its origins – they have often had to pay for it, as will be seen.

From about 1966 onwards, matters began to improve and in fact until the end of 1969 there were no systematic attempts to curtail the study privilege. Almost all prisoners who applied to study were allowed to do so and they could study the subjects of their choice, provided such subjects could be studied under the technical conditions prevailing on the Island. Certain exceptions will be noted presently. During these four years, there was a distinct development in an enlightened direction and one prisoner[20] was even moved to appeal to the COP to 'let the atmosphere of a university prevail' at Robben Island. Alas, this euphoria was not to last. As will be pointed out, the present direction is the exact reverse of the 'happy' years.

It is time to enumerate the technical details relevant to the administration and the tenure of the study privilege at Robben Island.

Firstly, no prisoner is allowed to *apply* to study unless the full costs of the tuition fees and prescribed literature are already credited to his prison account. Except in rare cases of leniency, if a prisoner is temporarily short of even a small sum to cover this requirement, he cannot apply or he has to cut out some of the courses he intended studying, which may not always be possible. And this, even if the institution makes provision for payment by instalment, as most of them do. Of course, this is in some ways a sensible arrangement but the rigidly bureaucratic implementation thereof has often tended to undermine the letter and the spirit of the Act, which enjoins the authorities to 'encourage', and not to obstruct, prisoners' studies.

Secondly, once a prisoner has been granted permission to study, he is obliged to sign an undertaking, the crucial provision of which states that should he abuse his study privilege by using his material for anything unrelated to his studies he may be compelled to forfeit this privilege for the rest of his period of incarceration. Initially, prisoners were unwilling to sign this undertaking as it could clearly be interpreted in the wildest possible manner. Only after the COP himself gave assurances that it would not be implemented in a petty manner did most prisoners agree to sign it.

Technically, of course, this undertaking represents an attempt to free the authorities from any liability for damages arising from the deprivation of studies. For most of the period under review the authorities have in fact honoured the assurances given by the COP, but during 1971/1972 and occasionally before then these assurances were openly ignored. The period 1971/1972 will be referred to below.

One instance may be quoted of the whimsical manner in which a prisoner could be stymied in his endeavour to study. One of the prisoners[21] in the general section had (in 1967) written with a ball-point pen a few points on the palm of his hand to remind him of what he wanted to discuss with a visitor (a relative) he was to see on that Saturday. It should be noted that at the time the authorities rigidly refused to allow prisoners to carry any memoranda on paper to the visitors' cubicles. Instead of charging, reprimanding, or punishing the prisoner concerned for contravening this (customary rather than legal) prohibition, the officer responsible at that time pettily and vindictively deprived the prisoner of his study privileges summarily. The result was that until 1970 this prisoner was not allowed to study. There were many such episodes later, underlining the arbitrary manner in which the privilege was administered in certain periods.

Lastly, since approximately 1966 prisoners are allowed to register with only four correspondence colleges, to wit, UNISA, Rapid Results College, Transafrika, and Volks Correspondence College.[22] The last-mentioned three institutions cater for the pre-university students. Right at the beginning prisoners could also register with London University or with ICS but this permission was gradually abolished and at present no prisoner is registered with any but these four colleges. It has been one of the great complaints of the prisoners that in thus limiting them the authorities restrict their choice of subjects quantitatively and of tuition qualitatively. In some instances, especially at university level, this has meant that subjects that it would otherwise have been possible to study under prison conditions had to be abandoned or simply passed over. Certain officials have made no secret of the fact that their objection to overseas colleges such as London University stems from their lack of influence on such institutions. It is well known to the prisoners that many things, both positive and negative from their point of view, have been done by the authorities 'via the backdoor', as it were, in that government departments were involved in the ultimate analysis and consequently the prisons department could make its influence felt.

In recent years the education of political prisoners has come under fire. For years it was very obvious that their permitting political prisoners to study was a kind of diplomatic trump card which the authorities were using in and out of season to refute allegations of ill-treatment of such prisoners. For reasons which are still obscure to some extent there seems to have been a moving away from this position, and the present tendency is to curtail, and possibly even to abolish, any serious study by the political prisoners.

An account of some of the obstacles, some of them integral to the prison situation, others created by policy, will show how this attack on prisoners' education has developed.

There are, firstly, the physical conditions in prison. To study systematically in prison demands much perseverance, inspiration, and discipline. After a hard day's tedious and tiring labour – especially in winter – it is not to be expected that most men would sit down conscientiously to their books. Fortunately, those in communal cells can inspire and encourage one another to a certain extent, but the tendency to fall into idleness, or at least into some not-so-demanding routine is very great for most of the men who, of course, have not been scholars outside.

The disciplined student can put in up to five hours of solid work every night but in fact most prisoners cannot do this after an ordinary day's work since they require one or two hours' sleep or relaxation. No prisoner is allowed to study after 11 pm, even though the lights must burn throughout the night in all cells (as Robben Island is an ultra-maximum security prison). This means that whereas most men would prefer to sleep immediately after a day's work for six to seven hours and to study thereafter, they are compelled to study when they are tired. This has often been pointed out to policy-making officials who have as often replied most unconvincingly that any other arrangement would lead to prisoners being too tired or too sleepy to do their work during the day. The answers to this – unless one assumes a completely irresponsible set of prisoners – are too obvious to mention. In fact, of course, this is just one more way of making the prisoner feel all the time that he is not free to do as he pleases, that he is controlled, and also to ensure for the authorities an opening should they wish to 'tighten the screw'.

It should be clear by now that 'the swinging of the pendulum' has much bearing on whether or not work becomes a serious obstacle to studies. In bad periods prisoners can virtually be prevented from studying by being overworked during the day; in good periods prisoners may have more time and leisure than many a full-time student in the free world outside. At examination time prisoners have customarily been granted a day off from work immediately before every paper or subject which they write, unless such a paper is written on a Monday or immediately after a public holiday observed in prison. In bad periods or under vindictive regimes prisoners have often been forced to work harder at examination time.

Secondly, certain obstacles to studying are deliberately placed in the way of prisoners. Of these, one of the oldest and most effective is prevention or obstruction from access to finance. As indicated above, the prisons department, partly to cover itself, insists that a prospective student should have to his credit in prison the total costs of the course he wishes to study. In the case of university students, this often runs into hundreds of Rands. Consequently, no matter what kind of assistance many prisoners may receive, they are in this way debarred from studying altogether, or at least from what and how they wish to study. It should be stressed again that all the colleges have provision for payment of their courses by instalment.

Relevant to this is the scrapping by UNISA, as of April 1968 with or without the connivance of the department of prisons, of the discount allowed to prisoners. Until April 1968 prisoners were expected to pay the full registration fee but only 50 per cent of all the tuition fees and it is understood that this concession was originally negotiated by the department of prisons itself, acting in accordance with the spirit of the Prisons Act. Needless to say, this was of great assistance to all prisoners and was much appreciated by them. The withdrawal of this concession was, therefore, a heavy blow and a decided indication that the mood of the department concerning education was changing. All subsequent attempts to get the department to renegotiate this concession have been in vain; yet it could not be maintained seriously that UNISA would suffer any financial loss considering the negligible number of prisoners who are pursuing university studies. Or was it that once again the authorities had to act with an eye on the reactions of envious warders and a reactionary electorate, which might ask awkward questions about facilitating education for 'murderers' and 'traitors'?

Many organisations, including NUSAS, the churches, and overseas organisations, were (and are) prepared to finance the studies of political prisoners.[23] NUSAS originally wanted to run a book scheme as well. While the authorities allowed financial assistance to be given by such *bona fide* organisations for the first three years or so, they stopped it abruptly thereafter, and all monies which did not come from friends or relatives were either returned or frozen for long periods, thus making it impossible for a prisoner to register for a year or more. Even monies sent by attorneys on behalf of relatives or organisations were treated similarly. Most families, of course, cannot afford the sums involved especially since the person needing funds was invariably the breadwinner of his family before his incarceration. It is also well known that the security police have time and again interrogated and intimidated people (even relatives) who have sent money (especially relatively large sums) to prisoners. In this way there has in recent years been a systematic campaign to cut off prisoners from financial resources for purposes of education and *this campaign has succeeded to a painful degree*. This matter requires careful study and possibly even needs to be tested in a court of law.

Payment of fees for another prisoner is strictly prohibited and this prohibition is rigidly implemented.

Finally, the original criterion for permission to study a subject was the technical feasibility of doing so, and in rare instances obvious security considerations played a part. Hence certain science subjects requiring laboratory experimentation were impossible. Post-graduate research for production of a thesis was apparently also out of the question since the reason given to Neville Alexander by the COP why his application to do a doctorate in German was turned down was that this would involve the writing of a thesis, and even if no archival research were necessary it could not be allowed.

The situation changed dramatically as from about 1969. From that time onwards there was a distinct attitude of suspicious parsimony towards prisoners' studies on the part of the authorities.

Certain measures tending to curtail and restrict the study privilege (e.g. financial measures) have already been referred to. Choice of subjects also came under fire. Political science and history were forbidden in 1969 though they were partly reinstated later and are at present very vulnerable subjects.

All post-graduate studies, including law, were forbidden at the end of 1969, Minister Pelser stating in parliament in answer to one of Mrs Suzman's questions that it was not the policy of the department to 'produce specialists'. But in private Brigadier Aucamp told some prisoners that 'the Whites' in Pretoria had 'abused' post-graduate studies for purposes of continuing to study guerrilla warfare. Probably he told the Whites the same thing about the Blacks. One can speculate about the actual reasons for this irrational, small-minded ban, but one factor is certainly the fact that it is much more difficult for the authorities to restrict and control the books used by post-graduate students, most of whom have to roam freely in the relevant literature, than it is to do the same as regards undergraduates. In the case of at least one prisoner, this ban meant that he had to abandon his LLB studies in his final year when he still had another four years to serve.

Of course, this ban was not difficult to conceive since hardly any White criminals would be affected by it, and no Blacks either. The only prisoners who could suffer were in fact political prisoners. As of 1971, no law subjects whatsoever could be studied. Even Nelson Mandela, who was given special permission to complete his LLB with London University (with which he was registered almost from the time he entered prison in 1962), was eventually given the deadline of June 1974, after which he would no longer be allowed to study either law or any other post-graduate courses and, of course, he would have to register with UNISA.

The latest subject to be brought into jeopardy is 'native administration'. As will become evident in the next section, the main reason for the banning of these subjects appears to be the fact that certain categories of books can enter the prison legally to form the basis of studying these subjects. At one stage all foreign languages were banned, i.e. only languages spoken in South Africa could be studied, but after a few years this ban became inoperative (incidentally because of changes of administration – regularly prohibitions and injunctions of previous years became null and void after such a change of staff). Again, the main reason seems to have been that access to books is frowned upon by the authorities, but through the grapevine it was learnt that the study of a language such as Portuguese was forbidden to prevent contact between FRELIMO and other anti-Portuguese Imperialist organisations, and prisoners on Robben Island.[24]

Since approximately 1970, all students, including university students, have to apply annually for permission to study in the year concerned. Whereas previously a prisoner wishing to study for the BA degree would be given permission for the whole period required to complete the degree, he is now given permission only for the year in which he applies. This enables the authorities to deprive a prisoner of his studies much more easily and, more important, this method increases the prisoner's feeling of insecurity. In fact, this measure is in line with the general tendency of the department to use studies as a lever with which to impose their kind of discipline on the political prisoners, the idea being that most prisoners will go to almost any lengths in order to retain their study privileges. This tendency became marked and in fact fully entrenched in the bad period of 1971/1972 under the regime of Badenhorst. We have already referred to the arbitrary demotion of prisoners on 4 January 1971.

The method of summary demotion was consciously adopted as a strategy by the authorities in order to bypass the provision in the Regulations regarding the prisoners' right to legal representation on their being charged. This point will be discussed in due course. But the first wave of prisoners to be demoted were actually ambushed by the authorities. Only after they were demoted (and it must be remembered that whatever the legal status of the demotions, the prisoners were *not* demoted for alleged abuse of study privileges but for quite different alleged offences) were the prisoners told that a special ministerial decree had been authorised after the minister himself had visited the Island (not, of course, to speak to any of the prisoners) whereby any prisoner demoted from a higher classification group to the D-group (i.e. the lowest group a prisoner can be in) was automatically deprived of his study privileges, until such time as by 'good behaviour' he once more merits promotion to the C-group. At that stage, the prisoner may reapply for permission, which permission may or may not be granted to him.

This malicious and inconceivably petty measure by men who have never even considered what it is to live under prison conditions had catastrophic results in a catastrophic situation. The worst warders came into the spotlight, haunting and hunting the most disciplined prisoners precisely because of their independence and their lack of concern with their 'custodians', in order to show them who really wielded power. Prisoners had to consider seriously whether there was any point in 'nursing their studies' (as it was dubbed), when the conditions of treatment deteriorated consistently. It was the easiest thing on earth for a vindictive, inferior-minded warder to provoke a prisoner so that he could march off the latter to the office and thus have him demoted on his say so.

It is learnt that in the single-cells section alone, out of a group of prisoners of about 30 only 8 prisoners managed in this period to retain the study privilege. The rest lost it through demotion to the D-group and with one or two exceptions none of them could in any sense be said to have abused his study privilege. This method of using studies for disciplinary purposes has since been used frequently if not blatantly as in the first months of 1971.

The now well-known Hassiem-Venkatrathnam cases against the Robben Island Prison authorities has a sequel in regard to studies which is very instructive and revealing indeed.[25] The Diemont Judgement ordered, *inter alia*, that Hassiem be registered for the BCompt for which he had originally been given permission. In actual fact, this instruction was carried out dilatorily after a lapse of months but it was clear that the authorities were extremely dissatisfied, especially as the learned judge in his *obiter dicta* had spoken scathingly of the prison department's curiously negative attitude towards legal studies by prisoners. Since it was clear that neither the legislature nor the judiciary could afford to tamper with the existing phraseology and interpretation of the Prisons Act without adverse consequences in the political and diplomatic spheres, an administrative subterfuge had to be found in order to hit back at the prisoners and to hit them in their most delicate spot.

Hence in 1974 the Prison Regulations were amended in such a way as to subvert the spirit of the Act. Now, the granting of permission is purely within the discretion of the OC, and unless lack of education was actually the cause of the prisoner's commission of the offence, he need not be allowed to study. Months before the amendment was formulated and made known to the prisoners, various officials indicated that there were radical changes in the offing in this regard. When asked to interpret the amendment after it was read to the prisoners, the head of the prison said that the department understood the amendment to mean that no post-matriculation studies would be permitted in the future. Those who were already registered would, however, be allowed to complete their degrees with UNISA. Thus, in effect, though it is wrong to assert that political prisoners are no longer allowed to study, it is very clear that should a policy decision be taken to do so, the department can stop all studies for political prisoners without in any way affecting other prisoners. Viewed thus, this measure is clearly in violation of the spirit of the Act, and there is good reason to believe that the regulation is *ultra vires*.

A clear pattern emerges. From an original position of boorish indifference and almost unbelieving unwillingness to consider it proper for *any* prisoner to study, the authorities progressed to a relatively liberal attitude, only to fall back into total opposition to studies for political prisoners. Apart from a political *trauma* which they acquired in this connection, there is no doubt that the authorities also have motives of vindictiveness. Knowing the importance of the privilege to prisoners, they have now decided to use it as a political weapon not only against the prisoners themselves but also against all those forces who plead their case and who support them to a degree. Just as assaults and physical pressures were used in the early days, the more experienced and more sophisticated administration has now resorted to pressures of a less tangible but none the less harmful kind.

It is not certain whether or how long political prisoners will be allowed to study. But if they are allowed, the central question in all matters relating to prison education, *viz.*, access to books, will require very serious study and systematic effort to bring about change. This has been a burning problem from the very beginning but, except for a brief period earlier on and occasional periods of relaxation, the situation has deteriorated to such an extent that the authorities need not ban a subject formally; they need only tell the prisoner that such and such a key work will not be permitted for him to decide that it would be a waste of money to pursue that particular course.

The position, therefore, needs to be described very carefully. To most people who have not had tertiary education one who has a large collection of books is looked upon as being extremely learned and (usually) therefore one to be respected. It is not difficult, therefore, to imagine in what a quandary the prison authorities were (and are placed *vis-à-vis* the White warders) when they realised that the necessarily book-lined cells of the prisoners registered with UNISA automatically subverted the distorted and weird image of these very prisoners obtained from the press and from government (including the department's own) propaganda. While only a few prisoners were studying with UNISA the situation was not intolerable for them, but soon there was a large group and a resultant flood of books and other literature. From being something to show off to foreign visitors these books became a source of acute embarrassment to the authorities who, consequently, began to restrict the number of books entering the prison in every possible way. It should be remembered also that the authorities came to be faced with a very real problem of lack of staff to handle studies. For years they would not appoint more than one studies officer with the result that as more and more men began to do post-matric studies, long delays in censorship of material occurred.

There is no scientific library on Robben Island. The prison library cannot even be compared to a mediocre high school library. The selection of books is purely fortuitous since it depends basically on charity. The greatest fault from the point of view of a student is the total lack of any serious reference works and encyclopaedias. This makes the library virtually useless as a tool of learning which, no doubt, it was not meant to be. All attempts to get the authorities to obtain or to allow the prisoners to obtain such a respectable series as the *Encyclopaedia Britannica* and the *Cambridge Modern History* have been met with point-blank refusals.

For books related to their studies, the prisoners are, therefore, almost entirely dependent on the authorised libraries and on purchases from bookshops. The University of South Africa's library, of course, supplies its registered students with books relevant to assignments excluding prescribed books (except in very special cases); in addition, the prisons department allows prisoners to obtain books from the 'Non-European Division' of the State Library in Pretoria. This latter facility was extremely useful and important to the prisoners until 1973 when, for reasons unknown to the prisoners, they were informed by the State Library that in future only books *prescribed* for courses for which the prisoner was registered would be supplied. Since then, of course, this concession has been quite empty as most prisoners in fact have to buy prescribed works which must be consulted constantly.

The buying of books has two limitations placed on it, *viz.*, censorship (common also to books obtained from libraries) and funds. Most prisoners try to provide before registering for sufficient funds to purchase at least prescribed books; but in view of the rudimentary and inconvenient library facilities they are compelled to buy also as many recommended books as possible. Quite naturally, only very few prisoners can in fact afford to do this. The majority of prisoners have therefore to make do with prescribed material and borrow from others and from libraries (where, in extreme cases, they may have to wait up to two months for books to arrive). There are many problems of a technical nature connected with the buying of books and though these are basically trivial they are often irritating and disruptive in their effects. Prisoners often have to wait for months before a book is delivered, even from official stockists of UNISA. It has happened on many occasions that books have arrived long after the assignments or the examinations for which they were needed had been written.

Censorship of books and of reading matter in general is a permanent problem and it is one that has become worse instead of better over the course of the years. Initially, mainly because of ignorance on the part of the studies officers, almost any book not banned in South Africa was allowed. The COP himself gave the prisoners permission to obtain both *prescribed and recommended* literature. Soon, of course, the precise definition of 'recommended' became an issue, one which has never been satisfactorily resolved.

Today, it appears, the censors have rule-of-thumb criteria which strike the outsider as being totally contradictory and inconsistent. In effect, only those books may be obtained which the censor permits. Since in all cases he never knows the contents of a book until he has read at least the blurb or the foreword, this means that prisoners have to get books from libraries and shops only to be told after the arrival of such books that they may not have them. Books bought from shops are then placed on the prisoners' property to be kept until they are released.[26] Thus whole libraries of innocuous matter have been placed on the property of prisoners. It seldom happens that the censor is persuaded to reconsider his decision and to issue a prohibited book. For those serving long terms and life sentences, this is a draconian measure that has led to much tension and frustration.

The attitude of prisoners in general has been that any book not banned in South Africa should be permitted with the possible exception of books that may undermine prison security; but while some prisoners are prepared to consider this last restriction as a reasonable possibility, the majority refuse to countenance it because of the obvious ways in which it may be abused by unscrupulous administrators.

Censorship of books in the South African context has always been farcical and degrading, but whereas the official South African censors are expected to have a modicum of formal education, the prison censors cannot, unfortunately, and do not, fortunately, have any pretensions about their level of understanding. They are obviously told by higher-ranking officials, and possibly in crash courses, what kinds of books, or rather, titles, to disallow. Any book containing any reference to any of the following concepts are almost automatically withheld: (i) Marx, Marxism; (ii) Lenin, Leninism; (iii) Russia, China, Cuba, etc.; (iv) Socialism, Communism; (v) Revolution, War, Civil War, Violence; (vi) Africa; (vii) Anti-Apartheid Literature; and (viii) Historic-Political Literature written by Blacks.

The consequences need not be spelt out, for they are readily imagined. One could write an entertaining satirical essay on the astonishing obtuseness of censors in general and of Island censors in particular.

A book by Croce on Marxian economic theories caused a first-class row; textbooks on history and politics are replete with lengthy chapters on communism, Marxism, etc. *The Role of Missionaries in Conquest* by Noispho Majeke and many other books are refused merely because they are ostensibly written by Blacks.[27] But no matter how conservative a writer may be, the mere fact that he treats such subjects is enough to shut the gates of Robben Island on his book.

One instructive example involved Neville Alexander, one of the prisoners who, it would appear, suffered most under the insanity of the censors, as he was doing a post-graduate degree in History. During 1968, after the row about Croce's book (involving another prisoner) the then studies officer, a certain Lieutenant Naude (himself not yet a matriculant) announced vindictively and impulsively that in future *no* books dealing with Marxism or communism would be permitted. Alexander was then working on two papers on historiography and philosophy of history, both of which dealt extensively (from an anti-Marxian point of view naturally) with the materialist conception of history and its contribution to historiography and historical science in the twentieth century. Faced with this threat, Alexander drew up a list of prescribed and recommended literature on the basis of UNISA's printed lectures, explaining the relevance of the works and asking that the list be sent to headquarters whence, after months a letter came which Naude read out to Alexander.

In this letter, the COP confirmed that he had read Alexander's request and informed the prisoner that he had consulted the UNISA department of history, which had told him that the prisoner could comfortably complete the papers and the course without the books concerned! To add insult to injury, the COP informed the prisoner that his list was suspect (*'verdag'*)! As though the list had not been necessitated by Naude's asinine threat. One must assume, of course, that if for some unfathomable reason the department of history in fact made such an unacademic assertion, it could have done so only because the facts were misrepresented to it; however, it is extremely difficult to understand why *any* department of history should consider that *any* book is unnecessary for a post-graduate student of history, of all subjects.

To demonstrate the complete Alice-in-Wonderland nature of the situation, it should be said that apparently Alexander applied to the UNISA library for some of these books a few months later despite this official refusal and he received them without the censor so much as suspecting that they were banned.

Recently, another prisoner had the whole list of books prescribed for 'native administration III' (his major) turned down (after having bought the books), even books (such as GD Scholz's work *'n Swart Suide-Afrika*) which were already in the possession of other prisoners! But the quotation of examples cannot add any more to the clarification of the dilemma faced by those prisoners engaged in university studies.

Whatever has been said above about books applies equally to prescribed and recommended scientific journals. With the exception of the *South African Journal of Economics* and *African Studies*, all other scientific journals (legal, historical, economic, anthropological) have at one time or another been proscribed. Those journals that are permitted are usually heavily censored. The most notorious example is the *Financial Mail* (a South African weekly for businessmen and students of economics) which has been stopped on a number of occasions, and if it is allowed in at all nowadays comes with almost all items cut out except some advertisements! Previously, the subscribers continued taking it in the hope that a change of policy would occur, and because they could at least study the weekly stock-exchange reports, until the authorities decided that even these reports were political dynamite! The British *Economist* was banned in 1968 but not before it had arrived for months in an unrecognisably mutilated condition.

From time to time, in order to harass prisoners, the local authorities implement a vicious regulation, in terms of which no prisoner may hand *any* article to any other prisoner without the permission of an authorised person, i.e. of a warder. Naturally, this nonsensical rule is a dead letter at most times, but it is very handy in crisis situations or for the purpose of provoking a crisis. Prisoners are then prohibited from exchanging books, which concession is an obviously indispensable condition of study in the circumstances. It could happen – as it did – that a student of law, needing a copy of the Constitution of the Republic of South Africa, and sleeping only a few feet away from a prisoner possessing a copy of this document (in pursuance of his studies in public administration) would have to buy or order a copy from the library. In either case, he would have to wait weeks to obtain a reference book which he needs for a few minutes at most and which he has but to stretch out his arm to obtain! The incongruousness of all this must have struck the authorities but in their viciousness they implemented the rule rigidly. This, in spite of specific permission from the COP for the exchange of books among prisoners!

On the credit side, it must be noted that throughout the years the authorities have sent off library books used by prisoners at state expense. Prisoners pay for letters and assignments sent off in connection with studies.

The difficulties and frustrations of studying in prison should have emerged clearly from the above notes. Prisoners have nonetheless fared extremely well – in fact, some of them have drawn forth the highest possible praise from the departments in which they were registered.

Apart from the prisoners' maturity and the goal-directedness of their efforts, one of their great advantages has been the possibility of discussing their educational problems among themselves, i.e. having tuition classes regularly (unlike many other external students). Though such 'classes' are officially non-existent, and prohibited, it is well known that they are held. From time to time warders intervene pettily to break up classes, but the force of circumstances is such that they cannot be abolished altogether. Many efforts have been made to get official permission to hold classes and discussions on academic work but such permission has been consistently refused, certainly not for any valid reason but rather as a safeguard in the eventuality of anything occurring where the prisoners might be able to use as an excuse the fact that permission had been granted.

Official permission for holding classes was given only in the case of literacy classes, an innovation, it is believed, deriving from one of the first visits of the IRC representatives. There was a small minority of such illiterates among political prisoners and the appointed tutors went at their task with gusto until by May 1973 there were no longer any illiterates left, except among the Namibians, in whose case a policy of vindictiveness was pursued especially after 1971. As far as is known there is at present no official permission to hold literacy classes among the Namibians even though it is known that there is a need for such classes. Permission to hold literacy classes was used so effectively that one can only hope that the lessons of this experiment will be learnt and implemented generally.

From the above broad exposition of the situation as regards the education of political prisoners at Robben Island it will be seen that this privilege, one of the most important to the prisoner, has been subject to the same miserly policy of giving with one hand and taking with the other.

It is also clear that very probably the 'heyday' of education at Robben Island belongs to the past. There is a definite movement towards the abolition of the privilege in practice, if not in law. In any case, it is to be expected that this will be one of the major areas of confrontation in the immediate future.

In order of priority, the following tasks present themselves: (a) Struggling to retain the privilege to study – and to get it defined as a 'right' rather than a 'privilege'. Reference to South Africa's signature of the International Standard Minimum Rules of the UNO needs to be clarified.[28] (b) Facilitating outside assistance to prisoners needing funds. (c) Restoring the right to pursue post-graduate studies. (d) Liberalising conditions of study in prison.

Related to the question of education in prison are two peripheral issues which can be dealt with conveniently at this point.

Firstly, the Regulations permit prisoners to purchase up to two approved books per week. Some officials interpret this regulation to the effect that the books shall become prison property on the release of the prisoner (but in practice – for purely technical reasons – this is not insisted upon). The latter contention is legally questionable. Initially, the regulation was a dead letter but at present it is operative in a rather sporadic manner. Books purchased are of course subject to censorship and the problems raised in that connection are also relevant here. There is a great need to insist on a more liberal interpretation of the regulation and on obtaining permission for private persons (or organisations) to send books to prisoners, if necessary directly from bookstores, for the simple reason that people outside prison have easy access to bibliographies and the latest developments in any particular field, and can thus guide prisoners in their reading so that they do not lose touch with social reality altogether.

Secondly, a prisoner classified in the A-group is normally entitled to subscribe to a paper and to obtain a radio; but this privilege, among others, is denied to political prisoners. The main reason quoted is that 'for security reasons' the department of prisons (read the Special Branch) cannot allow prisoners to have access to news, in spite of the fact that the department would censor the papers if permitted. This unreasonably vindictive and persecuting attitude is one of the major causes of discontent on Robben Island. For a political prisoner especially, access to news is virtually indispensable (for which reason – as will be shown – they obtain it illegally). Comparison with almost any other comparably-situated country shows that there is simply no valid reason – other than mere vengefulness – for such a prohibition. Department officials, including the present OC, have on occasion indicated that the question is 'under constant review' but this is probably no more than a formal verbal concession. The denial of this privilege is, of course, the surest sign that the South African government in fact recognises the category of 'political prisoner', all Alice-in-Wonderland denials to the contrary notwithstanding. Ironically enough, in many other countries it is the enjoyment of this privilege that distinguishes political prisoners from non-politicals!

It should be noted that certain magazines (e.g. *Farmer's Weekly, Huisgenoot, Reader's Digest, SA Panorama, Lantern,* and *Archimedes*) are allowed in. All these are from time to time heavily censored, the worst sufferers being *Huisgenoot* and *Reader's Digest*, both of which often carry news articles or political surveys. However, it should be noted that often even the cultural pages are mutilated, for reasons which ought to be obvious.

An example will illuminate the tragic situation. One of the prisoners, Ahmed Kathrada,[29] once complained to the then studies officer, Major Huisamen, about the fact that even photos of women are cut out of such kosher reading matter as the *SA Panorama*. Huisamen said '*Wat wil julle dan met 'n klomp kaalgatmeide doen?*' (What do you want to do with a lot of bare-assed trollops? – but the vulgarity of all this cannot be conveyed in words!). Kathrada then showed him that in the anthropology textbooks he was using there were many photos of completely naked women, only to be stunned by the reply, '*Ja, maar dis mos maar 'nklompi Bantoemeide*' (Yes, but that's only a lot of Bantu women). Comment is superfluous!

From every angle, it can be seen that the prisoners are up against a wall held together by a concrete of ignorance, prejudice, vindictiveness, and especially fear. Anything done can only be palliative (but palliatives in gaol can be vital) – hence this document – for the whole structure of society and the concrete persons constituting it must be altered before this kind of astonishing idiocy can be eradicated.

One Azania One Nation[1]

Nationality and the Relationship between Theory and Strategy

In this study, I examine the theory of nationality which has been propagated by the ideologues and theoreticians of the National Party in South Africa since the mid-1950s. This theory, the official justification for Bantustans and for the policy of Separate Development, purports to be of general validity and in line with political thought and practice throughout the modern world. Theoretically, it involves the question of what the nation of South Africa is, i.e. who constitutes the nation? Since the answer to this apparently simple question is the stuff of political controversy in this country, it is necessary to investigate the historical evolution of the theory of the National Party, to reveal the reasons for its propagation, to show whose interests it serves, to consider alternative theories, and to examine all these in terms of their relation to the class struggle in South Africa.

The Balkanisation of South Africa by means of the ruling party's Bantustan strategy has often been pilloried as fraudulent, monstrous, ludicrous, and so forth. Yet the very term 'Balkanisation' bears within it a historic judgement. For the centrifugal rupture of the Russian, Turkish, and Austro-Hungarian Empires shortly before, during, and after World War I resulted in state formations which have been accepted universally as constituting viable and legitimate nations. In a sense, therefore, the use of the term 'Balkanisation' imparts to the Bantustans a quasi-legitimacy which is at variance with the critique it is meant to express. The National Liberation Movement in South Africa finds itself today in a situation analogous to that which faced the precursors of the First International in the middle of the last century in Europe. There, the Pan-Slavonic policy of Balkanisation pursued by the Tsarist regime was aimed at weakening the Austro-Hungarian Empire and especially its Turkish rival in the Balkan peninsula. The incipient nationalism of the East European nationalities, created under the impulsion of a politically aspirant bourgeoisie was the main tool of this imperialistic drive to expansion. Since

Tsarist Russia was the symbol and bulwark of all that was reactionary
and backwards-looking in Europe, Marx and Engels and other socialists
and liberals were implacably opposed to Balkanisation, and many went
so far as to deny outright the legitimacy of the nationalisms of Eastern
Europe.[2] The encouragement of these reactionary nationalisms was
seen by the representatives of both the liberal bourgeoisie (e.g. Mazzini)
and the working classes to be in direct conflict with the real interests of
these classes. But, as Lenin later realised, the emancipation of the serfs
(1861) neutralised the historic reactionary character of Russia: the Tsarist
empire became in all important respects a colony of Western Europe and
was unable (after the crushing of the Polish Revolt of 1863) to play its
previous counter-revolutionary role. This altered the character of these
Eastern European nationalisms. Indeed, they came to be a vital dimension of the struggle against capitalism and feudalism in Russia itself.

South Africa is the Tsarist Russia of the southern African subcontinent. Whether in Namibia, Zimbabwe, or South Africa itself, its apartheid
policy of separate 'nationhood' for so-called 'Bantu' and other 'nations'
serves an analogous purpose. Hence political strategy dictates that this
nefarious policy be opposed by all possible means. The alleged success of
the Turnhalle conference in Namibia in 1978, and the claims made for the
'independent' Transkei as representing a model of peaceful decolonisation, are indications that, in certain quarters of the 'Free World', there are
influential people waiting to latch on to anything that will lend respecta-
bility to a policy and theory that have called forth universal abhorrence.
Already the liberation movement itself has had to witness the desolat-
ing spectacle of some of its supposedly staunchest members defecting to
the Bantustans amid a blaze of publicity. Men such as Joe Matthews (formerly of the ANC), T.T. Letlake (ex-PAC), and Digby Koyana (ex-Unity
Movement) have thrown in their miserable lot with the partitionists and
supine followers of the National Party's formula for South Africa – the
Matanzimas, Mangopes, etc. They, more than any others, have revealed
the counter-revolutionary potential of the Bantustan strategy.

The National Liberation Movement, i.e. the various organisations of
which it is composed, has presumably developed a counter-strategy. Ille-
gality of operation has by and large prevented this strategy from being put
forward explicitly. Very often that which is written does not reflect the
real views of the leadership who have to protect their membership and
supporters inside the country. However, strategies can also be inferred
from political acts, be they of a literary, mobilising, or military charac-

ter. The success or failure of such strategies will not be discussed in this work; what this book is concerned with is the fact that there does not seem to exist any systematic refutation of the theory of nationality which the National Party has been propagating. Yet such a refutation has to be undertaken.

In general, it is not sufficient to state what the objective effects and aims of the Bantustan strategy are or will be, and simply for that reason to reject it – i.e. because it happens to contradict one's own conception of the solution of the 'racial problem' in South Africa. For although the systematically expounded refutation of the theory by which the Bantustan strategy is interpreted to the world and to its victims is not a precondition for the formulation of possible alternative liberation strategies, it remains the task of the theorist to undertake such a refutation, the obverse side of which is the theoretical elucidation of the correct strategy of the National Liberation Movement.

An example will clarify the matter. Every organisation in the National Liberation Movement has rejected the Bantustan strategy because, amongst other reasons, it will 'divide the people'. Of course, it is implied or explained that this divisive process has economic, cultural, and political disadvantages for 'the people'. I know of no example, however, where the full ideological implications of such a statement have been worked out. I know of no document where the interconnections between the ideological dimension (implied by the words 'people', 'nation', etc.) and the politico-economic dimensions of our political practice have been explicated. Yet this has become a fundamental necessity. Practical decisions of far-reaching strategic and political importance depend upon the clarity of the leadership and membership of the liberation movement over this question – decisions such as whether 'Indians' are part of the 'nation', whether 'Coloureds' are a 'minority', whether only 'Africans' should belong to a given organisation. These have become questions of practical political importance, the answers to which require theoretical clarity and precision.

Strategy necessarily implies a theory. At a certain point, however, it becomes necessary for the very implementation of a strategy that the theory behind it be articulated explicitly. This book has tried to do this precisely because I felt that this point has been reached by the movement for national liberation in South Africa. It becomes daily more obvious that, unless this theoretical-historical task is initiated, the movement must continue to suffer one strategic defeat after another.

It is a conspicuous and ironical fact that neither the liberal nor the radical Marxist opposition to the present regime has formulated any reasonably systematic theoretical-historical analysis of the sociological assumptions and explicit propositions of the National Party's theory of nationality. There seem to be two reasons for this omission. In the first place, all liberal and surprisingly many Marxist critics of the National Party's theories share the latter's mystified conception of 'race' (notwithstanding many excellent analyses of the objective socio-economic basis of racist ideology in South Africa). The inevitable result is that they are unable to produce at the theoretical level a decisive argument against the National Party's theory of nationality, which takes as one of its points of departure the myth of 'race'. In the second place, the subject of nationality (nationalism, the nation, etc.), viewed from a bourgeois sociological perspective, is one of the most controversial fields of scientific investigation. Even in the Soviet Union, where there has been a long tradition of theoretical debate on the subject and almost as long a period of implementation of strategies concerning nationality, there is no definitive view on the subject – in fact, there is a constant revision of apparently well-founded principles. Methodological problems, such as the problem of definition, make a mockery of most work on the subject to such an extent that – especially on the so-called extreme left – many people actually question the very reality of the category 'nation' and all that goes with it.[3]

But far from being 'nonsense', nationality is a historic force. This is the reason for the propagation and proliferation of bogus nationalisms, the main purpose of which is to dissipate the force of the class struggle by deflecting it into channels that will nurture the dominant classes. The Bantustan strategy is precisely such an attempt to harness the creative and revolutionary energies of the National Liberation Movement in order to use them against the emergent nation by dividing it into warring and antagonistic groupings graced with the tainted robes of *One Azania, One Nation* 'independent nations'. These groups, be they language groups, religious sects, colour castes, or administrative units, have, in the South African context, a reality at a certain level. To deny this is to behave like an ostrich. It is much more important to recognise them for what they actually are, to characterise them as such and to analyse the dynamic, embedded in the class structure of the South African social formation, by which they have been and are being brought into motion. Only in this way, and not by mere negative assertion or inane ridicule, can the bogus claims of the National Party's theory and practice be exposed. This theory which postulates the existence in South Africa of eight (sometimes nine) 'Bantu nations', one 'White nation', one 'Indian', and one 'Coloured nation-to-be', has thrown into sharp relief the need to characterise scientifically these groups of people. Anyone who realises that theory is a guide to action will not doubt that future policies and strategies will be influenced by the existence of an articulated theory concerning the nature and possible direction of development of the groups concerned. The practical proof of this in South Africa is the National Party's theory and the impact it has had on government policy.

In a country like South Africa, where social relations have for generations been treated as 'race relations', the need to arrive at a practically illuminating description of the character of these relations, i.e. the real (socio-economic) basis of social inequality and the real (ideological) forms in which it is expressed, cannot be evaded by those who take on themselves, or on to whom is thrust, the political responsibility for planning the post-apartheid, post-colour-bar society now evolving there. It should be clearly understood, therefore, and I wish to state it as bluntly as possible, that this work is intended to meet both theoretical and practical political needs; it is not intended to be a mere juggling of words in the greyness of 'theory'. Only insofar as it is itself the result of, and capable of being a guide to, the action of the oppressed people is the writing of it to be understood at all.[4]

The central concepts which will be discussed in relation to the way they apply in the South African context are 'race', nation, 'ethnic group', colour-caste, and class. The basic thesis of this work is that the population groups (as they are officially called) which now inhabit South Africa are historically evolved colour castes; that a complex combination of caste consciousness, class consciousness, and class interests under definite but constantly changing material conditions of production and reproduction of relations of production determines the specific forms which historical development in South Africa has taken. The historical product of this development will be a single, democratically constituted nation which, unless counter-revolutionary strategies prevail, will not come into being as long as capitalist relations of production are dominant. Whether or not this single nation does come into being will depend on the extent to which a working-class leadership of the National Liberation Movement succeeds in determining the political ideology of the revolutionary people. On the other hand, this book argues that the imposition of Bantustans as alleged

nation-states can under specific circumstances (in particular a demoral
ising defeat of a revolutionary uprising) influence historical development
so that the solution of the national question will be retarded and distorted, albeit temporarily, in important ways. I stop short of formulating
a counter-strategy to that of the National Party, as this is more specifically
the task of political practice. However, I do believe that a strategy based
on the theoretical position expounded here represents the only viable
alternative for the National Liberation Movement.

'The Movement for National Liberation'[1]

The coming to power in 1948 of the National Party with its unambiguously reactionary programme and policy suddenly confronted the popular organisations of the oppressed with a challenge for which they were inadequately prepared. The declared anti-communist and anti-democratic aims of the ruling party put in jeopardy the continued existence of all working-class and democratic organisations. The assault on the few privileges and freedoms remaining for Black people, and the deliberate lowering of their living standards, implicit in the doctrine and practice of apartheid, meant that the radical intelligentsia, the urban and rural poor, and even some of the merchant classes and aspirant bourgeoisie among the Blacks clearly realised for the first time that they were faced with an immediate and common enemy. Moreover, the age-old distinctions drawn by the rulers between different sectors of the oppressed became less important since the Afrikaner sectionalists were now intent on disenfranchising every person not classified as white: The result was an unprecedented upsurge of nationalism among the oppressed people, stimulated by the realisation that the franchise was the only instrument whereby they could escape from the bondage of racist oppression.

The war years and the anti-imperialist victories, especially in Asia but including the stirring of independence movements in Africa, had much to do with this. The great miners' strike of 1946 on the Rand was a signal to the ruling class that the Black workers had become a force that could no longer be ignored. It only needed the challenge of the apartheid strategy to catapult the various organisations into action. In 1946, the progressives in the South African Indian Congress ousted the collaborationist Kajee leadership and launched a passive resistance struggle in conjunction with a diplomatic offensive by India in the United Nations. By 1948–1949, the Congress Youth League leadership had succeeded in gaining effective control of the ANC and ridding the organisation of Dr Xuma's braking tactics. These years were also the heyday of the Unity Movement which until the mid-1950s grew from strength to strength and radiated an influence and ideological challenge much larger than its actual membership. In particular, its advocacy of Non-European Unity based on a programme of minimum demands to be implemented through a policy of non-collaboration with the institutions of oppression could no longer be ignored. Events themselves were willy-nilly pushing all political activity in this direction. The simultaneous, strategically conceived assault on all 'Non-European' groups by the National Party – the Suppression of Communism Act, the Group Areas Act, the Bantu Authorities Act, the Bantu Education Act, among many other legislative invasions of the meagre rights of Black people – telescoped the process of oppression and compelled all sectors of the oppressed, irrespective of caste, to realise that they were the victims of a common subjection. Simultaneously, many political leaders and militants realised that they would have to fight this oppression jointly, not severally. But the caste-bound horizons of the majority of the people's organisations, the leaders' assessment of the depth of caste prejudice among the oppressed, as well as the leaders' own limitations and reformist aspirations, still made it impossible for them to think in terms of a single undivided National Liberation Movement. The South African Indian Congress and the African National Congress still concentrated on their own particular caste groups. Their unity was still a tactical affair born in different centres. There was still no strategically based unity, and certainly no theoretically conceived unity based on unalterable principles derived from a study of the history of freedom movements throughout the world and applied in the particular South African context.

Hence, the first great mass struggle after the war, the 1951–1952 Defiance Campaign against Unjust Laws was directed by a tactical united front of the two Congresses plus the South African Coloured People's Organisation and the South African Congress of Democrats, specifically for the abolition of the six Unjust Laws selected as the target of civil disobedience. This experience, together with the growing influence of ex-Communist Party[2] members within the Congresses, and the criticism from organisations of the Unity Movement, led to the 1955 Congress of the People, at which the now-celebrated Freedom Charter was conceived as the basis of the Congress Alliance. This Alliance consisted of organisations of the African, Coloured, and Indian sectors of the oppressed and the (white) Congress of Democrats. These organisations remained separate, caste-restricted organisations each with its own programme, but all expected to be guided by the demands formulated in the Charter. It is clear that at this stage the non-violent tactics of direct action – modelled on the approach of Gandhi and Nkrumah – were designed to create a climate of confrontation between the government and the oppressed people in which the leaders of the organisations of the Alliance would step forward as the 'valid interlocutors' on behalf of the oppressed. The subsequent Treason Trial and the events leading up to Sharpeville, the banning of the ANC and the PAC, the virtual smashing of their (and other) organisational networks, are a matter of history and represent the collapse of this strategy. Some of the implications of the consequent turn to armed struggle will be discussed below.

For our purposes it is to Point 2 of the Freedom Charter that we have to turn:

All National Groups Shall Have Equal Rights

There shall be equal status in the bodies of state, in the courts and in the schools for all national groups and races;

All national groups shall be protected by law against insults to their race and national pride;

All people shall have equal rights to use their own language and to develop their own folk culture and customs;

The preaching and practice of national, race or colour discrimination and contempt shall be a punishable crime;

All apartheid laws and practices shall be set aside.[3]

It is immediately obvious that this idea of four 'national groups' has persisted from the pre-war caste interpretations of the national question which were shared, from different theoretical points of view, by liberals, many Marxists and petty-bourgeois reformists. The influence of Soviet theories of nationality is also evident, especially in the guarantee for the use by each 'national' or 'racial' group of its own language and for the development of its own folk culture and customs. Though the concept of the nation advocated here was clearly based on the pluralist approach of taking the 'races' as given, unalterable entities, it was nevertheless clearly insulated against any beckonings from the National Party's Bantustan theory. In 1953, I. I. Potekhin, later to become Director of the Moscow Africa Institute, had written:

There are … two characteristic threads which run through all these stages [of the National Liberation Movement]. The first, all the Bantu peoples are opposing imperialism on a united front. There is no Zulu or Bechuana movement, there are no Zulu or Bechuana organisations, but there is a united Bantu movement led by organisations common to all. In this mutual struggle the idea of a single Bantu nation of South Africa and the Protectorates has arisen and become strong. In literature, particularly in the old ethnographic literature, one can come across 'the Zulu nation', 'the Basuto nation', and so forth. But usually now the reference is to a Bantu or African nation … 'A new people is being born which calls itself African … the small isolated worlds of the Zulu, Xhosa or Basuto have been left behind in the past and they will never return', writes … Dholomo.[4]

From this astounding document (in parts it could almost have been written by a member of the Afrikaner *Broederbond*, but for its anti-tribal point of departure) it becomes obvious that the prevailing theory on the national question in South Africa espoused by the Communist Party, which in this respect seems to have relied on the views of people like Potekhin, intersected neatly with that of the Africanist leadership of the African National Congress and the caste-orientated leadership of the other groups. Basing himself on a lifeless, logic-chopping interpretation of Stalin's definition of a nation, Potekhin, amidst unpardonable confusion of historical and cultural facts, arrives at the unadulterated liberal bourgeois conclusion that:

Today in the Union of South Africa the process of forming two national societies continues, that of the Bantu and of the Anglo-Afrikaner. There are no grounds for assuming that one nation can be formed which would embrace the Bantu, the Coloureds and the Anglo-Afrikaners. The Coloureds could not at the present time become a component of the national Bantu group, they do not know the Bantu languages and in language, cultural forms and self-consciousness they tend to identify themselves with the Anglo-Afrikaners. The Indians are a completely separate group.[5]

In actual fact, it is clear, Potekhin's theory is merely an *ex cathedra* benediction of the pro-Congress tactics finally decided upon by the Communist Party of South Africa after World War II, and especially after the dissolution of the CPSA in 1950.[6] In 1962, when the CPSA emerged again as the SACP, it adopted the Freedom Charter as an adequate expression of the short-term aims of the Party.[7] Potekhin's concluding remark in the above work holds within it a fatal ambivalence both as to the concept of the nation and as to the class leadership of the struggle for national liberation. Again it is necessary to quote him in full, lest paraphrasing him appear like distorting the real meaning of this celebrated 'Africanist':

> The South African Bantu have not yet united as a nation. At present we emphasise only that there are potential possibilities and grounds for assuming that the process that will lead to the formation of a nation has begun. These nations do not as yet have clear concise contours and it would be unjust to try to give a precise answer to this question now. The question of national boundaries will be decided by the peoples themselves once they have freed themselves from the imperialist government. *At this given stage of development the chief task of all Bantu peoples must be to unite their strength in one national front; and together with the progressive forces of the Anglo-Afrikaners, Indians and Coloureds, to liquidate the regime of racial discrimination* and to conquer political rights equal to those of the European section of the population.[8]

With a single significant exception, to which I shall refer below,[9] the ideas expressed in this document have remained the stock-in-trade of the Congress Movement and the SACP ever since. Indeed, in some respects, it has been rigidified into a dogma which has a significant point of intersection with the dogma of the Afrikaner sectionalists on the national question – their characterisation of South Africa as a 'multi-national' polity. Thus, for instance, a leading member of the ANC executive, and later the director of the Luthuli Memorial Foundation, wrote circa 1971 in answer to Minister M. C. Botha's claim that the Bantu-speaking people of South Africa consisted of eight different nations, that in fact there is only one African nation based on a community of oppression:

> Those who know something about South African history will remember that long before it was fashionable to speak about white unity and the white nation, the African people from different tribes, the Xhosas, Zulus, Sothos, Swazis, Shanganes, Tswanas and others met in Bloemfontein in 1912 and *decided to form themselves into one nation – an African nation* and then and there formed the African National Congress, their political mouthpiece.[10]

It is also clear that this ANC leader accepts the validity of the concepts: 'White nation', a 'Coloured nation', and an 'Indian nation'.[11] Similarly, in the important Political Report adopted by the Consultative Conference of the ANC at the Morogoro Conference, Tanzania, in May 1969, the idea of the four 'national groups' is entrenched, but with the incipient emphasis on the 'African nation' as the 'majority nation', the national liberation of which is 'the main content of the present stage of the South African revolution'. The report maintains that:

> The African, although subjected to the most intense racial oppression and exploitation, is not the only oppressed national group in South Africa. The two million strong Coloured community and three-quarter million Indians suffer varying forms of national humiliation, discrimination and oppression ... Despite deceptive and often meaningless concessions they share a common fate with their African brothers and *their own liberation* is inextricably bound up with *the liberation of the African people.*[12]

Although the question of the class leadership of the national liberation struggle is raised later on in the Morogoro Political Report, there is no attempt to explain how working-class leadership of this struggle is consistent with the idea of several nations each consisting of antagonistic classes, and the privileged classes of which are pulled in the direction of the ruling classes in the South African state. There is no attempt at all to analyse the idea of the nation theoretically, to consider for instance the link (if any) between the assertion of nationhood and the right of self-determination. This lack, which is evident in almost all writing on the question by South Africans, I shall examine in more detail below.

At the same Morogoro Conference an analysis of the Freedom Charter was presented whose purpose was to update the interpretation of the Charter in the context of the tactical changes brought about by the armed struggle. Moreover, ever since the adoption of the Charter in 1955, many individuals, especially people from the Western Cape where Unity Movement influence was greatest, had questioned the validity of the assumptions inherent in the Charter's formulation of this question. At Morogoro in 1969 the question came to a head, since it also involved the problem of organisational structure and non-racial membership of Congress organisations, specifically of the ANC It is significant, therefore, that despite concessions at Morogoro to the 'equality of rights of all national groups', the primacy of the 'African people' is still asserted unambiguously:

> The African people as the indigenous owners of the country have accepted that all the people who have made South Africa and helped build it up, are *components of its multi-national population*, and are and will be in a democratic South Africa people inhabiting their common home.[13]

An interesting, but by no means peripheral, development here is the ANC's discovery of new 'national groups'. For it is asserted that 'At the moment the Afrikaner national group is lording it over the rest of the population with the *English group* playing second fiddle to them'.[14] This tit-for-tat response to Bantustan theory ('If you split up the "African nation" we'll split up the "white nation"') not only does not illuminate the national question but leads away from the question of the class leadership of the struggle. This approach also presents the struggle as one being waged by various 'nations' against especially the 'Afrikaner nation', a conclusion that leads potentially to strategic errors of catastrophic dimensions.

In view of these unambiguously liberal bourgeois formulations of the question in South Africa, it is ironic that Ben Turok, a member of the SACP, who himself postulates the existence of 'large national minorities of whites, Coloureds and Asians', should claim that 'no final definitive formulation on the national question has ever been laid down' by the ANC.[15] This claim is all the more astounding since Turok says himself, in his brief review of ANC and CYL statements on the national question, that:

> The thrust of all these statements is for national liberation in the sense that white domination must be ended and that *the African people who in some way constitute a national entity* will establish a democratic society in which people of all colours will be able to participate.[16]

The uncomfortably close parallel between Bantustan theory and the essentially pluralist theory of the Congress Movement and the SACP, together with mounting criticism both inside and outside these organisations, *has led in recent times to soul-searching and reassessments which may still prove to be of great significance to the whole liberation movement in South Africa.* Ironically enough, the (temporary) upsurge of Black Consciousness as an organised movement lent an agonising urgency to this reassessment since, as I shall show, the Black Consciousness Movement

rejects the pluralist thesis in favour at least of Black solidarity. Lest, therefore, the theoretical paralysis of the Congress Movement (and the SACP)
on this question lead to its being outflanked inside the country by this
new tendency, it has had to pause for a reappraisal. This was indubita-
bly one of the main reasons for the series of contributions on the national
question run in *The African Communist* in 1976–1977.

The first contribution to this new debate is a letter signed *Maatla Ke A
Rona!!!* (Strength is Ours). The author, avowedly a member of the ANC,
stresses that:

> The situation in our country is changing very fast, and if we are not
> careful we shall be caught napping. There is still time to remedy the
> situation, and that is through a critical appraisal of our work in propa-
> ganda and publicity.[17]

He/she boldly rejects Stalin's definition of the nation as irrelevant to the
Afro-Asian colonial struggles and insists that it refers to 'mature' European nations, in contrast to the African peoples who are still building
their nations. Consequently, the author arrives logically at the position
that there is no South African nation in existence as yet; 'The South
African nation is in the process of being born, and we, in the ANC – in an
embryonic form – represent the unborn South African nation'.[18]

Though this brief contribution does not enter further into the
theoretical implications of this statement, it does open a completely new
perspective from within the Congress Movement. This is particularly
clear when one recalls that the letter is prompted by a criticism of various
assertions made in *Mayibuye*, one of the organs-in-exile of the ANC.
Maatla Ke A Rona!!! is especially bothered by the suggestion that the
author of these assertions seemingly thinks that 'the Boers are a "nation"'
and, therefore, the question 'how many "nations" do we have in South
Africa?' is posed. Moreover, the original *Mayibuye* author's rejection
of the demand for self-determination as 'counter-revolutionary in the
specific historical and social conditions of South Africa' moves *Maatla Ke
A Rona!!!* to remind him of the 'internal colonialism' thesis (with which I
deal in the next section).[19]

Whether intended by the editors of *The African Communist* or not,
it is nonetheless clear that the letter is flying a kite, an interpretation
borne out by the fact that it was followed up by further contributions.
On the other hand, the letter is clearly in conflict with the received Con-

gress tradition, which it studiously avoids dragging into the bullring. This problem, though not explicitly stated, is treated by Joe Ngwenya in 'A Further Contribution on the National Question', published in *The African Communist*, No. 67. The uneven quality of this article should not obscure its real purpose, which is twofold: to demarcate clearly the difference between the ANC's multi-nationalism and that of the Afrikaner National Party ideologues; and to show that the ANC's theory is not at variance with that of Black Consciousness, at least on the national question. The confusions, contradictions, and obfuscations in the article need not be dealt with in detail. It suffices to enumerate them: Ngwenya equates 'racial group', 'national group', and 'nationality': he does not consider it contradictory to speak of 'national groups' and 'the nation' in the same breath (a fault common to many writers on the question, as must have become evident by now); he stresses repeatedly the idea of the Africans as the majority national group, in the process falsifying the history of the country by claiming that they are the 'indigenous owners of the land'. (If this refers only to people descended from Bantu-speaking tribes, it is patent nonsense, for it is well known that the Khoi- and the San-speaking people inhabited southern Africa even before Bantu-speaking people appeared there. Not that this is of any significance in itself, but it makes nonsense of the idea of 'ownership' by 'Bantu-speaking Africans'.)

This attempt to cast the ANC's conventional views in terms that would meet the changing situation at home without altering the core of the theory leads to absurd, even mutually contradictory, formulations. An example in Ngwenya's article is the following:

Their [the 'Africans'] acceptance of other groups with open arms clearly shows their non-sectarian approach. The South African nation can only be formed on the basis of democratic processes firmly based on majority rule or more correctly the leading role of the majority, in a non-racial society where the skin of a person will have no role.[20]

At the same time, Ngwenya stresses the correctness of the ANC's multi-racialism which has nothing in common with the so-called multi-racialism of the Liberal Party, or the National Union of South African Students ... which is 'multi-racialism' based on minority rule or direction, ignoring the leading role of the African people as the core and the moving spirit of the South African people and NATION.[21]

On the theoretical level, the author tries to do what is virtually impossible – to distinguish between the 'multi-national' approach of the ANC, on the one hand, and that of the Afrikaner 'nationalists', on the other, in the same way as he had tried to distinguish between the two supposedly different multi-racialisms. He is embarrassingly conscious of this theoretical dilemma:

> The component parts of the South African nation consists of differing racial or national groups. *We have no intention of over-emphasising the racial origin of the various communities*; on the contrary, we reserve the term nation to emphasise the direction in which we are moving. South Africa is one country in which all groups are economically interdependent and integration is taking place in spite of government policy. *It is only recognition of the fact that the government is depicting tribalism as a manifestation of the nation that makes us cautious to use the term national group.* Many of the national groups – in fact all of them – are dispersed all over the country and intermingled ...[22]

This is pitiable stuff to say the least. It is contradicted by a brief burst of unrestrained great nation chauvinism when he maintains that the ANC 'seriously takes into consideration *the grievances of the other national groups* in the formulation of the overall revolutionary strategy ... and closely works with the other sister organisations.'[23]

Even on the question of the class leadership of the national struggle, confusion creeps in when he attempts to show that the danger of bourgeois deviations from the ranks of the African oppressed is almost non-existent.[24] It is not that the point itself is wrong; *the point of departure* is wrong, because he attempts to equate the African 'national group' with the working class, so as once again to underpin the leading role of this 'national group'.

Although this contributor eschews the question of whether Stalin's famous definition is applicable to the South African case (i.e. he refuses to argue his case theoretically), his major assertion is extremely important, if one ignores the flagrant contradictions between the various assertions made in the article. For it is a great step forward, spurred on by Black Consciousness and the growing criticism from other wings of the National Liberation Movement, to state roundly that 'In our opinion, the South African nation is the totality of all its people, Black and White, who pay allegiance to South Africa as their homeland'[25] and even that the consciousness of the African 'should be broadened so that in it the African should understand not only his being African but more his being South African. This is the surest blow to Bantustanisation'.²⁶

All in all, however, it does not appear that the Congress's contributions to the continuing discussion on the national question have taken the matter much further on the theoretical level, and the patent confusions concerning concepts such as national groups, national minorities, racial groups, nationalities, bear this out clearly. This is reflected in the other major contribution to *The African Communist's* series on the national question.

This second contribution – by Ben Molapo – (which only became accessible to me after I had written the above) does go some way towards posing the correct questions. And although he does so very briefly, he subjects previous writings by Communists and others to an extremely relevant questioning. In some respects, e.g. the trap of a mechanistic application of Stalin's definition, he anticipates, even if only in outline, some of my own findings. As such, therefore, the article provides a valuable point of departure. However, since many of his propositions are repetitions of views already criticised by me and since the general approach in this book should help one to read it critically, I have chosen to comment briefly only on those aspects that appear to be new or important.

It is noteworthy that Molapo makes no attempt to establish any connection between the holding of different views on the national question and the respective interpretation and theory of class struggle in each case. No attempt is made to show the effects, in terms of the class struggle, of a 'one nation', a 'two nations', or a 'many-nations' approach to the national question in South Africa. Yet this is the crucial point, an omission which, if it occurs, leaves analysis merely at the level of superficial pigeon-holing.

Moreover, Molapo, apart from the now obligatory swipe at Stalin and equally obligatory genuflection to Lenin, cannot free himself from the fatal SACP thesis of 'colonialism of a special type'. The result is once again lamentable confusion, an opening of many doors to opportunism and even betrayal, as we have seen. Let us quote him:

> The great disadvantage of the one nation thesis is, then that it obscures the colonial nature of our society and in consequence the national character of our liberation struggle. It is this flaw that the two nations thesis is deliberately designed to counter ... This view holds essentially that South Africa is a colonial situation of a special type in which two

nations, an oppressing nation and an oppressed nation, live side by side within the same territory ... The two nations thesis is, in my view, the correct one, but it is not always clear what is meant by 'nation' in this context. Both the oppressing nation and the oppressed nation fail to meet the general conditions stipulated by Stalin's classical definition of the nation, a definition that continues to enjoy wide currency in Marxist writings ...[27]

Quite consistently with this thesis, Molapo characterises the 'Coloured and Indian communities in South Africa' as 'minority groups', largely on the grounds that they possess neither actual nor potential economic viability as groups. The static and mechanistic character of this argument should be obvious to anyone who has read my book with care.

Tragically, Molapo, after feigning an attack on Stalin's 'entirely mechanical' definition, tries to save it in a kind of 'facing-both-ways' exercise that is almost incredible. By way of demonstrating the resultant confusion let us cite a few sentences from Molapo:

It may be that it is preferable to reserve the term 'nation' as such for a fully developed national community that satisfies all four components [of Stalin's definition] rather than for a community that is advancing along the lines of national organisation. In this case the two nations thesis in South Africa while designating the general character of the class struggle in South Africa needs slight adjustment, for neither of the nations is complete in the fullest sense.

As though this attempt to salvage the implications of the internal colonialism thesis for the analysis of the national question were not unfortunate enough, Molapo continues with a passage that bristles with contradictions manifest even in his terminological confusion and inconsistency:

Whether one accepts this refinement or not, however, the centring of the national question on the class struggle and the formation of an economic community confirms the general approach of the two nations thesis in South Africa. *While the white nation* (or proto-nation) has not achieved (and may not achieve) a single national language and homogeneous culture, *the white alliance* based on certain cultural and racial criteria has been more important objectively than English/Afrikaans differences. These differences have been subordinated to white national supremacy. This oppressor nation ... has through the control of state power carried through the normal democratic reforms within the confines of *the white nation* ... This white national framework has long since performed its national democratic tasks, and from a democratic point of view, it has become an anachronism, which is not to say that it is therefore about to wither away of its own accord. Further meaningful democratic advance in South Africa can only be achieved within the framework of another national entity, *the African South African nation. This nation already exists, at least partially*, in the objective alliance between the great majority of the proletariat, the peasantry and fractions of the petit-bourgeoisie who are all subjected to the same national oppression ...[28]

From the above excerpts it is clear that Molapo's article, however stimulating it might be, remains an incomplete and confusing document, primarily because, being imprisoned within the framework of the internal colonialism thesis of the SACP, he is unable to perceive the national question from the point of view of the revolutionary working class.

In conclusion, from what has been said earlier concerning the pluralist thesis of liberalism in South Africa it is obvious that only through a consistent emphasis on working-class leadership of the national struggle can the Congress Movement cease to be prone to a reformist alliance with the liberal bourgeoisie (as it had been throughout the 1950s). But in that case, its very concept of the nation and its analysis of the national question needs change.

THE INTERNAL COLONIALISM THESIS

Ngwenya, like the previous contributor to *The African Communist's* series on the national question, bases himself on the thesis that 'In fact, the white minority has established a special colonialist system differing from the classical model in that the coloniser and the colonised share the same country'.[29]

The immediate source of this internal colonialism thesis is the 1962 programme of the Communist Party in which it was stated that:

South Africa is not a colony but an independent state. Yet the masses of our people enjoy neither independence nor freedom. The conceding of independence to South Africa by Britain, in 1910, was not a victory over the forces of colonialism and imperialism. It was designed in the interests of imperialism. Power was transferred not into the hands of the masses of people of South Africa, but into the hands of the white minority alone. The evils of colonialism, insofar as the Non-White majority was concerned, were perpetuated and reinforced. A new type of colonialism was developed, in which the oppressing white nation occupied the same territory as the oppressed people themselves and lived side by side with them.[30]

The programme, called *The Road to South African Freedom*, climaxes in the assertion that 'Non-White South Africa is the colony of White South Africa itself'. It is worthwhile quoting the whole of the relevant passage:

On one level, that of 'White South Africa', there are all the features of an advanced capitalist state in its final stage of imperialism. There are highly developed industrial monopolies, and the merging of industrial and finance capital. The land is farmed along capitalist lines, employing wage labour, and producing cash crops for the local and export markets. The South African monopoly capitalists … export capital abroad … But on another level, that of 'Non-White South Africa', there are all the features of a colony. The indigenous population is subjected to national oppression, poverty and exploitation, lack of all democratic rights and political domination by a group which does everything it can to emphasize and perpetuate its alien 'European' character. The African Reserves show the complete lack of industry, communications, transport and power resources which are characteristics of … territories under colonial rule … Typical, too, of imperialist rule, is the reliance by the state upon brute force and terror, and upon the most backward tribal elements and institutions which are deliberately and artificially preserved. Non-White South Africa is the colony of White South Africa itself.[31]

Harold Wolpe, in his study of this question, has pointed to the fact that the notion of internal colonialism has been used by many writers to describe the politico-economic domination of white people over Black people and stresses correctly that 'Used in this way, the term "internal colonialism" is interchangeable with the notion of "pluralism"'.[32] In regard to the SACP's propositions Wolpe concedes that the Party Programme's use of the term internal colonialism is linked with capitalism, but the programme 'fails to clarify the nature of the imperialist relationship between the two South Africas' and, more importantly, 'despite the reference to capitalism, and no doubt to the failure to specify the crucial relationship, the analysis slides into an account in terms of white and Non-white South Africa which is very similar to that provided by the pluralists'.[33] Up to this point, Wolpe's findings concerning the position of the SACP are congruent with what I have repeatedly stressed concerning the pluralist core of Congress-orientated theories of the nation which are accepted by the SACP. The Party's internal colonialism thesis is, in fact, not much more than a neo-pluralist thesis which, though prefigured in its much earlier slogan of the 'independent native republic', is clearly tailored to suit the post-war alliance between the Communist Party and the ANC. Because a pluralist position on the national question carries the inevitable implication of a two-stage revolution, it also – objectively – says something about the position of its advocates on the question of class leadership of the national liberation struggle. In the South African context, a 'multi-national', i.e. pluralist, position, however defined, is inextricably linked with the proposition that the national struggle shall be led by the liberal bourgeoisie and the aspirant bourgeoisie, rather than by the working class.

Wolpe attempts to salvage the internal colonialism thesis by reinterpreting it in terms of the reserves ('pre-capitalist mode of production') and metropolitan South Africa ('capitalist mode of production') somewhat on the model of the centre-periphery literature that has proved to be so stimulating in recent years. In the process, however, he jumps from the frying pan into the fire and creates an opening not towards an alliance with the liberal bourgeoisie (which the neo-pluralists have done) but with the Afrikaner sectionalists themselves! His thesis is simply that the real colonial relationship in South Africa exists between the capitalist ruling classes in the 'metropolitan area' of South Africa itself on the one hand, and the reserves ('homelands' in the official nomenclature), on the other. These latter, by reproducing labour power cheaply, i.e. at a cost which is forcibly kept at a minimum through the perpetuation ('conservation') of the underdeveloped state of these reserves, are the 'colonies' of the metropolis, which benefits from the resultant increased rate of capital accumulation.

It is this feature, the introduction into the capitalist circuit of production of labour power produced in a non-capitalist economy, that denotes one important feature of imperialism. This 'crossing' of different modes of production modifies the relationship between wages and the cost of reproducing labour power in favour of capital. The uniqueness or specificity of South Africa, in the period of capitalism, lies precisely in this: that it embodies within a single nation-state a relationship characteristic of the external relationships between imperialist states and their colonies (or neo-colonies).[34]

This thesis raises a host of controversial and interesting questions, but these cannot be allowed to detain us. More relevant to our focus are the comments of Molteno who points out that Wolpe's 'picture of the articulation of a capitalist mode of production with a non-capitalist mode of production is a mere translation of the pluralist notion of a *dual economy* into the "Marxist" code of language he sometimes uses';[35] and that he in effect 'concedes to National Party ideology the possibility of decolonization via political "independence"'.[36]

It is this latter aspect that is especially relevant to the present study. For the logic of Wolpe's theoretical position leads to the possibility of acceptance by men and women in the liberation movement of the legitimacy of 'homelands' and of Bantustan independence as a form of national liberation. The example of Joe Matthews is the most instructive. This one-time almost legendary and long-standing executive member of the ANC and the SACP, having abandoned his faith in the efficacy of the armed struggle, regressed along the whole spectrum to a position that is now no different from that of Matanzima or Buthelezi. Although this episode deserves much detailed inquiry, I shall refer to only two aspects of Matthews' justification of his change of position and betrayal of former colleagues. He stressed throughout his interview with journalist J. H. P. Serfontein, his commitment to capitalism and his opposition to the pro-communist 'anti-West posture' of the ANC:

> The crux of the programme of reform in South Africa lies in the fact that while there are two or three pieces of legislation against communism, the South African Statute Book has about 150 laws preventing the emergence of a capitalist class among Africans.[37]

Hence despite an obligatory genuflection to the possibility that Bantustan 'independence' may be only a temporary detour to a possible federation of southern African states at a later stage, his main concern is the reform of the system in such a way that capitalism can flourish without limitations imposed by considerations of 'race'. He conceives of the various language groups as constituting 'nations', each entitled to the right of independent state creation. According to Matthews, 'The right of any group to establish a state is a most fundamental one. The right to a state cannot be counterposed to hypothetical rights in a future united South Africa whose emergence might still be far off'. Bourgeois leadership of a pluralised South Africa: this is the logic of the multi-national position, whether in the versions of the SACP or those of Wolpe or even Matthews.

A recent attempt by Joe Slovo, a leading member of the Communist Party, to salvage the pre-Wolpean SACP thesis of internal colonialism or 'colonialism of a special type' does not carry the matter further. Indeed, if anything, it renders the colonial analogy, used in this way, more risky, since it opens wide the portals of the liberation movement to the very kind of opportunism of which a Joe Matthews is such a significant example. Against Wolpe, Slovo holds that:

> In South Africa the thesis of internal colonialism sees class relations in an historically specific context in which internal group domination has lent shape to, and influenced the content of, the exploitative processes. The thesis, however, stresses the existence of internal class divisions in both the dominant and subject groups, with these class divisions influencing political and ideological positions in the struggle for social change. To identify 'White South Africa' with an imperialist state and 'nonwhite South Africa' with the 'colony' is undoubtedly a useful shorthand, *at one level*, to depict the reality of the historically specific race factor in both the genesis and the existing nature of class rule.[38]

The italicised phrase does not serve to answer Wolpe's main contention. Moreover, the cat is let out of the bag when the author attempts to annex Wolpe's thesis to that of the SACP and thus to show that the latter is the necessary progenitor of the former. But, ironically, by doing this Slovo shows up precisely the danger in Wolpe's amended thesis, because he thereby confirms the view that Wolpe lends an air of legitimacy to the National Party's myth of decolonisation à la Bantustan:

> What general purpose is the re-structured Reserve system designed to meet and how will it alter the relationships of internal colonialism? In brief, *it is an attempt partially to externalize the colonial relationship in the shape of ethnic states*, eventually having all the attributes of *formal* political independence. In other words, the ruling class is, under pressure, searching for a neo-colonial solution especially adapted to South

African conditions ... These new steps to transform the Reserve system reflect a policy which is, therefore, in the direct line of succession from the present internal form of colonialism, showing the strains of its lack of sufficient geographic definition. It is an attempt to legitimize the foreign conquest in a new way.[39]

Thus we see how Wolpe's brand of internal colonialism has become Slovo's neo-colonialism. This neo-colonialism continues to coexist peacefully with the original SACP's 'colonialism of a special type'. While Slovo accounts in a manner of speaking for the Bantustan strategy (the Bantustans are, at least in the National Party's view, neo-colonies) he fails to realise that the very same process is taking place within the metropolitan centre of the National Party's 'white' South Africa. The Tom Swartzs and the Reddys are, like the Matanzimas and Buthelezis, the agents of this 'neo-colonialism'. Similarly, the Coloured Development Corporation, for example, plays the same role as the Bantu Investment Corporation and its offspring in the 'Bantu homelands'. But – to continue in Slovo's metaphor – these Coloured and Indian 'neo-colonies' have no foreseeable hope of eliminating 'the strains of [their] lack of sufficient geographic definition' and are therefore doomed to be forever examples of 'neo-colonialism of a special type'(or perhaps of 'internal neo-colonialism') as too, are those 'homelands' that have yet to choose *formal* political independence.

There is simply no logic in maintaining, on the one hand, that South Africa's inhabitants of European descent are no longer a settler population, that they have become indigenous to Africa, and so are *Africans*, while on the other hand attempting to stretch the colonial analogy to the point where it negates this valid assertion. There is a great difference between saying for the sake of descriptive vividness, and for understanding certain politico-ideological manifestations of the liberation struggle, that the Black people suffer under an oppression *akin* to that associated with colonially subjugated peoples, and maintaining, as the SACP (and Slovo) do, that 'Non-White South Africa *is* the colony of white south Africa itself'. The colonial analogy, used in this way, legitimises multi-nationalism and, in the final analysis, therefore also legitimises partition in the guise of independence. Slovo argues that the pre-1910 colonial status and subjection of the Black people has continued, whereas for the whites it came to an end in that year and that 'The ruling and exploitative establishment has always been drawn from the dominant white group (either local or foreign), and the Blacks as a group have always had a subject or colonial status'.[40]

One might as well argue that the bourgeoisie and peasantry nurtured in the womb of European feudalism became, after the bourgeois-democratic revolutions of the eighteenth and nineteenth centuries, 'imperialists' and 'colonised subjects', respectively. The historical coincidence that in the case of Europe, we had people of the same skin colour, whereas in the South African case we have people of different skin colour merely exposes the fact that those who characterise the latter case as a 'colonialism of a special type' are the prisoners of the pluralist thesis which is based on a mystified conception of 'race'. I do not, of course, contend that the 'racial' factor in the South African case is non-existent or unimportant. On the contrary, it is of the greatest importance. But unless one sees it in a proper perspective, unless one's theory can account for its significance in a scientific manner, one's political strategy remains vulnerable to the winds of sectionalist opportunism.

This is evident from the very consistency of the advocates of the internal colonialism thesis. They really *do* perceive of the colour-caste groups, the four so-called 'racial' groups of South Africa, as nations or national groups who are nationally oppressed like overseas colonials. That national oppression can conceivably have a different meaning is not properly understood. It *is* understood in part, because the consistency breaks down at the fundamental point concerning the right of nations to self-determination. This right – for *nations* – involves the right to secede from the multi-national state. In this, the Afrikaner sectionalists are – theoretically – more consistent than the other multi-nationalists who baulk at the spectre of the logical conclusion of their theory. Yet the National Party's 'multi-national' frame of reference is completely congruent with the colonial analogy used by the SACP and – as the example of Matthews shows – constitutes the point of tangency between 'Afrikaner nationalism' and 'African nationalism' interpreted in this way. Consistency, on the other hand, is found for instance in 'Trotsky's Letter' quoted above. The former Soviet leader, whose ignorance of South African history absolves him from responsibility for his incorrect conclusions, also believed that the 'races' were nationalities.[41] Hence he held that:

We must accept with all decisiveness and without any reservations the complete and unconditional right of the Blacks to independence. Only on the basis of a mutual struggle against the domination of the white exploiters can be cultivated and strengthened the solidarity of Black and White toilers. It is possible that the Blacks will after victory find it unnecessary to form a separate Black State in South Africa; certainly we will not *force them* to establish a separate State ... The proletarian revolutionaries must never forget the right of the oppressed nationalities to self-determination, including a full separation, and of the duty of the proletariat of the oppressing nation to defend this right with arms in hand if necessary.[42]

The contradictions of the multi-national approach to national liberation have been sufficiently revealed. It is clear that the internal colonialism thesis needs to be recast and that the discourse of 'nationalities' and 'minorities' needs to be rephrased if the liberationist intentions and strategic conceptions of many members of the Congress Movement are not to come into irreconcilable conflict with their theory. Moreover, it needs to be stressed that any bourgeois or aspirant bourgeois leadership which takes to heart these theories could without much effort persuade its following that self-determination means 'national' territorial separation from the South African state. The option of 'Black majority rule' in a unitary South African state can only remain an effective mobilising slogan in the current southern African climate of revolutionary optimism. But – as the example of Matthews shows – disenchantment with the tortuous and hazardous road of armed struggle can lead to mass and debilitating defections to the enemy, *using the theory of the National Liberation Movement itself.* The pluralist thesis – which is what multi-nationalism is – lays the movement open to a fatal alliance with the liberal bourgeoisie.

PART II

Reaping the Whirlwind:
The 1970s and the 1980s

Introduction to Part II

Although written in 2007, the first article is reflective and insightful of events in the 1970s and the strategies of resistance organisations primarily in the Black Consciousness Movement but also other organisations. It also speaks to the divide-and-rule policies of the Bantustan 'leaders'. It is written in a biographical register and an elegiac tone since Steve Biko 'was ambushed by the apartheid police and murdered on his way back from a visit to Cape Town ... One of the purposes of that visit was to discuss with our group some of the apparent obstacles that had emerged with respect to the planned intervention for unification of the armed formations and of the liberation forces more generally'.

Biko was stopped with another activist Peter Jones at a random police checkpoint on his way back from Alexander's house in Cape Town on 18 August 1977. Both Alexander and Biko were under restrictive banning orders. Taken to a police station and although in disguise, Biko was recognised by the police. He was jailed in Port Elizabeth (now called Gqeberha), severely assaulted by the security police, then driven naked and shackled in a police van to Pretoria (a distance of 740 miles), where he died of a massive brain haemorrhage on 12 September 1977.

In the second article, Alexander uses (possibly for the first time in his writings) the concept of 'racial capitalism' which has now achieved considerable attention internationally and is the subject of many contemporary writings on the subject. It is clearly intended to explicate the nature of the relationship between apartheid's racist regime and capitalism in South Africa, a relationship which remains hidden from view in liberal interpretations of apartheid. The latter interpreted capitalism as separable from and dysfunctional to the racist system. Such a perspective, however, conflicted with the enormous body of evidence to the contrary.

Central to his approach to the national question were the many concepts used in its discussion and this required Alexander to explore and clarify his use and understanding of them and especially to distinguish his approach from those against whom he directed his critique. Thus his explanation of concepts like 'race', 'nationality', 'national group' 'ethnicity', and the struggles against racial capitalism from conceptions of 'multi-racialism' and 'non-racialism'.

Arguably the best and succinct analysis of the 1976 Uprising, the third article pays homage to the hundreds of students who were killed by the apartheid police but also the crisis in apartheid education. Alexander lyrically asserts, 'the fact of the matter is that the rifles and ammunition that laid low Hector Peterson and his comrades and that sent the Tsietsi Mashininis into exile and the Dan Montsitsis into prison, put an end to all illusions about achieving equality of conditions and of educational content as long as the system of racial capitalism obtained in South Africa'.

The final article provides the background to the adoption of a socialist document, the Azanian Manifesto, which called for a struggle against racial capitalism. He also discusses the formation of the National Forum, a united front against attempts by the apartheid regime to divide the oppressed. In the article, Alexander is keen to correct what he considers distortions and the need to correct the historical record.

The final article has important historical significance, especially in the light of the tendentious writing of history from the perspective of its 'victors'. Alexander sets out here to 'illuminate' and to counter the falsifications about the National Forum, in which he was a key figure, and its adoption in 1983 of the Azanian Manifesto as a socialist programme for a united front against racial capitalism. He was especially concerned to counteract the 'distortions' about the National Forum by the media, political and academic commentators, and its 'disappearance from the national canvas'. He argues that the Forum constituted an alternative approach to the liberation struggle to that of the prevailing dominant view which largely ignored any perspective about the struggle against apartheid – other than that of the ANC.

An orientation to socialist ideas was important to the development of the National Forum whose major purpose was to promote the unification of the liberation movement as a whole in a 'long-term strategic alliance' for the overthrow of the apartheid state and to overcome the pervasive sectarianism that marred such a possibility. Alexander provides the background to the decision to send Steve Biko and himself to 'discuss with the armed movement in exile' the idea of forming a united front in opposition to the apartheid regime. He refers also to the tragic circumstances of Biko's murder. Alexander also provides an analysis of the principles which informed the programmatic demands of the Azanian Manifesto and the political pledges and commitments associated with it.

'Steve Biko's Last Attempt at Uniting the Liberation Forces'[1]

A MOMENT OF POIGNANCY

I am profoundly moved and honoured by the invitation from Rhodes University to me to deliver this tribute to Bantu Stephen Biko. For very many reasons, this is a moment of poignancy for me. I never met Steve Biko even though I had ample opportunity to do so at one of the turning points in contemporary South African history. That fact is an integral part of the story I want to tell this evening. I am motivated to do so because I believe that we should review our recent past in such a manner as to foreground the complexity of the historical process and to counter the impression that there was some inevitable trajectory that had been predetermined by some unknown trans-historical 'intelligence'.

A MOMENT OF NATIONAL REFLECTION

Anyone who sets out to recount a segment of contemporary history has to accept that his or her version of events will be challenged, denied, or corrected in various ways. When the events recounted refer to periods of violent political contestation, the danger that such an account might be condemned as deliberately falsifying is very great. If one is as conscious as I am of the traps that are strewn in the path of those who engage in the writing of contemporary history, it is obvious that one must have good reasons for attempting to write about such events.

I have chosen the occasion of the commemoration of the death of Comrade Bantu Stephen Biko at the hands of the brutalised killers of the apartheid regime in order to make two essential points. But, before I say what these are, let me say quite simply that the remembrance on the part of the entire South African nation of one of the darkest periods of our recent history should not be wasted on mere pomp and ceremony. Today, we are facing a social crisis of such crucial significance for the future of the new historical community that we are trying to create in this country that not to use this moment of national reflection for the purpose of reviewing and reconsidering the direction in which we are moving would be tantamount to a second national suicide. Beyond the obvious and much eulogised political, economic, social, and cultural achievements of post-apartheid South Africa, all of us know from very personal experience that fundamental issues, including many that were central to the philosophical understandings of Steve Biko, remain unresolved. They are manifest in the numerous social pathologies that we are afflicted by, whether we think of the rampant crime, violence, abuse, individualism, corruption, AIDS, TB, or the basic socio-economic inequality from which most of these ills derive. The growing gap between rich and poor is like the elephant in the room, an overwhelming presence that everyone tries to ignore, one which will sooner or later wreck the entire edifice.

This is the reason why I want to focus our attention this evening on two fundamental insights of the Biko generation, namely, the need for unity of the liberation forces and the need to build our communities on the basis of the socialist values intrinsic to the concept of *ubuntu*. In doing so, I shall avoid the analytical discourse that we have come to associate with these occasions and proceed, rather, to tell you two related stories about the relations between Biko, the Black Consciousness Movement and tendencies that were critical of, but not hostile to, the BCM. The ability to do this and to emerge from the exercise with a sense of constructive understanding of the issues and, thus, of a way forward is, for me, the litmus test of a democratic dialogue. In the early 1950s, a short pamphlet by the Chinese Communist Party leader, Li Shao-Chi, entitled 'How to Handle Contradictions Among the People', was very popular in radical circles and it had a strong influence on my own thinking. Its thrust was that it is essential to recognise whether specific contradictions are antagonistic or non-antagonistic, since this will determine one's strategy and tactics. This is the reason why it was possible for us to work closely at many different levels with the BCM.

A PERSONAL NOTE

When we emerged from Robben Island Prison in April 1974, we had no knowledge at all of the BCM. Though under house arrest, which was the fate of all released political prisoners at the time, we immediately set about regrouping, and contacted those of our organisation or persuasion who had survived the waves of repression of the early 1960s, in order to get to an understanding of the political dynamics in

the country at a time when FRELIMO and the MPLA were rapidly liberating the former Portuguese colonies in southern Africa and having
a tangible influence on people's spirit and their willingness to engage
politically. We quickly understood that the cadres of the BCM were, if
not the only, then certainly the main, activists in the Western Cape and
elsewhere in the country. Like other graduates of Robben Island University from diverse political backgrounds, we began engaging with these
activists, many of whom had approached us to help them in the study
of political theory and South African and African history. Our interactions were of exceptional use and significance to all concerned. All of
us knew that we differed on grounds of philosophical orientation and
political strategy but it was our common understanding of the need for a
united front that made us explore together the possibilities of joint action.
In this way, a sense of mutual respect and trust evolved among us and we,
who had been involved in adult literacy projects during the 1950s and on
the Island itself, came to appreciate and to understand the importance
and the significance of the Black Community Programmes as a means of
community building and, thus, an instrument of political mobilisation.
Elsewhere,[2] I have analysed these activities of the BCM in terms of Gramscian and Freirean theories of the war of position and the pedagogy of the
oppressed. There is no doubt in my mind that although this was not the
first time in twentieth-century South African history that these tactics
were employed by political activists, it was the first time that they were
employed as part of a systematic strategy that was integrated in a political
vision and a programme of action inspired by the need for the unification
of the oppressed and exploited masses of the people who, for reasons of
history, were organised in and paid allegiance to different and contending
political organisations. Of these, in the 1970s, the most important were
the ANC and the PAC. The Unity Movement in its various instantiations
had become all but invisible even though, as subsequent developments
showed, it had not expired.

Be that as it may, this explicitly political analysis is not the subject of
my address this evening. Instead, I should like to refer, by way of practical
example, to the fact that a number of the activists who were organised in
the underground independent socialist group we had established almost
as soon as we were jettisoned from the prisons where we had spent the
previous decade, among other things, worked in the community projects established by BCM, including especially the Zanempilo Clinic in
the Eastern Cape and the clothing factory in the Western Cape. It was,

as I have indicated, through these activities and through the joint study groups that we got to know and trust one another.

A POLITICAL NOTE

It was because of this bond that it became possible for us to consider joint political activity. The event that first made this feasible was the projected 'independence' of the Transkei Bantustan in October 1976. As soon as this possibility became known, we began discussing the ways in which the people could be mobilised against this overt Afrikaaner Nationalist strategy of partitioning South Africa. In the context of the repression at the time, it was clear that a protest action would have to mark our rejection of this violation of territorial integrity of the country, even though none of us for one minute believed in some kind of chauvinist manner in the national entity that Britain with the complicit agreement of the *Boer* generals had created in 1910. Indeed, our common acceptance of the name 'Azania' for this entity was meant, among other things to give expression to the pan-African aspirations that were an integral part of radical political action at the time. Incidentally, since we are busy renaming streets, towns, cities and other places, this might be the moment to think about renaming the country we live in, given the etymology of its current appellation.

As I remember it, the call for such a demonstration originated in Ginsberg/King William's Town, but it may well have started elsewhere. The fact is that all of us were thinking along the same lines and the idea was completely consonant with the spirit of the time. We agreed to establish joint organising committees that would include people from all political tendencies in the liberation movement even though most of the members were necessarily affiliated to the BCM via the Black People's Convention or other BC structures. The details have faded, I am afraid to say, and I doubt whether much, if any, documentation might substantiate these assertions in detail, because such documentation would have been perilous at the time. However, I have no doubt that there are people in this very audience who will vouch for the truth of what I am recounting here. On the other hand, although I do not hope so, I assume that such acknowledgement may well be inconvenient today for some of those who came from all over South Africa and met with me and others in illegal nocturnal meetings in Cape Town and elsewhere in order to discuss principles, tactics, and logistics for the realisation of this protest demonstration that would have been held in the vicinity of Pretoria on 26 October 1976. As it turned out, the unexpected events of June 1976 that we now commemorate as the Soweto Uprising cut across this dynamic and set in motion the wave of mobilisations and uprisings that eventually brought the apartheid regime to the negotiation table.

In the aftermath of the Soweto Uprising, we began to discuss in all seriousness a practical strategy for bringing together the liberation forces, including the armed formations, of the movement. This was in accordance with one of the fundamental tenets of the BCM and had been articulated on many occasions and in different forms by Steve Biko himself. In one of his very last interviews a few months before he was murdered, he addressed the issue in the clearest possible terms with reference to the divide-and-rule function of the Bantustan leadership:

> We are of the view that we should operate as one united whole toward attainment of an egalitarian society for the whole of Azania. Therefore, entrenchment of tribalistic, racialistic or any form of sectional outlook is abhorred by us. We hate it and we seek to destroy it. It is for this reason therefore that we cannot see any form of coalition with any of the Bantustan leaders, even the so-called best of them like Gatsha Buthelezi, because they destroy themselves by virtue of the kind of arguments that one has put up.[3]

And, with reference to the armed formations, he was equally clear though guarded because of the legal constraints on freedom of speech:

> I think in the end there is going to be a totality of the effect of a number of change agencies operating in South Africa. I personally would like to see fewer groups. I would like to see groups like the ANC, PAC and the Black Consciousness Movement deciding to form one liberation group. It is only, I think, when Black people are so dedicated and so united in their cause that we can affect the greatest results ...[4]

REFLECTION ON THE BCM

Which brings me to reflect on one of the most significant practical political lessons of the Biko generation. To put it in a nutshell: they taught us that the struggle for liberation has to encompass all dimensions of society and of the individual. Economic reductionism which, among other things, sees the trade union and other economic struggles as the totality of the struggle is neither enough nor even as fundamental in the long term as many previous theoreticians and strategists of the movement have maintained. This practical insight which led, among many other things, to some of the most innovative artistic work of the second half of the twentieth century, was the source of the emphasis on community development projects, for which the BCM became so well-known and so firmly planted in the grassroots across the country. It was the socio-political counterpart of the struggle against the slave mentality and for the decolonisation of the mind. Education for liberation meant that the young university and high school students had to roll up their sleeves, get down on their knees and help to promote that sense of self-reliance that is the beginning of all liberation and of all liberated zones.

Today, as we commemorate the death of one of the most charismatic individuals of our struggle against colonialism, apartheid, and capitalism, it is essential that we recall these valiant efforts of the BCM to return not merely to the African source of *ubuntu* as a means of undermining the rampant individualism and destructive competition that are inherent in the capitalist system but more generally to all the springs of a true humanity. In the words of Biko himself:

> We see a completely non-racial society. We don't believe, for instance, in the so-called guarantees for minority rights, because guaranteeing minority rights implies the recognition of portions of the community on a race basis. We believe that in our country there shall be no minority, there shall be no majority, just the people. And those people will have the same status before the law and they will have the same political rights before the law …[5]

Asked whether the Black majority would not be motivated by feelings of resentment and desires for revenge, Biko responded to the journalist just a few months before his death:

> We believe it is the duty of the vanguard political movement which brings change to educate people's outlook. In the same way that Blacks have never lived in a socialist economic system they've got to learn to live in one. And in the same way that they've always lived in a racially divided society, they've got to learn to live in a non-racial society. They've got many things to learn.

In paying tribute to Steve Biko and through him to all those who were called upon to make the supreme sacrifice to get us to this stage in our long march to freedom, equality, and solidarity, I can do no better than to suggest that this remains our primary task: to learn and to teach one another how to live in a democratic non-racial society based on anti-capitalist economic and humanist social and cultural principles. We have to protect and rebuild our communities and our neighbourhoods. The blight of a decaying epochal culture is infecting our country in all strata and in all dimensions. These words of Steve Biko are at one and the same time an accurate diagnosis and a prescription for social and individual health. Let us once again create the conditions in which our youth and other activists can become the barefoot doctors that will restore our self-respect and eradicate the conditions of our enslavement and of our debasement.

The struggle continues!

'Nation and Ethnicity in South Africa'[1]

The immediate goal of the national liberation struggle now being waged in South Africa is the destruction of the system of racial capitalism. Apartheid is simply a particular socio-political expression of this system. Our opposition to apartheid is therefore only a starting point for our struggle against the structures and interests which are the real basis of apartheid.

In South Africa, as in any other modern capitalist country, the ruling class consists of the owners of capital which is invested in mines, factories, land, wholesaling and distribution networks, and banks. The different sections of the ruling class often disagree about the best methods of maintaining or developing the system of 'free enterprise', as they call the capitalist system. They are united, however, on the need to protect the system as a whole against all threats from inside and outside the country.

During the past hundred-odd years, a modern industrial economy has been created in South Africa under the spur of the capitalist class. The most diverse groups of people (European settlers, immigrants, African and East Indian slaves, Indian and Chinese indentured labourers, and indigenous African people) were brought together and compelled to labour for the profit of the different capitalist owners of the means of production.

Now, during the eighteenth and nineteenth centuries in Western and Central Europe, roughly similar processes had taken place. But there was one major difference between Europe and the colonies of Europe. For in Europe, in the epoch of the rise of capitalism, the up-and-coming capitalist class had to struggle (together with and in fact on the backs of the downtrodden peasantry and the tiny class of wage workers) against the feudal aristocracy in order to be allowed to unfold their enterprise. Through unequal taxation, restrictions on freedom of trade and freedom of movement and in a thousand different ways the aristocracy exploited the bourgeoisie and the other toiling classes.

In order to gain the benefit of their labours, to free the rapidly developing forces of production from the fetters of feudal relations of production, the capitalist class had to organise the peasants and the other urban classes to overthrow the feudal system. In the course of these struggles of national unification, this bourgeoisie developed a nationalist democratic ideology and its cultural values and practices became the dominant ones in the new nations. The bourgeoisie became the leading class in the nation and were able to structure it in accordance with their class interests.

In the twentieth century in the colonies of Europe, however, the situation has been and is entirely different. In these colonies, European or metropolitan capitalism (imperialism) had become the oppressor who brutally exploited the colonial peoples. In some cases, the colonial power had allowed or even encouraged a class of colonial satellite capitalists to come into being. This class, being completely dependent on London, Paris, Brussels, Berlin, or New York could not oppose imperialism in any consistent manner. If it had done so it would in effect have committed class suicide because it would have had to advocate the destruction of the imperialist-capitalist system which is the basis of colonial oppression. After World War II, especially, the imperialist powers realised that this situation (backed up by the existence and expansion of the Soviet system) would put a great strain on the capitalist system as a whole. Consequently, we had a period of 'decolonisation' which as we now know merely ushered in the present epoch of neo-colonialism which Kwame Nkrumah optimistically called the 'last stage of imperialism'.

In South Africa, a peculiar development took place. Here, the national bourgeoisie had come to consist of a class of white capitalists. Because they could only farm and mine gold and diamonds profitably if they had an unlimited supply of cheap labour, they found it necessary to create a split labour market – one for cheap Black labour and one for skilled and semi-skilled (mainly white) labour. This was made easier by the fact that in the pre-industrial colonial period white–Black relationships had been essentially master–servant relations. Racialist attitudes were therefore prevalent in one degree or another throughout the country. In order to secure their labour supply as required, the national bourgeoisie in South Africa had to institute and perpetuate the system whereby Black people were denied political rights, were restricted in their freedom of movement, tied to the land in so-called 'native reserves', not allowed to own landed property anywhere in South Africa and their children given an education, if they received any at all, that 'prepared them for life in a subordinate society'. Unlike their European predecessors in the eighteenth and nineteenth centuries, the colonial national bourgeoisie in South Africa could not complete the bourgeois-democratic revolution. They compromised with British imperialism in 1910 in order to maintain their profitable system of super-exploitation of Black labour.

They did not incorporate the entire population under the new state on the basis of legal equality, they could not unite the nation. On the contrary, ever since 1910, elaborate strategies have been evolved and implemented to divide the working people into ever smaller potentially antagonistic groups. Divide and rule, the main policy of any imperial power, has been the compass of every government of South Africa since 1910.

In order to justify these policies the ideology of racism was elaborated, systematised, and universalised. People were born into a set-up where they were categorised 'racially'. They grew up believing that they were 'whites', 'Coloureds', 'Africans', 'Indians'. Since 1948, they have been encouraged and often forced to think of themselves in even more microscopic terms as 'Xhosa', 'Zulu', 'Malay', 'Muslim', 'Hindu', 'Griqua', 'Sotho', 'Venda', etc. To put it differently: at first, the ruling ideology decreed that the people of South Africa were grouped by God into four 'races'. The ideal policy of the conservative fascist-minded politicians of the capitalist class was to keep these 'races' separate. The so-called liberal element strove for 'harmonious race relations in a multi-racial country'. Because of the development of the biological sciences where the very concept of 'race' was questioned and because of the catastrophic consequences of the racist *Herrenvolk* policies of Hitler Germany, socio-political theories based on the concept of 'race' fell into disrepute. The social theorists of the ruling class then resorted to the theory of 'ethnic groups', which had in the meantime become a firmly established instrument of economic and political policy in the United States of America as well as elsewhere in the world. It is to be noted that this theory of ethnicity continued to be based on the ideology of 'race' as far as South Africa was concerned.

From the point of view of the ruling class, however, the theory of 'ethnic groups' was a superior instrument of policy because, as I have pointed out, it could explain and justify even greater fragmentation of the working people whose unity held within itself the message of doom for the capitalist apartheid system in this country. The fact of the matter is that the Afrikaner National Party used ethnic theories in order to justify Bantustan strategy whereby it created bogus 'nations' and forced them to accept an illusory 'independence' so that the working class would agitate for political rights in their own so-called 'homeland'.

The idea, as we all know, was to create, revive, and entrench antagonistic feelings of difference between language groups (Xhosa, Zulu, Sotho, Tswana, etc.), religious groups (Muslim, Hindu, Christian, etc.), 'cultural' groups (Griqua, Malay, Coloured, etc.), and of course 'racial' groups (African, Coloured, Indian, white, etc.). I need not show here how this theory was designed to serve the interests of the ruling class by preserving apartheid (grand and petty) and how ruthlessly it was applied. The literature on apartheid is so large today that no single person could study all of it in the span of one lifetime. What we need to do is to take a careful, if brief, look at how the liberation movement has conceived of the differences between and the unity of the officially classified population registration groups, the different language groups and religious sects that constitute our single nation.

MULTI-RACIALISM, NON-RACIALISM, AND ANTI-RACISM

Those organisations and writers within the liberation movement who used to put forward the view that South Africa is a multi-racial country composed of four 'races' no longer do so for the same reasons as the conservative and liberal ruling-class theorists. They have begun to speak more and more of building a 'non-racial' South Africa. I am afraid to say that for most people who use this term 'non-racial' it means exactly the same thing as multi-racial. They continue to conceive of South Africa's population as consisting of four so-called 'races'. It has become fashionable to intone the words a 'non-racial democratic South Africa' as a kind of open sesame that permits one to enter into the hallowed portals of the progressive 'democratic movement'. There is nothing wrong with the words themselves. But, if we do not want to be deceived by words we have to look behind them at the concepts and the actions on which they are based.

The word 'non-racial' can be accepted by a racially oppressed people if it means that we reject the concept of 'race', that we deny the existence of 'races' and thus oppose all actions, practices, beliefs, and policies based on the concept of 'race'. If in practice (and in theory) we continue to use the word non-racial as though we believe that South Africa is inhabited by four so-called 'races', we are still trapped in multi-racialism and thus in racialism. Non-racialism, meaning the denial of the existence of races, leads on to 'anti-racism' which goes beyond it because the term not only involves the denial of 'race' but also opposition to the capitalist structures for the perpetuation of which the ideology and theory of 'race' exist. Words are like money. They are easily counterfeited and it is often difficult to tell the real coin from the false one. We need, therefore, at all times to find out whether our non-racialists are multi-racialists or anti-racists. Only the latter variety can belong in the National Liberation Movement.

ETHNIC GROUPS, NATIONAL GROUPS, AND NATIONS

The theory of ethnicity and of ethnic groups has taken the place of theories of 'race' in the modern world. Very often 'racial' theories are incorporated into 'ethnic theories'. In this paper, I am not going to discuss the *scientific validity* of ethnic theory usually called pluralism of one kind or another. That is a job that one or more of us in the liberation movement must do and do very soon before our youth get infected incurably with these dangerous ideas at the universities. All that I need to point out here is that the way in which the ideologues of the National Party use the term 'ethnic group' makes it almost impossible for any serious-minded person grappling with these problems to use the term as a tool of analysis.

It has been shown by a number of writers that the National Party's use of the terminology of ethnicity is contradictory and designed simply to justify the apartheid/Bantustan policies. Thus, for example, they claim amongst other things that:

The 'African' people consist of between eight and ten different 'ethnic groups', all of whom want to attain 'national', i.e. Bantustan, 'independence'.

The 'coloured' people consist of at least three different 'ethnic groups' (Malay, Cape Coloured, Griqua, and possibly 'other Coloured'). On the other hand, 'Coloureds' are themselves an ethnic group, but not a 'nation'.

The 'Indian' people constitute an ethnic group as do people of Chinese origin, but these are not 'nations'.

The 'white' people consist of Afrikaans, English and other ethnic groups but constitute a single nation, the white nation of South Africa.

In all this tangle of contradictions, the most important point is that every 'ethnic group' is potentially a so-called 'nation' unless it is already part of a 'nation' as in the case of the whites.

We have to admit that in the liberation movement ever since 1896, the question of the different population registration groups has presented us with a major problem, one which was either glossed over or evaded or simply ignored. I cannot go into the history of the matter here. We shall have to content ourselves with the different positions taken up by different tendencies in the liberation movement today. These can be summarised briefly as falling into three categories:

For some, the population registration groups are 'national groups or racial groups, or sometimes ethnic groups'. The position of these people is that it is a 'self-evident and undeniable reality that there are Indians,

Coloureds, Africans and whites (national groups) in our country. It is a reality precisely because each of these national groups has its own heritage, culture, language, customs and traditions'.[2]

Without debating the point any further, let me say that this is the classical position of ethnic theory. I shall show presently that the use of the word 'national group' is fraught with dangers not because it is a word but because it gives expression to and thereby reinforces separatist and disruptive tendencies in the body politic of South Africa. The advocates of this theory outside the liberation movement, such as Inkatha and the PFP, draw the conclusion that a federal constitutional solution is the order of the day. Those inside the liberation movement believe contradictorily that even though the national groups with their different cultures will continue to exist they can somehow do so in a unitary state as part of a single nation.

We have to state clearly that if things really are as they appear to be we would not need any science. If the sun really quite self-evidently moved around the earth we would not require astronomy and space research to explain to us that the opposite is true, that the 'self-evidently real' is only apparent. Of course, there are historically evolved differences of language, religion, customs, job specialisation, etc. among the different groups in this country. But we have to view these differences historically, not statically. They have been enhanced and artificially engendered by the deliberate ruling-class policy of keeping the population registration groups in separate compartments, making them lead their lives in group isolation except in the marketplace. This is a historical reality. It is not an unchanging situation that stands above or outside history. I shall show just now how this historical reality has to be reconciled through class struggle with the reality of a single nation.

The danger inherent in this kind of talk is quite simply that it makes room both in theory and in practice for the preaching of ethnic separatism. It is claimed that a theory of 'national groups' advocated in the context of a movement for national liberation merely seeks

to heighten the positive features of each national group and to weld these together so that there arises out of this process or organization a single national consciousness.[3]

Whereas the ruling class 'relying upon the negative features' of each national group 'emphasises ethnicity' or 'uses culture in order to reinforce separation and division'. We can repeat this kind of intellectualistic solace until we fall asleep, the fact remains that 'ethnic' or 'national group' approaches are the thin edge of the wedge for separatist movements and civil wars fanned by great-power interests and suppliers of arms to opportunist 'ethnic leaders'. Does not Inkatha in some ways represent a warning to all of us? Who decides what are the 'positive features' of a national group? what are the boundaries or limits of a national group? Are these determined by the population register? Is a national group a stunted nation, one that, given the appropriate soil, will fight for national self-determination in its own nation-state? Or does the word 'national' have some other more sophisticated meaning?

These are relevant questions to ask because the advocates of the four-nation or national-group approach maintain that a liberated South Africa will guarantee group rights such as 'the right of national groups to their culture' and that 'we have to accept that if the existence of national groups is a reality and if each national group has its own culture, traditions, and problems, the movement for change is best facilitated by enabling organization around issues which concern people in their daily lives, issues such as low wages, high transport costs and poor housing'. Or, as other representatives of this tendency have bluntly said, we need separate organisations for each of the national groups, which organisations can and should be brought together in an alliance.

These are weighty conclusions on which history itself (since 1960 and especially since 1976) has pronounced a negative judgement. To fan the fires of ethnic politics today is to go backwards, not forwards. It plays into the hands of the reactionary middle-class leadership. It is a reactionary, not a progressive policy from the point of view of the liberation movement taken as a whole. Imagine us advocating 'Indian', 'Coloured', and 'African' trade unions or student unions today!

There is a diametrically opposite view within the liberation movement even though it is held by a very small minority of people. According to this view, our struggle is not a struggle for national liberation. It is a class struggle pure and simple, one in which the 'working class' will wrest power from the 'capitalist class'.

For this reason, the workers should be organised regardless of what so-called group they belong to. This tendency seems to say (in theory) that the historically evolved differences are irrelevant or at best of secondary importance.

I find it difficult to take this position seriously. I suspect that in practice the activists who hold this view are compelled to make the most acrobatic compromises with the reality of racial prejudice among 'workers'. To deny the reality of prejudice and perceived differences, whatever their origin, is to disarm oneself strategically and tactically. It becomes impossible to organise a mass movement outside the ranks of a few thousand students perhaps.

Again, the historical experience of the liberation movement in South Africa does not permit us to entertain this kind of conclusion. All the little organisations and groups that have at one time or another operated on this basis have vanished after telling their simple story which, though 'full of sound and fury', signified nothing.

The third position is one that has been proven to be correct by the history of all successful liberation struggles in Africa and elsewhere. I have found no better description of this position than that outlined by President Samora Machel in a speech held in August 1982 in reply to General Malan's accusations that South Africa was being 'destabilised' by hostile elements in the subcontinent. In that speech, Machel said amongst other things:

Our nation is historically new. The awareness of being Mozambicans arose with the common oppression suffered by all of us under colonialism from the Rovuma to the Maputo. Frelimo, in its twenty years of existence and in this path of struggle, turned us progressively into Mozambicans, no longer Makonde and Shangane, Nyanja and Ronga, Nyungwe and Bitonga, Chuabo and Ndau, Macua and Xitsua. Frelimo turned us into equal sons of the Mozambican nation, whether our skin was Black, brown or white.

Our nation was not moulded and forged by feudal or bourgeois gentlemen. It arose from our armed struggle. It was carved out by our hard-working calloused hands.

Thus during the national liberation war, the ideas of country and freedom were closely associated with victory of the working people. We fought to free the land and the people. This is the reason that those, who at the time wanted the land and the people in order to exploit them, left us to go and fight in the ranks of colonialism, their partner. The unity of the Mozambican nation and Mozambican patriotism is found in the essential components of, and we emphasise, anti-racism, socialism, freedom and unity.[4]

This statement is especially significant when one realises for many years FRELIMO accepted that 'there is no antagonism between the existence of a number of ethnic groups and national unity'. This sentence comes from a FRELIMO document entitled 'Mozambican Tribes and Ethnic Groups: Their Significance in the struggle for National Liberation'. It was written at a time 'when the movement actually was under strong pressure from politicians who were consciously manipulating ethnicity in their own interest'.[5]

Even earlier in 1962 a FRELIMO document had stressed that:

> it is true that there are differences among us Mozambicans. Some of us are Makondes, others are Nyanjas, others Macuas, etc. Some of us come from the mountains, others from the plains. Each of our tribes has its own language, its specific uses and habitudes and different cultures. There are differences among us. This is normal ... In all big countries there are differences among people.
>
> All of us Mozambicans – Macuas, Makondes, Nyanjas, Changans, Ajuas, etc. – we want to be free. To be free we have to fight united. All Mozambicans of all tribes are brothers in the struggle. All the tribes of Mozambique must unite in the common struggle for the independence of our country.

The development of the Mozambican national liberation ideology through the lessons learnt in struggle is shown clearly by President Machel's August 1982 statement that

> Ours is not a society in which races and colours, tribes and regions coexist and live harmoniously side by side. We went beyond these ideas during a struggle in which we sometimes had to force people's consciousness in order for them to free themselves from complexes and prejudices so as to become simply, we repeat, simply people.

Every situation is unique. The experience of FRELIMO, while it may have many lessons for us, cannot be duplicated in South Africa. Certainly, the population registration groups of South Africa are neither 'tribes' nor 'ethnic groups' nor 'national groups'. In sociological theory, they can be described as colour castes or more simply as colour groups. So to describe them is not unimportant since the word captures the nature or the direction of development of these groups. But the question of words is not really the issue. What is important is to clarify the relationship between class, colour, culture and nation.

The economic, material, language, religious, and other differences between colour groups are real. They influence and determine the ways in which people live and experience their lives. Reactionary ethnic organisation would not have been so successful in the history of this country had these differences not been of a certain order of reality. However, these differences are neither permanent nor necessarily divisive if they are restructured and redirected for the purposes of national liberation and thus in order to build the nation. The ruling class has used language, religious and sex differences among the working people in order to divide them and to disorganise them. Any organisation of the people that does not set out to counteract these divisive tendencies set up by the ruling-class strategies merely ends up by reinforcing these strategies. The cases of Gandhi and Abdurrahman are good examples. Middle-class and aspiring bourgeois elements quickly seize control of such colour-based 'ethnic' organisations and use them as power bases from which they try to bargain for a larger share of the economic cake. This is essentially the kind of thing that the Bantustan leaders and the Bantustan middle classes are doing today.

Because they are oppressed, all Black people who have not accepted the rulers' Bantustan strategy desire to be free and to participate fully in the economic, political, and social life of Azania. We have seen that the national bourgeoisie have failed to complete the democratic revolution. The middle classes cannot be consistent since their interests are, generally speaking and in their own consciousness, tied to the capitalist system. Hence only the Black working class can take the task of completing the democratisation of the country on its shoulders. It alone can unite all the oppressed and exploited classes. It has become the leading class in the building of the nation. It has to redefine the nation and abolish the reactionary definitions of the bourgeoisie and of the reactionary petty bourgeoisie. The nation has to be structured by and in the interests of the Black working class. But it can only do so by changing the entire system. A non-racial capitalism is impossible in South Africa. The class struggle against capitalist exploitation and the national struggle against racial oppression become one struggle under the general command of the Black working class and its organisations. Class, colour, and nation converge in the National Liberation Movement.

Politically in the short term and culturally in the long term the ways in which these insights are translated into practice are of the greatest moment. Although no hard and fast rules are available and few of them are absolute, the following are crucial points in regard to the practical ways in which we should build the nation of Azania and destroy the separatist tendencies amongst us.

Political and economic organisations of the working people should as far as possible be open to all oppressed and exploited people regardless of colour.

While it is true that the Group Areas Act and other laws continue to concentrate people in their organisations – geographically speaking – largely along lines of colour, it is imperative and possible that the organisations themselves should not be structured along these lines. The same political organisations should and can function in all the ghettos and group areas, people must and do identify with the same organisations and not with 'ethnic' organisations.

All struggles (local, regional, and national) should be linked up. No struggle should be fought by one colour group alone. The President's Council proposals, for example, should not be analysed and acted upon as of interest to 'Coloureds' and 'Indians' only. The Koornhof Bills should be clearly seen and fought as affecting all the oppressed and exploited people. Cultural organisations that are not locally or geographically limited for valid community reasons should be open to all oppressed and exploited people.

The songs, stories, poems, dances of one group should become the common property of all even if their content has to be conveyed by means of different language media. In this way, and in many other ways, by means of class struggle on the political and on the cultural front, the cultural achievements of the people will be woven together into one Azanian fabric. In this way, we shall eliminate divisive ethnic consciousness and separatist lines of division without eliminating our cultural achievements and cultural variety. But it will be experienced by all as different aspects of one national culture accessible to all. So that, for example, every Azanian child will know – roughly speaking – the same fairy tales or children's stories, whether these be of 'Indian', 'Xhosa', 'Tswana', 'German', or 'Khoikhoi' origin.

The liberation movement has to evolve and implement a democratic language policy not for tomorrow but for today. We need to discuss seriously how we can implement – with the resources at our disposal – the following model which, to my mind, represents the best possible solution to the problem of communication in Azania.

All Azanians must have a sound knowledge of English whether as home language or as second language. All Azanians must have a conversational knowledge of the other regionally important languages. For example, in the Eastern Province every person will know English; Afrikaans-speaking persons will have a conversational knowledge of Xhosa and Xhosa-speaking persons will have a conversational knowledge of Afrikaans. In an area like Natal, a knowledge of English and Zulu would in all probability suffice.

These are sketchy ideas that have to be filled in through democratic and urgent discussion in all organisations of the people and implemented as soon as we have established the necessary structures and methods.

THE HISTORIC ROLE OF THE BLACK WORKING CLASS

The Black working class is the driving force of the liberation struggle in South Africa. It has to ensure that the leadership of this struggle remains with it if our efforts are not to be deflected into channels of disaster. The Black working class has to act as a magnet that draws all the other oppressed layers of our society, organises them for the liberation struggle, and imbues them with the consistent democratic socialist ideas which alone spell death to the system of racial capitalism as we know it today.

In this struggle, the idea of a single nation is vital because it represents the real interest of the working class and therefore of the future socialist Azania. 'Ethnic', national group or racial group ideas of nationhood in the final analysis strengthen the position of the middle class or even the capitalist oppressors themselves. I repeat, they pave the way for the catastrophic separatist struggles that we have witnessed in other parts of Africa. Let us never forget that more than a million people were massacred in the Biafran War, let us not forget the danger represented by the 'race riots' of 1949. Today, we can choose a different path. We have to create an ideological, political, and cultural climate in which this solution becomes possible. I believe that if we view the question of the nation and ethnicity in this framework we will understand how vital it is that our slogans are heard throughout the length and breadth of our country.

One People, One Azania!
One Azania, One Nation!

'Ten Years of Education Crisis:
The Resonance of 1976'[1]

In the seamless web of South African history, 16 June 1976 represents both an end and a beginning. Those great events, which began as innocently and undramatically as most significant moments in the history of a nation, were the culmination of decades of relatively peaceful protest by Black students against the inequities of segregation and apartheid in the educational institutions of South Africa. The most striking feature of all the years of protest and resistance since the introduction of a modern system of schooling for Black people after the inauguration of the Union of South Africa, was the fact that all the students' actions were motivated by the desire on their part for equality of the conditions of learning and of the content of education with those enjoyed by whites.[2] This feature was enhanced after the introduction of Bantu education and other forms of tribalised schooling. The systematic and provocatively articulated Verwoerdian policies of retribalisation of the oppressed, industrially orientated people of South Africa generated the most intense opposition ever on the part of almost all Black parents, teachers and students at all levels of the schooling system. So much so, indeed, that even the paternalistic missionary education of previous years began to seem desirable. Some of the middle-class beneficiaries of that system, in fact, began to present it as a kind of golden age of Black schooling by blurring over all the reactionary elements that inhere in all golden ages! Be that as it may: the fact of the matter is that the rifles and ammunition that laid low Hector Peterson and his comrades and that sent the Tsietsi Mashininis into exile and the Dan Motsitsis into prison, put an end to all illusions about achieving equality of conditions and of educational content as long as the system of racial capitalism obtained in South Africa.

But they did more than that. In a dialectical fashion, those events made ordinary school students begin to examine more attentively what it was that they were fighting for. The very hopelessness of the struggle for the will-o'-wisp of 'educational equality' made students and eventually many progressive educationists believe that education, properly so-called, was only going to be possible in a liberated South Africa. Education and liberation were seen to be clearly related, the struggle of students for better conditions in the schools, colleges and universities was seen to be inseparable from the struggle for liberation (i.e. the struggle for democratic rights for all) and eventually from the struggle for class emancipation. And, as these things go, once this link had been established in the consciousness of the new generation and in the concrete fact of thousands of Soweto students fleeing into neighbouring territories to find refuge in the guerrilla training camps of the African National Congress and the Pan-Africanist Congress as well as in transit and other shelters run by South African political organisations or by international relief agencies, the Freirean idea of Education for Liberation came to express precisely the dialectical shift that had, quite unintentionally, been brought to the surface by the volleys of rifle fire that drowned in blood one of the most heroic episodes in the history of our people.

From that moment, protest changed into challenge. The class of 1976 and every subsequent generation of Black South African school students rejected even the superficial legitimacy on which South African governments had until then prided themselves and in the faded garments of which they strutted about on the stage of world politics. What is called the battle for the hearts and minds of the Black youth was finally and decisively lost on the streets of Soweto and of every other major city in South Africa in the course of 1976 and 1977. And let it be said here once and for all: *there is simply no way in which this government or any other white minority government is going to regain the trust and the consent of the Black youth*. Neither the *sjambok* (now called the quirt) nor the *casspir*, and no amount of cooing and wooing is going to undo or reverse the thorough demystification of Black schooling begun by the bullets of 1976. Instead, the challenge to state power, state legitimacy inherent in the concepts and practice of liberatory education, people's education, or even alternative education will continue to grow ever stronger, no matter how many retreats will have to be made, no matter how many reverses are suffered.

It is not part of my brief to look back at the causes of the uprising of 1976; I am not expected to repeat the now well-known and even well-worn phrases about the role of the Black Consciousness Movement, of organisations such as SASO and SASM, or even of the link between the renewed stirrings in the urban Black proletariat and the actions and sentiments of their children in the schools of the ruling class. These and other relevant questions have been repeated *ad nauseam* in one conference after another and in one publication after another. Instead, I have been asked to summarise as succinctly as possible what we consider to be the most significant consequences of the uprising of 1976 and of the subsequent actions of Black students, parents, and teachers in the educational arena. By way of explanation, it is necessary to stress that this introduction to the subject is intended to do no more than to draw your attention to what I consider to be the most relevant resonances of those events. I have deliberately refrained from overloading the text with tables and graphs, since these are readily accessible in numerous publications. Moreover, I have to stress that this introduction represents no more than a summary of conclusions and ideas reached by very many scholars and activists in countless workshops and conferences. While I take full responsibility for the formulations I use, I want to insist that this is not an original document in the monadic sense of that term.

THE CRISIS

It is as well to begin with a statement of principle. For the sake of analytical convenience, we isolate particular phenomena in order to identify their specific qualities and features. In reality, however, all things are interconnected. The events in the educational arena since 1976, important as they obviously are, cannot be treated in isolation from the critical developments in the rest of the social formation and in southern Africa as a whole. Any monocausal approach leads to blatant distortion of reality and inevitably to disastrous interventions. In short, we have to be clear at all times that the then years of crisis in the educational arena represent at the same time ten years of crisis in the system of racial capitalism as a whole. The crisis in education both reflects and reflects back on the larger crisis in which the system is encoiled politically, economically, and ideologically.

Again, even though there are a few competing analyses of the crisis, the broad outlines are known well enough to permit us simply to state the obvious briefly. There is, first of all, the crisis of capital accumulation. The intensified labour-repressive option represented by apartheid in 1948 and chosen by the white electorate as against the gradualist liberalisation option recommended by the Fagan Commission in 1947, pushed up against ceilings inherent in that option, in particular shortages of skilled labour, a severely restricted domestic market that led to recurrent crises of realisation of value, and shortages of new (especially foreign) investment because of international political pressures against a regime that was seen increasingly as not only racist and genocidal but also dangerous to world capitalism insofar as it bred conditions conducive to socialist revolution in the industrial heart of Africa. This economic crisis has deepened to the extent that by the mid-1980s, the once unstoppable South African economic engine had not only come to a grinding halt but in some years was even going in reverse.

Socially, this has meant that the increasingly proletarianised Black population has been locked into the vicious circle of a kind of Third-World hell of unemployment and poverty, terrifying in the urban ghettos, unbearable in the rural slums. As is well known, even in some cities such as Port Elizabeth, unemployment among the Black youth (under 25 approximately) is placed as high as 70 per cent. And this is not exceptional today. Indeed, as I shall point out presently, this layer of young, mostly semi-schooled, unemployed Black workers is going to be the nemesis of our liberation struggle, the rock on which the solid future of a socialist Azania will be built or upon which the entire struggle will founder.

The existence of this layer of people reminds us that the rapid economic growth of the 1950s and 1960s brought about major changes in the class structure of South Africa. Today, only a few nostalgic analysts would still insist that the 'peasantry' (however defined) constitutes the majority of the oppressed people and thus the driving force of the struggle for liberation. Proletarianisation (and increasingly the urbanisation of the proletariat) has been the visible feature of social development in the post-war period.

By way of precluding any analytical short circuits, let me say parenthetically that the acknowledgement of this indisputable fact of South African history does not in any way detract from the importance of the agrarian question in our struggle or alter the fact of national oppression. New demands, new aspirations, new methods of struggle were placed on the agenda through this process of social evolution. The workers demanded a share of the commodities and facilities which their labour produced; they, therefore, demanded higher wages and better working and living conditions. In this, they were no different from workers anywhere in the world. But, in doing so, they were challenging one of the pillars of the alliance between maize and gold that ruled supreme before World War II. That is to say, they were demanding that the restrictions on the growth of the domestic market for the products of secondary industry be lifted, that the political economy of cheap Black labour be jettisoned and that the importance of the manufacturing sector be given legislative recognition. The trajectory of these demands and aspirations tended in practice towards the many manifestations of class struggle that have become the very ambience in which we live today. I refer, of course, to the struggle for the right to form independent trades unions and all the struggles attendant on that, the struggle for freedom of movement, for efficient and cheap transport, for decent and cheap housing and health care, and, above all, for free and compulsory education for all our children as well as for continuing education for those who are forced to leave the schools prematurely because of poverty and racial oppression.

These demands were, as we all know, made more urgent and more dramatic by historic events in the subcontinent. The victorious liberation struggles in Guinea Bissau, Angola, Mozambique, and Zimbabwe in the mid- to late 1970s and the ongoing saga of Namibia, have lent to the demands of the urban proletariat of South Africa, and especially of the more than 50 per cent of them who are younger than 20 years, an urgency and an impatience that were unknown in the previous decades. South Africa is often portrayed as 'the last colony'. This analogy happens to be very wrong and misleading, for we are not involved in an anti-colonial struggle but rather in a civil-war situation. Analysts and theoreticians may differ on this point but there is no doubt at all that the anti-colonial struggles against Portugal, Britain, and South Africa in neighbouring southern African countries have resonated in the liberation struggle being waged by the oppressed and exploited people of South Africa against the system of racial capitalism. They have, in short, made the Black people impatient to get rid of the racism that springs from the same colonial regimes overthrown between 1975 and 1980 on our borders.

The strategic answer of the ruling class to these socio-economic developments has been the inept attempt to encourage the growth and the co-option of the various Black middle-class elements ranging from Bantustan and other ethnic politicians to the upper echelons of their respective civil services, a large segment of their teachers and other professionals as well as the traditional middle class of small shopkeepers and other business people. In effect, the state has attempted to counter the strategic leverage which the Black working class has acquired within the South African economy by building up a Black middle class as a buffer. This has meant, among other things, doing away piecemeal with various aspects of Verwoerdian apartheid that are immediately repugnant to middle-class people. This, in turn, has meant effectively downgrading the white workers who were previously the junior partners in the class alliance that constituted the power bloc in South Africa.

We are living through the many tragi-comic contradictions that arise from this attempt to construct a neo-apartheid system that will successfully co-opt the Black middle class and simultaneously make the white minority regime more acceptable in the community of nations. Never mind that this is an impossible dream. It is one of those unavoidable adaptive mechanisms imposed by the dynamics of the unique history of nations by which ruling classes desperately attempt to salvage the old order. Sometimes, as in our own case for reasons that are too obvious to recite, such transitional moments seem to last an eternity. But this is all the more reason why it is essential to divine the limits as well as the possibilities of the historical moment. Miscognition so often leads to suicidal action or retreats along the line of march that previous generations have painfully established. There is no need for me to analyse all the manoeuvres and deceptions of a Heunis or a Pik Botha on the one side or of a Le Grange or a De Klerk on the other side by which the regime is trying to make the world believe that Tweedle-Dee and Tweedle-Dum are totally compatible elements of its total strategy of benevolent despotism. Suffice it to repeat that far from gaining legitimacy, this leprous regime instead taints everybody that chooses to collaborate with it. That is a story which every Bantustan leader, every community councillor, every member of a management committee and even the reprobates in the tricameral parliament and in the President's Council can tell in great and vivid detail.

Hegemony, according to Gitlin, is a relationship between the dominant and the dominated class in a social formation. It refers to

> the successful attempt of a dominant class to utilise its control over the resources of state and civil society, particularly through the use of mass media and the educational system to establish its view of the world as all-inclusive and universal. Through the dual use of force and consent, with consent prevailing, the dominant class uses its political, moral and intellectual leadership to shape and incorporate the 'taken-for-granted' views, needs and concerns of sub-ordinate groups. In doing so, the dominant class not only attempts to influence the interests and needs of such groups, it also contains radical opportunities by placing limits on oppositional discourse and practice.[3]

By this or by any similar definition, it is clear that even though the South African ruling class continues necessarily to be dominant, it has, since 1976, become progressively less hegemonic. Barring exceptional historic developments, this is a situation that cannot be reversed.

TOO LITTLE TOO LATE

The campaign of 1976–1977 was followed by the even more deep-going crisis in the schools in 1980. Since 1980, schooling for Blacks has been in a state of permanent disruption even though the focal points of the crisis have shifted from one region of the country to another and there has not yet been a situation where all regions have been equally disrupted. The climax, for the moment, was reached in 1985 when large parts of the schooling system simply collapsed under the sustained assaults of students and mobilised working-class communities. These are well-known facts. It is more important for us to understand, however, that the organic connections between the different arenas in which the crisis of the system becomes manifest lead to the intensification of contradictions in each of the arenas of struggle and thus to ever more radical solutions or proposed solutions. This has been the story of the struggle in the education arena since 1980.

Early on, i.e. before the emergence of the large trade union federations and the national political fronts and their active participation in the hurly-burly of township struggles, one of the consequences of this radicalisation was the belief among many students that students as a group constitute the vanguard of the struggle. In some respects, this was a legacy of the epoch of Black Consciousness and of the particular history of SASO during the repression of the 1960s and early 1970s. We are all familiar with the lament on the part of students that if their parents had acted while they were young, there would have been no need for them to wage 'the struggle' as they were doing. In a forum such as this, where some knowledge of the history of South Africa may be presupposed, it is unnecessary to discuss this assertion. The point to be made here is simply that there was, in historic-ideological terms, a long march ahead of the students out of this student-centric universe through the plains of the 'student–worker alliance' into the hard realities of the 'worker–student alliance'.

Those who are interested in what one may call the phenomenology of student boycotts in South Africa could hardly do better than to read the journalistic gem by Brian Pottinger and Siphiwe Ralo in *Front-line* of March 1981, entitled 'The Eastern Cape Boycotts. Where Crisis has Become a Way of Life'. Here is set out concisely but meticulously the causes, course and consequence of a particular regionally defined boycott of schools, a process described in a framework that could be applied to almost any similar boycott anywhere in South Africa since 1976. Here we find the stubborn statistics of educational deprivation and inequality from which all boycotts start, the general background of turmoil in the Black schools of the country, the specific grievances at a specific school in the region that become the proximate cause of the regional boycott campaign, the inept intervention of the authorities on the one side and/ or the activation of an existing or submerged infrastructure of pupil/ student representation, often the deposit of previous school boycotts and usually including student activists from neighbouring 'Bush Colleges', the rapid escalation of the conflict, the formation of a parents' (crisis) committee, often leading to negotiations or talks with the authorities to defuse the situation, generational conflict between parents and students over such supposed collaboration, and so forth. The rest of the story and all its repercussions must be present to the mind of every member of this audience!

As in the struggles of the Black workers at the point of production or in the townships, the response of the state – from the point of view of the exploited and oppressed – is either too little or too late. Of course, it has never been the intention of the rulers to satisfy the needs of the workers. What is for Botha and his National Party a giant leap is not even a small step towards the realisation of the goals to which the oppressed and exploited people of South Africa are committed!

Essentially, the actions of the generation of Soweto imprinted on our minds the invaluable lesson that the Black working class is the primary source of all radical change in South Africa. It marked the beginning of the end of the epoch of mere reactive strategies and tactics in which the liberation forces had been held captive for six decades and more. Parliament was no longer seen as the *fons et origo* of all socially significant initiatives. Instead, the ruling class was forced to react overtly to the initiatives of the working class. 'Reform' was placed on the order of the day. The liberal antennae of the ruling class in the guise of the South African Institute of Race Relations picked up the signals from the turmoil on the streets. They established the first of the series of reform-orientated ruling-class Commissions to investigate the education provision for Blacks. The report of this (Bozzoli) Commission was entitled *Education for a New Era* and was published in 1979. Neither the subsequent De Lange Commission Report published in 1981 nor the Buthelezi Commission's report, completed in 1982, despite their volume and detail, went beyond the reformist principles established by the SAIRR's Bozzoli Commission. Of these, the most relevant for our purposes is the stipulation that the acknowledgement of the 'multicultural nature of South African society'[4] should be the point of departure for all educational reform. Moreover, the Commission assumed that 'some form of consociational structure will evolve, possibly for a transitional period preceding the establishment of a unitary political system'.[5]

It is tempting to consider in detail the various panaceas that have been put forward by those who wish to reform the unreformable. But this would be a waste of the time of this gathering. These voluminous documents have generated numerous academic and political analyses according to the law whereby all paper produces more paper. We need not get onto that particular merry-go-round! More important, of course, is the fact that for the present the ruling party, out of a consideration of its power-political position, is not even prepared to transform all this paper into some kind of material reality. On the contrary, it has itself produced white papers in order to negate for the present, let us repeat, the recommendation of its own commissions! The point at issue is no more and no less than that the rulers have been forced to react to the historic initiatives of the oppressed and exploited even if only to conjure up the mirage of a slightly different future. In doing so, they have unwittingly strengthened the forces of liberation. The very recommendations of their commissions are found to be too few. Alternatives are, therefore, necessarily put forward and in this completely objective manner, the process of radicalisation is intensified. The regime, as has been often said, is in a no-win or catch-22 situation. It is a pre-revolutionary regime, clinging to the steering wheel of power for as long as it may but in no position to alter radically the fatal course on which its own policies have set the ship of state.

AK47S, PETROL BOMBS, DRIVER'S LICENCES, AND MATRIC CERTIFICATES!

Bearing in mind that we are always speaking of a situation of uneven development both in space and in time, it is nonetheless possible to main-

tain that in the present state of education in South Africa, schooling for
Blacks has become devalued to the extent that only a very few Black students in the urban areas expect to complete their secondary schooling.
Apart from the 'normal' economic political mechanisms that push out
whole phalanxes of Black pupils at the annual points of exit from the
system of tribalised schooling, since 1976 economic, political and ideological pressures generated by the crisis of the system and the maturation
of the struggle for national liberation have put in question profoundly
the legitimacy and usefulness of secondary schooling for the majority of
Black pupils.

There is, first of all, the rapidly growing army of young people who
leave school in order to join the guerrilla fighters, those who have come
to the conclusion that they will serve both themselves and their people
best by taking up arms. This group of young men and women, most of
whom go directly out of school boycotts into exile and – usually – into
training camps (which include further education, of course) numbers
several tens of thousands already and has become in many a township
the role models for our children. For them, sitting around in DET or
other tribalising schools is a waste of time; they represent the most conscious and impatient vanguard of the alienated post-1976 generation and
will become a factor of increasing significance in the overall situation.
Their option, or alternative, will present a challenge to all other proposed
or executed alternatives and it is, therefore, of national importance that
those of us who are concerned for the future socialist dispensation we
believe in consider the most appropriate ways and means whereby this
vanguard element can be synchronised with other equally important and
equally inevitable groups and layers of young (and older) South Africans.

A second 'alternative' is that in which more than a million young Black
South Africans find themselves trapped willy-nilly at any given moment.
This is the rapidly growing army of unemployed Black youths who have
begun to take control of the townships and rural slums of South Africa
at night and increasingly also in the day time. Insofar as their way of life
is not the result of a conscious decision, it does not represent an alternative in the normal sense of the term. On the contrary, they are the
pathetic by-products of the system of racial capitalism just as much as
are the fascist-minded young toughs that gravitate towards the *Afrikaner Weerstandsbeweging* (AWB), the vanguard organisation of the
counter-revolution. Some allegedly liberal journalists and commentators
have compared this army of young men and women with what they call

the Khmer-Rouge youth (a myth of modern journalism if ever there was one)! In doing so, they deliberately evoke the picture of a brainwashed, moronic, ant-like mass of youngsters who at a command from (usually 'ANC') activists will kill and destroy anything, even their nearest and dearest, a kind of debased, dehumanised mass that acts in a paroxysm of self-delusion for 'freedom', 'democracy', and for all the other noble words that we read in the pamphlet literature of every organisation engaged in the liberation struggle.

This is not only adding insult to the injury inflicted on our youth by the system; it is, in fact, a counter-revolutionary misreading of the sociology of modern South Africa. For this youth, as we all know, constitutes the basis of the militancy of the townships. They are the ones who wield petrol bombs, stones and even more lethal weapons usually in self-defence against the system and its agents. That some of them have on occasion been exploited and misled by criminal elements or by *agents provocateurs* does not detract from the overwhelming reality of the fact that they are the ones who have pushed the struggle across the Rubicon and that they and their successors will be in the front ranks of the victorious struggle. I shall show presently why I believe that they, more than any other groups of people, represent the most appropriate audience for any serious liberatory education projects regardless of the names by which they are called. There is certainly no reason to accept fatalistically that all these young people should become criminalised members of anti-social gangs as in the perhaps not untypical case of 'The Hobos' in Bonteheuwel in the Western Cape, whose members were 'too clever for the gangsters' because they were 'school boys dropped out of school during the demonstrations'.[6]

For this group, clearly, formal schooling does not represent an option anymore. They are the ones who have begun to realise that even a matric certificate does not lead to a guaranteed job as it did even ten years ago. They see their older brothers and sisters struggling to help their parents make ends meet in the situation of the well-known advertisement where the system is constantly pulling the ends further and further away from each other. Those who continue to try to find a job have realised that a driver's licence is more useful in South Africa today than is a matric certificate.[7]

There remain 'the lucky few' who make it to and remain in the senior secondary courses of our schools, including our schools in the 'independent' and self-governing Bantustans, let me stress, since the insidious process of talking about our country as though we accept the partitionist strategy of the ruling party has to be countered actively if we are not to aggravate our problems. This has become one of the most analysed and written about groups of people in South Africa since Black students (besides unionised Black workers) have been so visibly on the frontline of the resistance against the consequences of the system of racial capitalism. Indeed, it is difficult to summarise in a few paragraphs the complexity of the dynamics that structure the situation in which Black secondary and tertiary students find themselves today. However, certain features are crystal clear.

It is clear, for example, that the pressures on these students to discontinue or disrupt their schooling are constant and increasing. Conditions of crisis both inside and outside the schools simply make it impossible for Black students in South Africa today to enjoy the luxury of even the segregated inferior normality of yesterday. There are very many analyses of the reasons for this situation and I do not intend to repeat these here. Besides some of the reasons that have been implicit in what I have said hitherto, I should like to draw your attention to two factors that contribute to the shaping of the schooling environment of our children.

The first of these is, of course, the socio-political context. Schooling is seen to be, and is in fact, so inseparably part of the total situation of unequal life chances which defines racial capitalism, that almost anything can spark off a schools boycott. The then president of COSAS, Lulu Johnson, is reported to have said in October 1984 in an interview with the *Financial Mail*:

> Before they are students ... the students are members of their community. Students are affected by rent hikes because it affects the amount of money their families have for their schooling ... The schools and the community are inseparable.[8]

What had been in the 1950s and 1960s an insight shared only by a few thousand 'educated' Black people, *viz.*, the fact that a democratic and adequate system of education is only possible in a democratic non-racial and united South Africa, has become a fact of mass consciousness today. So much so indeed that it is spelt out clearly by academics at most universities, those seats of 'higher learning' which have so often obfuscated the simple truths of the South African situation. In the words of Professor Owen van den Berg:

Equal education is a fiction in an unequal society: schooling – any brand of schooling – will always be unacceptable to the majority if it occurs within an economic, social and political framework that is unacceptable to the majority. And that is the crux of the education debate.[9]

The demands put forward by progressive student organisations of all political tendencies have become more and more overtly political. Some, indeed, have become explicitly socialist or anti-capitalist. In such a context, given the reactionary intransigence of the ruling party, periodic disruptions of schooling for Black adolescents and university students are unavoidable. The Bush Colleges of yesteryear that were deliberately designed to mass-produce Eiselen men and women have instead become the centres of student militancy and political activism. Just as their Afrikaner counterparts of the 1930s and 1940s produced the *Herrenvolk* leaders of the 1950s and after, they are assiduously producing the political and cultural leadership of a free Azania. So much for the 'good' intentions of politicians and social engineers! Because so many of these students come from remote rural areas, their interventions simply guarantee that the political resistance and upheaval will continue to have a national, albeit uneven, spread.

The radicalisation of the student movement is predictable in the circumstances I have sketched. This is as it should be. Our students are no different from any other group of students similarly placed in other parts of the world. However, we would be failing in our duty if we did not point out certain dangers inherent in the relationship between the schools and society. False perceptions or analyses of what is going on in the society at large, a euphoric desire to see only the possibilities in the situation and to ignore its limits, can wreak havoc among the millions of our children at school. It has been said again and again by various progressive organisations and individuals since October 1985 that the optimistic perception of the South African regime as one that is ready to be toppled can only lead to demoralisation and apathy among our children. This false view of the situation generated, among other things, the Nongqause-like slogan 'Liberation Before Education' and beliefs such as that indefinite or long-term boycotts will weaken or even topple the regime. Fortunately, saner counsels have prevailed. A pamphlet underwritten by more than 100 organisations in the Western Cape in January 1986 put the matter clearly and prophetically:

Although most students have decided to 'return to school', there is much confusion about whether or not to return to formal classes. One view is that the boycott should continue until all our demands are met ...

This view is based on a completely false reading of the political situation in South Africa, since it supposes that the National Party government is about to fall and that an indefinite schools boycott will hasten this fall. While it is true that the apartheid state has never been as weak and as open to internal and external pressure as at present, it is a disastrous illusion to believe that the government is on its knees. We believe, instead, that the government will be forced to make certain 'reforms' but that it will be kept in power by its imperialist supporters in the Western world until a more suitable liberal government becomes possible. If this should prove not to be possible, we should prepare ourselves for an open military government supported in deed, if not in words, by all the imperialist powers for the salvation of capitalism in South Africa. In other words: let us not be misled into believing that freedom is already within our grasp. The struggle is going to be a long one yet and is going to demand many more sacrifices from us.

This may not be the popular thing to say but it is the correct and responsible thing to say. There is no moral, political or education reason for continuing the boycott of classes 'indefinitely'. Indeed, to do so would be like plunging a knife into the heart of our struggle. The boycott is one of the most important weapons of an oppressed and unarmed people. But it is not our only weapon. It is but one of a whole arsenal of weapons at the disposal of our people and of our movement. Like all weapons, if it is not used correctly, it can become a suicidal instrument.[10]

A similar assessment of the situation was articulated in the keynote address to the conference of the National Education Crisis Committee in March 1986. At various points in his address, Sisulu warned against euphoria and delusion:

It is important that we don't misrecognise the moment, or understand it to be something which it is not. We are not poised for the immediate transfer of power to the people. The belief that this is so could lead to serious errors and defeats. We are however poised to enter a phase which can lead to transfer of power. What we are seeking to do is to decisively shift the balance of forces in our favour. To do this we have to adopt the appropriate strategies and tactics, we have to understand our strengths and weaknesses, as well as that of the enemy, that is, the forces of apartheid reaction.[11]

On the general political level, I need merely refer here to the increasingly clearer realisation on the part of the student leadership that without the organised Black working class, their heroic struggles cannot bring about more than a few episodic improvements in the schools. I have already referred to the path of development from student-centric actions to the idea of a student–worker alliance and beyond that to the hope of a worker–student alliance. There have been and are many practical examples of these developments, spectacular ones like the November 1984 stayaway in the Transvaal and countless unpublicised examples of organised students helping at trades union offices or at crèches in working-class areas or at workers' conferences or meetings. It is such developments which are among the most hopeful signals of the future direction of the student movement in South Africa.

The second important factor that shapes the schooling environment of our students is the teaching corps. The situation of teachers in Black schools has become acutely problematical since 1976. The sharpening of the contradictions between the oppressed and exploited people and the ruling class has led to a situation in the schools where increasingly teachers have to decide to support the demands and actions of the Black students or face the fact that they are no more than agents of an oppressive and repressive state once all the pious prattling about 'vocation' and 'duty to our children' has been bracketed out. Again, this is an area that has been analysed often in recent years.

Among the earliest, quasi-contemporary analyses, I recommend two contributions to the compilation of the Centre for Extra-Mural Studies of the University of Cape Town on the *Education Crisis in the Western Cape in 1980*. I refer to the article by Trish Fledermann, 'Some Effects of the Boycott on the Role of the Classroom Teachers under the Department of Coloured Affairs', and that of Henry Joubert on 'Coping in a Crisis: A Headmaster's Case Study'. The latter, with a few deft strokes of the pen, paints what he calls 'the dilemma of the headmaster in a Black school' as follows:

Under normal circumstances he is seen as a tool of the state who has to implement government policy (or 'gutter education'). He has, in many cases, withdrawn himself from the community which he should serve, lives in an exclusive suburb and maintains a standard of living which few of his pupils can hope to achieve. Headmasters were therefore in the first line of attack by pupils, parents and the public in general. After an initial phase of an increased authoritarianism by principals and after the dismissal of certain principals in March, it was 'open season' on principals.

What emerges clearly from all these analyses is the fact that inside the Black schools as they are structured at present, the most fundamental need of all is the professional and academic training and the political and ideological retraining of the teaching corps. All attempts by students, progressive teachers and parents to insert and to widen the scope of liberatory education alternatives within the framework of the state schools will simply come to nought unless this process is taken in hand. The state, clearly, has a vested interest in obstructing the process. Hence, the struggle in this sector of the educational arena is going to be sharpened. Teachers are not inherently part of the enemy as young students have sometimes maintained. They constitute a layer of people for whose allegiance and commitment we have to contend with the ruling class. The developments since 1976 have led overwhelmingly to the conclusion that all progressive organisations of the people, political, civic and education, have to focus their activities on gaining the total commitment of the vast majority of our teachers. If we succeed in this, the educational arena, or at least the schools as institutions, will have been finally lost to the powers that be. The practical implications of this position need not be spelt out here.

ALTERNATIVE EDUCATION AND CULTURAL REVOLUTION

Other papers delivered at this National Consultation on Education for Affirmation will be dealing with the concept, problems, and practical manifestations of alternative education. I need only point to the fact, therefore, that particularly after 1980, the cry for alternative education went up until today, in the forms of 'people's education', 'workers' education', 'liberatory education', and 'popular education', almost every Black student and teacher and many a Black parent sees the realisation of this ideal as the answer to the crisis in education. It is as well, therefore, to insist on a sober appraisal of what is possible at present both inside and outside the schools.

We need, above all, to get rid of the naïve idea that an 'alternative education system' can be set up as long as the apartheid state lasts. At most, we can encroach on the control, content, and methodology of education within the schools. This is one of the fronts on which we are doing battle in the 'war of position' against the ruling class with a view to establishing a counter-hegemonic thrust that will shift the balance of forces in our favour. It is an extremely conflictual, see-saw process in which we will gain much and every so often be compelled to relinquish ground that we believe to be firmly controlled by our forces.

Outside the schools, opportunities are much greater, although we must not forget that

> [under] the present dispensation, our room for manoeuvre is very limited indeed, and some of our opportunities present serious problems of compromise.[12]

I wish to draw your attention to an area that has been hopelessly neglected by progressive educationists, *viz.*, that of the unemployed youth in the townships and rural slums, many of whom have attained a fair level of literacy and numeracy. Real alternative pedagogy is possible among these people. They have no faith in or desire for state-sponsored certificates. They *do* wish to acquire life skills for survival in and beyond the apartheid state. Their rebellious energies can be transformed into a power for radical and constructive change provided that they can be recruited into a cultural revolutionary movement that is integrally part of the movement for national liberation.

Another question that should perhaps be given special mention here is the need for development-orientated organisations to consider carefully and to implement long-term liberatory educational projects in towns and countries. I am thinking here of fundamental interventions that spring from fearless analysis of the structure and dynamics of a rapidly changing South Africa. Rural development projects of a cooperative kind, language projects, labour and community education projects, pre-school programmes, literacy programmes, distance education programmes: these are some of the more obvious and more important areas in which slow, plodding progress made today will ensure solid foundations for a democratic socialist Azania tomorrow.

We have a long way to go even though we have already come a long way. As in so many other areas of life in South Africa today, what is happening in the educational arena is unique, exciting, and creative in spite of the heartbreak and the suffering that accompanies every breakthrough and every advance. What we need to do above all else is to spread the consciousness of what is actually taking place and what can take place and constantly to weigh up these considerations against what we believe ought to take place. Only in this way will we be able to acquire and to sustain a sense of direction amid the turbulence and the confusions that have turned the educational institutions for Blacks into a minefield that can be negotiated successfully only by those who have clarity of vision and a realistic appraisal of the means at our disposal.

'An Illuminating Moment: Background to the Azanian Manifesto'[1]

SALVAGING ELEMENTS OF HISTORICAL TRUTH

Any political programme of principles has to be understood and assessed in the context of the times of its genesis. The terminology used, the underlying concepts or theory it expresses, as well as the strategy implicit in the formulations are all necessarily informed by the class character and the immediate and long-term objectives of the political movement or forces concerned as well as by the legal-political environment where they are operative. The Manifesto of the Azanian People is no exception. Accordingly, I want to describe and analyse as concisely as possible the social, political, and organisational background to the evolution of the Manifesto. This is especially important because of the furious but misguided attempts that were made from time to time to vilify the authors of the Manifesto and to falsify the circumstance in which the document came to be adopted in June 1983 by the National Forum (NF) as the unifying programme of principles of what was intended to be a united front against the apartheid strategy of divide and rule as manifested in, among other things, P.W. Botha's Tricameral Constitution.

Historians and political sociologists expect that victorious movements will attempt to represent the past as a trajectory that inexorably and uninterruptedly leads to the moment of their victory, the moment of the seizure, or, as in the South African case, the 'transfer' of power. Even so, the rapidity and the comprehensiveness of the process of recasting and rewriting South Africa's contemporary history that began sometime before 1994 is surprising. Although a certain cavalier attitude on the part of journalists and pseudo-historians can be understood within limits, it is not acceptable that reputable historians and political and other social scientists can satisfy themselves with versions of what happened in South Africa between 1960 and 1990 more or less, that are misleading and distorting, even if only because of omission of significant moments. Although some of the earlier, near-contemporary accounts attempt to situate the NF in a more open perspective,[2] by the time we reach the late

1990s it has virtually disappeared from the historical canvas. Some of the latest 'historical' writings are among the worst examples of contemporary history even if one takes into account the well-known limitations of the genre.

This essay, which is consciously formulated in a quasi-anecdotal rather than a strictly analytical mode, is an attempt to put forward a set of perceptions and an account of a particular dynamic moment in the early 1980s in South Africa that may help to correct the distorting mirror that has, by and large, been held up to the post-1994 generation hitherto. It is important therefore, to point out that there are hundreds of people who were party or privy to the events and processes I refer to here, who will either confirm or amend the picture I paint. Some, because of the twists and turns of their lives, might deny some or even all of what I have noted here. But should this occur, future historians will have to judge the merits of the respective versions.

BLACK CONSCIOUSNESS AND SOCIALIST INFLUENCES

Without explicit reference to, but basing myself on, the numerous accounts of the origins and development of the Black Consciousness Movement (BCM) in South Africa in the late 1960s, I want to highlight a few generalisations about this development that are relevant to the subject of this essay.

To begin with, the repression of the early 1960s, which was initiated with the proliferation of banning orders served on individuals under the Suppression of Communism Act of 1950 and intensified after Sharpeville by means of the General Laws and Amendment Act of 1962 and the Terrorism Act of 1967, appeared to bring down a blanket of silence and compliance on the oppressed people of the country. Of course, none of the organisations involved in and committed to the national liberation struggle abandoned that struggle, but their activities were effectively curbed and disrupted for more than a decade after 1963.

Steve Biko and his comrades were products of the apartheid university and secondary school system, notably of the network of Bush Colleges. Some of them had direct and indirect links, sometimes no more than familial bonds, with persons who were in prison, in exile, or in the underground political structures of the National Liberation Movement, properly so-called. It is also clear that, besides these natural influences on their thinking and their political universe, they were albeit by way of many detours, decisively influenced by developments in the rest of the world, especially by the rise of the student movement and youth activism in Europe and in the United States of the 1960s. Through the University Christian Movement and other sources, they came into contact with the pedagogical and social conceptions of Paulo Freire and the theology of liberation, among others, and all of these influences, in the context of the repression and against the background of the mixture of Christian philanthropy and African communal life that all of us who were adults in those days had experienced in the countryside, undoubtedly contributed to their formulation and conscious promotion of a strategy that was in fact a version of Gramsci's famous 'war of position'. The strategy of Black Community Programmes, together with the development of a modern labour movement, which had a more differentiated but related source and a sometimes converging, sometimes diverging, trajectory, was no less than such a war of position, one that eventually brought about a change in the balance of forces and helped to reshape the political space in the worst years of the repression.

There is also no doubt that the crucial element in the expansion and deepening of the BCM was the cadre of students that was strategically distributed across the country, especially in the countryside, through the mechanism of the Bush Colleges and related institutions. These young people, intended by white supremacist rulers whose sanity was compromised because of their simplistic racist preconceptions, to become 'Eiselen' men and 'Eiselen' women, that is, a collaborationist layer of intellectuals and professionals committed to tribal (so-called ethnic) communities became, instead, the Trojan horse of Afrikaner nationalism and the natural vanguard of this apparently reformist and, as they believed, potentially co-optable student and youth movement.

The politics of the BCM as a movement was complex and constantly changing. At first sight, it was informed by an Africanist ideology that was closer to the views of a Robert Sobukwe than those of a Nelson Mandela. The leadership tried to shape an inclusive Black identity that, in ruling-class South African terms, included all the oppressed people whether classified – in terms of the apartheid social categories – Bantu, Coloured, or Indian. In this respect, the BCM appeared on the surface and in the modalities of its operations, to be closer to the Non-European Unity Movement than to the Congress Movement. Whichever way one approaches the matter, however, it is very obvious that both the leadership and the membership of the BCM was strongly influenced by *all* the different tendencies that constituted the National Liberation Movement. This catholicity of the movement turned out to be a great strength initially, but also held within itself the danger of political fragmentation under pressure. In retrospect, this angle on the subject makes a lot of sense in the context of the repression and the consequent potential of any radical quasi-political grouping to serve as a pole of gravitation for impressionable young students of diverse backgrounds who could not but be politically orientated.

I will not expound any further on the ideological developments and contradictions within the BCM.[3] However, in order to understand the theoretical and ideological content of the Azanian Manifesto, it is essential that I say a few words about my perception of the relationship between the BCM and socialism as an ideology as well as specific socialist currents in South Africa.

When I emerged from prison in 1974, after serving ten years on Robben Island, I was placed under house arrest in my mother's home, where I have continued to live up to the present. It soon became obvious to me and my comrades that the activists of the BCM were the main group of political people among the oppressed who were trying, overtly and covertly, to organise them, mainly at the point of reproduction. The independent trade union movement, including those unions initiated by BCM activists, was in its infancy at that time and was, naturally, focused on conditions at the point of production. Because of our reputation as members of the 'National Liberation Front' and a certain measure of publicity locally and abroad, many BCM members gravitated towards us and soon we were involved with them in (illegal) study groups, in which mainly political and historical themes or developments were the subject. By way of example, I can vouch for the fact that, among other things, in our Cape Peninsula study groups we addressed the staple issues of the moment such as the land question, the national question, the language question, African culture, the economic system. Needless to say, similar patterns involving political activists and ex-Robben Islanders from different political organisations occurred throughout the country with more or less regularity and for similar reasons. It is in these study groups and, from what I was told by men such as the late Strini Moodley and Saths Cooper, among others, those that they attended on Robben Island, mainly in collaboration with Unity Movement comrades, that the BCM came, not necessarily for the first time, to engage directly and systematically with Marxist socialist thought. Up to that time, besides some reading of revolutionary socialist texts, most BCM activists were guided by the political concepts of Black communalism that, as I understood them, was an amalgam of notions of *ubuntu* and liberal-individualistic democratic principles.

There was never any explicit attempt on our part to 'convert' the BCM comrades to our version of socialist principles and strategy. I have no doubt that most of them would have resented and rejected any such agenda. Like us, they were interested in exchange of ideas, knowledge, and information in order to conduct the struggle better, as they saw it. However, the levels of trust and mutual respect that were established amongst us were of great importance subsequently. One specific moment that has never been recorded adequately should be noted explicitly. I refer to the planned public protest demonstration against the granting of so-called independence to the Transkei on 26 October 1976, that, at the initiative of the BCM, we set out as a united internal movement, to organise at Hammanskraal in the Transvaal on the national scale for the day of 'independence'. Although one of us, whether members of under-ground political structures of the Pan-Africanist Congress (PAC), the African National Congress (ANC), or of independent socialist groups, who were privy to this plan from its inception believed that there was any real danger of the country being partitioned by this self-delusional Act of the white South African parliament, we believed that it was essential that a public stand be taken by the oppressed people against the principle of partition and for the territorial integrity of South Africa. In addition, this was considered to be the ideal issue on which to reassert publicly the political aspirations and demands of the oppressed people and to test the resolve of the apartheid state. Committees were set up in different parts of the country in order to arrange for transport and other logisti-cal requirements. These committees, as far as I know, involved mostly people who were or considered themselves to be members of the BCM, but they included some people from other groups, including the inde-pendent socialist network we had begun establishing almost as soon as the prison gates were shut behind us.

Whether or not this particular initiative would have succeeded without much bloodshed belongs in the realm of speculation. As is well known now, the events of June 1976 rendered everything else irrelevant and rang in a new phase of the struggle for national liberation. It is also clear that some of the preparatory work that had been occasioned by the anti-Transkei 'independence' protest helped to spread the Soweto Uprising across the country much more rapidly than would otherwise have been the case. This is certainly true in respect of the Western Cape.

Also unrecorded but equally significant was the plan that we, in Cape Town, had worked out in conjunction with and the initiative of Steve Biko and his comrades in Ginsberg to send abroad myself and Comrade Steve in order to discuss with the armed movements in exile the suggestion to constitute a single united liberation army that would be complemented and 'represented' by the Black People's Convention (BPC) as the legitimate voice of the oppressed inside the country. Whether or not this exploratory talk was naïve is not the point here. It is quite possible that some of the individuals who were involved in this plan will now deny that it was ever considered. If so, they would, quite simply, be guilty of selective amnesia. It is certainly a matter of historical fact that Biko, in taking this initiative, was acting in terms of existing positions of the BPC and in line with the general political orientation and of specific discussions within the BCM after the Soweto Uprising had exploded. By way of example, I quote at some length from a 'position paper' discussed at a BPC executive meeting not long after December 1976:

Who then are the people involved in the liberation process? It is quite clear that the frontline role is now played partly by the banned movements ANC, PAC, UMSA and partly by the Black Consciousness Movement. Over and above the frontline role, there are those groups who are merely important in so far as they can form useful or destructive alliances with the frontline groups. The following features ought to be recognised in the further analysis of those involved in the liberation process:

(a) There is a need for the resolution of conflicting interests in pursuit of this the following options are open:
   – We can form a new front operating both internally and externally;
   – We can form a basis for future unity encompassing all liberation movement;
   – We can form an exclusive frontline alliance with one group at the expense of others;
   – We need to be ready to form alliances with non-frontline groups of particular importance to us.

The strategist who drafted this document goes on to suggest the following course of action:

> Of all the available options there is no doubt that going for amalgamation of all groups under one banner would be the best option in the interests of the struggle. It would appear though that preferable though this option might be it is full of limitations which we will impose on other groups and which they in turn would impose on us. Reluctantly therefore one is forced to suggest that for the time being the only option available to us is to be on our own both internally and externally, but all the same to maintain a positive neutrality with regard to other groups which operate outside and underground internally in the hope that in future we might be a useful unifying force.[4]

In the light of what happened subsequently but without having been privy to the relevant discussions, I can only conclude that Steve Biko and his comrades had to decide (with or without mandate, I have no way of telling) to explore the 'preferred option'. Hence, the plans they were busy working out with our group and others. In any case, it is now a matter of history that before Biko's projected departure and by the time I managed to get to Europe in 1978–1979, he had been murdered in detention as the result of a series of catastrophic events, the definitive account of which remains outstanding. As I have noted elsewhere,[5] one of the objectives of his fateful journey to Cape Town, a few days before he was murdered in detention, was to meet with our group and others in order to discuss this plan in Cape Town, he in fact stayed with one of our underground operatives. As recounted there, that meeting was, tragically, aborted. It is also important to record here, against the detractors of Steve Biko, that whatever one's critique of the BCM in general and of Biko in particular, he died, literally, in quest of the unification of the forces of liberation in South Africa.

A UNITED FRONT OR A 'THIRD FORCE'?

The point of this all too brief reference to a potentially revolutionary moment in our contemporary history is to underline the fact that the BCM leadership, whatever the contradictions and disagreements in its ranks, together with other organisations including underground socialist groups such as the one to which I belonged, was actively exploring ways and means of establishing a united political front not merely as a tactical alliance but as a long-term strategic alliance for the attainment of the overthrow of the apartheid state. Another significant step along this path was the systematic underground circulation in 1982 of 'the Stuurman document', of which I myself had written the original draft and which is referred to below.[6] This well-considered move, however, was prevented from gaining momentum and actively opposed by, among others, leading members of the South African Communist Party, who spread the vicious rumour that this was a manifestation of the activities of a so-called 'Third Force' that was being nurtured and funded by American imperialism.[7] This contemptible political nonsense helped to create an atmosphere of suspicion and rivalry between the BCM and many cadre of the ANC and was, without any doubt, part and parcel of the strategy of gaining for that organisation the spurious United National Organisation (UNO) and Organisation of African Unity (OAU) accredited status of 'sole authentic representative' of the oppressed people of South Africa, a fashionable and patently anti-democratic 'divide and weaken' tactic used by 'liberal' as well as some 'communist' organ grinders in order to control 'their' particular monkey.

This episode does, however, provide the necessary background to understanding how the Azanian Manifesto came to be conceptualised and eventually adopted by the NF in June 1983. By the time the South African Students' Organisation (SASO) trialists emerged from prison, there was a history of close cooperation between the BCM and some of the revolutionary socialist groups that were operating in the country. The early 1980s was a period of intense agitation and mobilisation in Western Cape, beginning with the 1980 Schools Boycott campaign and the establishment of the Parents Teachers Students Association (PTSA) movement, followed by the militant opposition to the 'Koornhof Bills' by the *ad hoc* Disorderly Bills Action Committee (DBAC) that culminated in the formation of the broad united front that came to be known as the Cape Action League (CAL). In this context, the sterling political work that was being done on a countrywide basis in the diverse structures that were accountable to the South African Council on Sport (SACOS) has a place of honour. Like all the other initiatives and organisations referred to here, these structures worked on a strictly non-sectarian basis in accordance with the united front ethos that characterised this phase of struggle. It was undoubtedly this wave of militant and overt political action that attracted the Azanian People's Organisation (AZAPO) leadership to those of us who were known to be sympathetic to cooperation with the BCM. It was, moreover, in this context that the Stuurman document that, from many accounts, had an important catalytic effect, was widely disseminated in samizdat fashion. After a careful analysis of the idea of the united front, the document called on the active cadres of all the organisations of the oppressed to band together in a fighting front for liberation from racist oppression and class exploitation. It is appropriate in this context to quote the concluding paragraphs:

> The intensification of the struggle in southern Africa and the mortal danger of disunity and civil war among the oppressed people have created a situation of urgency. Ever since the historic events of 1976 it has become clear to all serious-minded militants that we can work together and that we can have unity in action even though we have not reached full agreement on all principles.
>
> Although some recent developments appear to contradict this tendency of people's organisations to work together, it is clear that most serious militants realise that such developments would constitute a modern-day national suicide. There is a great need for a national debate on the principles and practice of the united front.
>
> The time has come to combine our forces in a united front that represents the vast majority of the Black workers and of the radical Black middle class. The challenge to the oppressed and exploited people has never been greater in our entire history. Against this background of the heroic events since the Soweto Uprising, there is no doubt that the organisations of the people will rise to the occasion and will create through united action the instruments required to meet this challenge.
>
> Let us make 1982 into the year of the united front and raise our struggle for liberation from apartheid and capitalism on to a higher level. Let us unite for a non-racial, democratic and undivided Azania-South Africa![8]

Informal and formal discussions with various political tendencies and groupings initiated and coordinated by the AZAPO leadership, which included well-known and prominent comrades such as Lybon Mabasa, Strini Moodley, Saths Cooper, Muntu Myeza, Pandelani Nefolovhodwe, Ish Mkhabela, and Zithulele Cindi among many others, eventually led to the decision to organise the first NF. A provisional NF Committee was established that included non-AZAPO members, and, among others, Bishop Tutu, Rev. Alan Boesak, Frank van der Horst (SACOS), and myself. The decision to establish a 'Forum' was calculated to appeal to the broadest possible constituency among the oppressed people as well as to individuals classified 'white' but committed to the liberation of South Africa. It was in respect of this latter objective, insisted upon by groups such as ours, that contradictions arose at various times during the months preceding the conference as well as during the conference and its successive gatherings.

It is unnecessary to delve into the details of the organisation and mobilisation of the first NF. However, a few noteworthy features of this event should be mentioned here.[9] The first is the fact of the participation of the two clerics – Bishop Tutu and Rev. Boesak – who subsequently played such a prominent role in the United Democratic Front (UDF).[10] As soon as the UDF move was initiated, Rev. Boesak abandoned ship and devoted all his time to promoting, funding, and strengthening the UDF. Bishop Tutu, to his credit, tried for a few years to straddle both formations and to get them to work together. In his trademark ironic manner, he both lauded those who had initiated the Forum and warned against the dangers of divisive, sectarian approaches and practices:

> We all know that we Blacks, as they say, are slow thinkers. We could not think for ourselves that it was high time we held such a National Forum worried as we must have been by the fragmentation of the Black community making it easier for the enemy of the struggle to apply the old ploy of divide and rule ... We do their dirty work for them. We wash our dirty linen in public. What does it really matter whether you say you are an exponent of Black Consciousness and somebody else is an upholder of the Freedom Charter, whether you are AZAPO, COSAS or Committee of Ten – isn't the most important thing the struggle itself for the total liberation of all the people of South Africa, Black and White to live where the rule of law obtains with *habeas corpus* holding sway, where all have full citizenship rights and obligations ...[11]

Other clerics affiliated to the South African Council of Churches – with warm thoughts for Rev. Manas Buthelezi – stayed the distance until the overwhelming material and political support for the UDF eliminated the NF as a notional rival.

To come back to the Manifesto: for the historical record, it should be noted that I was given the task of preparing the draft document on the basis of the resolutions put forward for adoption at the first NF. This task was completed during the night before the final day of the Forum. Inevitably my political background and my political stance influenced the specific formulations that now comprise that document, although it was, naturally, amended in decisive ways before it was unanimously adopted by the hundreds of Forum delegates. It is essential, if one is interested in getting a sense of the many-stranded texture of the Forum and of its social matrix, to go back to the actual resolutions that were proposed.

Lest the leadership of the Forum be accused of blatant manipulation, it ought to be stressed that this phenomenon is generic to all such gatherings. Some of the laughable strictures to which we have been subjected by Stalinist critics of the Forum over the years are disingenuous at best and downright mendacious at worst.[12] The Manifesto is usually – implicitly rather than explicitly, lest it be dignified by the very act of juxtaposition – compared to the Freedom Charter that is presented as a 'sacred' text that was 'written' by 'the people' themselves. On reflection, it is obvious that the manner in which the Freedom Charter came to be formulated is reflective of a particular historical moment in the mid-1950s before the full repressive might of the apartheid state was brought to bear on the liberation movement. It is, therefore, invidious to suggest, as Comrade Mzala does, that unless a political programme has evolved in the manner of the Freedom Charter, it cannot have any validity. Besides the obvious ahistorical character of this argument, one need only apply it to a world-historic document such as the Communist Manifesto to realise how fallacious it is.

RETROSPECT

Today, 23 years after the event, with all the advantages of hindsight and of the volumes of analysis that have tried to explain the geopolitical shifts that took place in the period 1985–1989, it is easy to understand why the NF and its brave attempt at placing an overtly socialist alternative on the political agenda of the South African revolution had to fail. That is not the subject of this chapter. It is relevant, however, to conclude by referring to the contemporary analysis of the Manifesto and of the NF that I made at the second NF during the Easter weekend of 1984. In retrospect, the following judgement seems to have been as accurate as it was possible to be at the time:

The [National Party (NA)] government's New Deal strategy, which embraces at the same time the Koornhof Acts and the relocation of the African people in Bantustan concentration camps, threatened to unleash a flood of working-class militancy and action. Since 1980, almost every significant mass action in South Africa has carried the imprint of the Black working class. Socialist solutions to the system of racial capitalism were becoming common coinage among the youth and in workers' organisations. This development was and is feared by the petite bourgeoisie and by the liberal bourgeoisie.

Liberals of all colours and shapes thus tried to ensure that the mass movement against the New Deal would not be placed under the leader-ship of the working class. The instrument they chose for this purpose is the so-called United Democratic Front... [Despite] the fond illusions of some self-proclaimed leftists in the UDF, the reins of that bandwagon are firmly in the hands of middle-class leaders whose vision and prac-tices do not extend beyond opposition to the superficial symptoms of apartheid. Men have been built up through the newspapers and by other means who can now steer the bandwagon almost in any direc-tion they choose ...[13]

In the same stocktaking I also looked at the achievements and failures of the NF under the motto: *Tell no lies, claim no easy victories*, but still in the belief that an albeit conflictual constructive interaction between some of the UDF formations and the NF was possible and necessary. With respect to the Manifesto itself, we were still brimming with hope and did not realise that as we were speaking, developments around the ascent to power of Mikhail Gorbachev in the USSR were going to squash for a long time any hopes of a successful socialist revolution anywhere in the world. So, in the light of the profound technological, economic, polit-ical, and general social changes that have occurred during these past 25 years, although the principles of the Manifesto remain relevant because, like similar documents that proclaimed the socialist alternative at a par-ticular socio-historical moment, new approaches to strategy and tactics are essential, indeed, a new 'language' has to be forged, in order to reveal the relevance and the feasibility of realising those principles. It is as clear now as it was then that the struggle continues. *Aluta continua!*[14]

MANIFESTO OF THE AZANIAN PEOPLE

This historic conference of organisations of the oppressed and exploited people of Azania held at Hammanskraal on 11–12 June 1983 and convened by the National Forum Committee, having deliberated on vital questions affecting our nation and in particular having considered the implications of the Botha government's 'new deal' strategy (the President's Council, constitutional proposals, and Koornhof Bills), resolves:

1. To condemn the murder of freedom fighters by the racist minority regime.
2. To issue the following manifesto for consideration by all the organisations of the people to be reviewed at the second National Forum to be convened during the Easter Weekend of 1984.

Our struggle for national liberation is directed against the system of racial capitalism which holds the people of Azania in bondage for the benefit of the small minority of white capitalists and their allies, the white workers and the reactionary sections of the Black middle class. The struggle against apartheid is no more than the point of departure for our liberation efforts. Apartheid will be eradicated with the system of racial capitalism.

The Black working class inspired by revolutionary consciousness is the driving force of our struggle. They alone can end the system as it stands today because they alone have nothing to lose. They have a world to gain in a democratic, anti-racist, and socialist Azania. It is the historic task of the Black working class and its organisations to mobilise the urban and the rural poor together with the radical sections of the middle classes in order to put an end to the system of oppression and exploitation by the white ruling class.

The successful conduct of the national liberation struggle depends on the firm basis of principle whereby we will ensure that the liberation struggle will not be turned against our people by a treacherous and opportunistic 'leader'. Of these principles, the most important are:

- Anti-racism and anti-imperialism.
- Non-collaboration with the oppressor and its political instruments.
- Independent working-class organisation.
- Opposition to all alliances with ruling-class parties.

In accordance with these principles, the oppressed and exploited people of Azania demand immediately:

- The right to work.

- The right to form trade unions that will heighten revolutionary worker consciousness.
- The establishment of a democratic, anti-racist worker Republic in Azania where the interests of the workers shall be paramount through worker control of the means of production, distribution and exchange.
- State provision of free and compulsory education for all and this education be geared towards liberating the Azanian people from all forms of oppression, exploitation and ignorance.
- State provision of adequate and decent housing.
- State provision of free health, legal, recreational and other community services that will respond positively to the needs of the people.
- Development of one national progressive culture in the process of struggle.
- The land and all that belongs to it shall be wholly owned and controlled by the Azanian people.
- The usage of the land and all that accrues to it shall be aimed at ending all forms and means of exploitation.

In order to bring into effect these demands of the Azanian people, we pledge ourselves to struggle tirelessly for:

- The abolition of all laws that discriminate against our people on the basis of colour, sex, class, religion or language.
- The abolition of all influx control measures and pass laws.
- The abolition of all resettlement and group areas removals.
- Reintegration of the 'Bantustan' human dumping grounds into a unitary Azania.

The Transition to Democracy: 1990 to 1994

Introduction to Part III

In the first article, Alexander sets out to examine explanations about how the South African 'system of institutionalised racism' has been approached relative to its relationship with 'the system of class exploitation'. He examines the variety of approaches to its historiography ranging from conservative interpretations to what he calls 'liberal pluralist explanations of race relations' to the revisions made by radical scholarship. He also considers developments around the debates about class and 'race' reductionism – the proclivities of social and political analysts to privilege either of these categories of analysis to the exclusion of the other, together with the critique of such reductionist approaches.

The second article reviews and comments on the plethora of writings about political transitions to liberal democracy globally – the study of 'transitology'. These studies refer to geopolitical and technological changes as the motive forces for such transitions all of which have led ultimately to the global dominance of a neoliberal ideology propelled by the collapse of the Soviet Union and the end of the armed struggles which it had supported. Alexander argues that such transitions as were witnessed in post-colonial states followed a similar pattern of development through, in each case, a process of negotiation and compromise.

The specifics of the South African transition lie in the role of the ANC and its engagements with the Nationalist Party government of the white minority propelled by the power and influence of the global neoliberal regimes of power and a combination of local and international factors. Alexander also examines the role of leaders on both sides of the negotiations and in particular the influence of the 'Madiba factor' a reference to the influence of Nelson Mandela and his role together with other leaders who fashioned the contours by which the ANC was assimilated into the compromises of the post-apartheid state.

Africa and the New World Order situates Africa in its historical context as a continent that has been violated by the enslavement of Africans and the process of colonial expansion of European nations as part of the evolution of European capitalism. The explicit purpose of his paper is to convey the 'message that it is out of Africa, by virtue of the depths of its suffering, that a new world order will be born, no matter how improbable that may appear at present'. It is reminiscent of Steve Biko's view[1] in his collected essays *I Write what I Like*: 'The great powers may have done wonders in giving the world an industrial and military look, but the great gift still has to come from Africa – giving the world a more human face'.

Alexander takes account of the contemporary technological developments, the imperialist ambitions of the US through its 'monopoly of force', the collapse of the Soviet bloc of countries, and other contemporary developments as setting the context for an evaluation of Africa's place in the world. Against this background, he sketches the possible trajectories of global political and economic development and especially the developments in the African continent, some of which had recently transited from authoritarian regimes to 'democratic systems' but not without a contextual re-examination of the very concept of democracy as it applies to the African continent. It was in this regard that the concept of pan-Africanism had also to be reconceptualised as that related to questions about development, aid and sovereignty against the imprimatur of global 'development' agencies like the World Bank and its associated institutions of power and control. Their policies and effects reinforced the rampant global inequalities in which 'some are more equal than others'. Alexander points especially to alternative views to counteract the power and influence of the prevailing global order and to the insightful writings about it which held the possibilities for a fundamental reorientation of the trajectory of African history and development.

Alexander's foreword to the translation into isiZulu of the Communist Manifesto by Lwazi Brian Ramadiro is simultaneously about the historical importance of the Manifesto and about the question of its appearance in an African language given the dominance of the languages of the 'colonial master' in the 'political education of the emerging leadership of the working class in colonial and postcolonial Africa'. The translation was therefore a 'benchmark' defining what might be called an African Renaissance – referring to the use of an African language in the 'important domains of life' and as a print language. The translation was important for the development of democratic practices based on the recognition of the languages used in daily life, signalling, as it were, a return to the source 'to revive the belief' in an alternative to the violence of capitalist oppression prefigured in the Manifesto. Alexander felt that the translation had potential in supporting the development of an emergent working-class leadership because of the 'treasury of theoretical and strategic wisdom' contained in the Manifesto and its continued relevance to the struggles against the power of neoliberal globalisation.

Taking South African Education out of the Ghetto is an example of Alexander's constant search for concrete alternatives in the present supporting the Gramscian notion of the 'war of position'. Collaborating with progressive urban planners, he promoted the feasibility of 'clustering' of schools to address the issue of spatial apartheid and the imperative to genuinely desegregate schools and work toward quality education. The detailed plan for overcoming the spatial apartheid nature of the city of Cape Town was meant to function as a pilot for other cities in South Africa. The plan argued in considerable detail how the establishment of well-equipped schools at important nodal points on the main transport arteries of the city could enable 'all children, regardless of colour, language group or place of residence' to attend such schools. Alexander lamented that:[2]

Although complimentary copies of the book were made available to some individuals in the new bureaucracy, and the approach was discussed with and positively received by cabinet ministers and urban planners involved in rethinking the apartheid city in Cape Town, it had very little impact at the time because of the timidity and tentativeness, i.e. lack of clarity and vision, that characterised the first years of the transition. Yet, unless we get back to this approach, complemented by and working in tandem with some of the other foundational changes that are required, social and racial integration among poor and working-class children will remain a dead letter for decades, if not centuries ...

'"Race" and Class in South African Historiography: An Overview'[1]

The colonial history of South Africa differs radically from the history of other European settler colonies which were established in the course of the sixteenth and seventeenth centuries in that, with one important exception,[2] it did not eventuate in the genocidal eradication of the indigenous population. As against this astonishing fact, however, it is notoriously the history of a system of institutionalised racism, one which lasted formally until the very last decade of the twentieth century.

The actual course of the 'discovery', conquest, and colonisation or settlement by Europeans is not the subject of this chapter.[3] Instead, I want to consider the more important and relevant attempts at explaining why the system of institutionalised racism developed and, in particular, how it articulates with, or relates to, the system of class exploitation. This is important because my purpose is to help us understand where we are today and how we can move 'beyond racism'. It is analytically convenient to deal with the different explanatory frameworks which have been used by scholars and activists under the broad rubrics of *conservative*, *liberal* and *radical* paradigms. In particular, the second and third of these paradigms, which have given rise to illuminating debates during the past 30 years, will be considered in some detail.

CONSERVATIVE APPROACHES

The first attempts at partial or total descriptions of the history of South Africa were, understandably, written from a completely Eurocentric point of view. Indeed, in most cases,[4] the angle of vision is myopically *Anglo-centric*. Of the very first historians who based their work on archival and field research, only G. M. Theal broke a lance for the *Boers* (that is, those settlers of 'Dutch' descent).[5] None of the earliest historians, again for understandable reasons, ever thought of looking at the history of the colony from the point of view of the indigenous African peoples whom the Europeans found living here. All of this history was, in the spirit of Trevor-Roper, the history of Europeans in Africa.[6]

Besides a few episodic propositions of a general character, which in their crudity now have no more than antiquarian significance,[7] there are essentially two socio-historical complexes which the conservative historians analysed or tried to 'explain'. The first complex pertains to the relations between the people of European descent who had interest in the colony, on the one hand, and the people of African or Asian descent, whom they had conquered or enslaved, on the other hand. The second complex is connected to the relations between the two groups of people of European descent who, notionally competed with each other for hegemony on the subcontinent. The entire set of complexes was viewed and treated in terms of an ideology of promoting 'Western Christian Civilisation' in Africa.

In the view of the conservative historians, the 'white man' conquered and settled South Africa in the course of the 'expansion of Europe', which was the direct result of the emergence of mercantilism or mercantile capitalism and the development of weaponry (after the 'discovery' of gunpowder). Some historians explicitly, and all of them implicitly, described the events associated with these processes in teleological terms, usually as the unfolding of a 'divine will', that is, 'God's plan', but always in terms of the march of 'progress' and the civilising mission of the Europeans. Consequently, the indigenous people were portrayed as savages and barbarians who had no culture that was worthy of emulation or adoption. The technological and scientific superiority of the Europeans over the Africans of southern Africa was so great that it was taken as not only a gift of God but as bestowing on Europeans the moral right to rule over all other peoples anywhere on the planet. These are inarticulate premises which inform the writing of even the most critical and philanthropically sensible historians who wrote during the mid-to-late nineteenth century in South Africa. In all cases, the settler-colonial ideology in terms of which the conquerors saw themselves as 'God's Chosen People' who had been called upon to subdue the 'heathen' and teach them 'the discipline of toil', was tacitly affirmed by these chroniclers of the res gestae of their forefathers.

For our purposes, those features in the historical situation that led to the evolution of the system of racial oppression and discrimination are the most significant. To begin with, the original Dutch mariners and traders, for whom the Cape of Storms was, like the rest of the continent of Africa, no more than a nuisance that had to be circumnavigated so that the wealth of India could be accessed, were dependent on the fresh fruit, vegetables and meat that Van Riebeeck's halfway-house was exclusively designed to secure. The burgomasters of Holland and Zeeland had no intention of colonising the barren and inhospitable land at the southern tip of this unknown continent. Consequently, there was no reason to kill off, or even to enslave, the natives provided they were willing to 'trade' in the wares required by the Dutch East India Company (DEIC). In this way, and as the natives became accustomed to the trinkets and gadgets as well as the addictive drugs from Europe, a relationship of mutual dependence evolved. Native interpreters and eventually, after the reluctant decision by the DEIC to undertake limited colonisation, native domestic servants and agricultural labourers grew in number and in subordinate stations along with the 'free' burgher colonists in a process that was punctuated by slave revolts; passive resistance by Khoi clans, who increasingly began to experience the pressure of colonial demand and expropriation on their land and livestock; as well as outright guerrilla struggles by desperate San hunters and gatherers whose livelihood of small game and other animals was being exterminated systematically by the Dutch farmers.

Conservative historians, such as Theal and Cory, as well as most of the early Afrikaner nationalist historians, described the process of colonisation in Darwinian terms. They implied, and often explicitly postulated, a gradient of human evolution valued or measured in terms of intellectual and moral worth that ranged from the barely human[8] San hunters and gatherers at the bottom, to the almost divine European males at the top. In their paradigm, if the domination of the natives by the colonists was not *necessary* in socio-historical terms, the manifestation of divine will which had ordained that the Dutch, and later the British, should bring the light of civilisation to the people of southern Africa. In this paradigm, the fundamental values of early capitalist society were never questioned. Private property in the means of production, appropriation of the economic surplus (in terms of certain agreed-upon rules and limitations) by the owners of the means of 'wealth creation', as well as the unlimited accumulation of capital, were taken as the natural order of things. The Social Darwinist principles of 'might is right' and 'survival of the fittest' were accepted as the allocative mechanisms whereby human beings were classified and located in the unavoidable hierarchy of social inequality. The men and, to a much less extent, the women, who tamed the wilderness of Africa, Christianised its native people and created outposts of

European life and manners at the tip of the 'Dark Continent', were pioneers, martyrs and heroes and their story was told in hagiographic terms to their descendants, and all those who came after them were encouraged to follow in their footsteps.

Corresponding to the socio-economic and political structures of inequality, cultural stereotypes were generated through the mechanisms of ideology which, as the colony 'progressed', were increasingly equated with alleged racial characteristics of individuals and groups.[9] To put it differently, the social division of labour found its ideological deposit in a hierarchy of racial stereotypes which reinforced the relations of domination and subordination that had been inaugurated by colonial conquest and colonial settlement. Indeed, it can be said that the period and the manner as well as the location of the integration into the prevailing labour processes of the different groups of people who came to constitute the permanent population of the political unit now known as the Republic of South Africa, determined not merely the class but also the racial 'place' of the group and its descendants. We shall return to this proposition below. As far as the conservative chroniclers of the history of South Africa were concerned, the social place of the different groups and individuals was determined by inherent biological and especially intellectual characteristics. In this, they were merely following the tradition of British and much other European historiography of the late nineteenth century, which instrumentalised historical writing for the purpose of 'explaining', that is, justifying, the class divisions in Western European capitalist societies. In South Africa, though, this historical practice both affirmed and consolidated racial ideology and obscured the class element in the evolving social scale. Thus, the enslavement of East Indians and East Africans during the period of Dutch rule, the enserfment of the Khoisan peoples, the importation of Indian plantation labour on the basis of the cruel contract of indenture, and the large-scale recruitment of migrant African labour right up to the present was seen as the inevitable accompaniment of the modernisation project which, initially, was conceptualised and justified in religious (Christianisation) and moral (civilisation) terms.

LIBERAL-PLURALIST EXPLANATIONS OF RACE RELATIONS

The conservative historiography initiated by Theal and Cory overlapped with the emerging liberal-pluralist explanations of South African history before and for a few decades after the Second World War. In particu-

lar, Afrikaner nationalist historians[10] continued to write in this vein long
after most English-speaking historians of South Africa had jettisoned the
crude analytical frameworks of the late nineteenth century. The disaster of Hitler's national socialism and of the Holocaust marked a turning
point in the history of fascism in general and in the historiography of
all racist societies. Besides the numerous declarations of the United
Nations Organisation (UNO) in which the belief in and the practice of
racism were condemned and exposed as having no foundation in human
biology, the changing social division of labour necessitated by both technological developments and by the exigencies of war had begun to do
away with the iron barriers that had kept most 'non-white' people out of
the modern industrial sector of the South African economy above the
level of unskilled labour.

In the inter-war period, however, the salience of 'race' as a factor in the
formulation and the implementation of the policy of segregation under
Smuts and Hertzog, whose governments were responding to the gradual
development of a secondary (manufacturing) industry in South Africa,
and to the concomitant demand for semi-skilled and skilled Black labour,
led to professional, specifically liberal, historians rewriting the history of
the country in terms of a 'race-relations', later a 'plural-society', paradigm.
Of these, the most significant were without any doubt Eric Walker,[11]
W.M. Macmillan,[12] and C.W. de Kiewiet.[13] Although both Macmillan
and De Kiewiet went very far in order to introduce notions of class into
their historical research, in the final analysis, their writing entrenched
the perception of modern South Africa as being a 'dual economy', in
which whites and Blacks were neatly cordoned off into a relatively
wealthy 'modern' sector and a poor or 'traditional' sector, respectively.
However, the decisive issue is that they perpetuated the view that racial
ideology, racial prejudice, and racial discrimination were inimical to capitalist development and economic growth. Conversely, they held that the
rational, colour-blind logic of the market would, even if only in the longer
term, lead to the disappearance of 'race' as a factor in South Africa. In
this, they were followed by a generation of historians and other social
scientists who consolidated this liberal-pluralist orthodoxy of the period
between approximately the 1920s and 1970s Most of the best-known
South African social scientists of this period, men and women such as
Edgar Brookes, Eric Walker, Jean van der Poel, Monica Wilson, Sheila van
der Horst, Ellen Hellman, Leo Marquard, J. S. Marais, Leonard Thompson, and Rodney Davenport, worked within this paradigm.

In certain respects, this scholarship was no more than the continuation of the Anglo-Boer War by historiographical means. For these scholars and their political counterparts in what the sociologist, Pierre van den Berghe, called the 'Herrenvolk democracy' instituted by the Act of Union in 1910,[14] it was the Boers and their descendants, or what Macmillan dubbed 'the frontier tradition' (of a kind of South African wild west),[15] that had given rise to racial prejudice and racial discrimination. This thesis was to hold sway in South African historical writing and in the social sciences in general right into the 1970s. While the relevance of social class was not denied by the liberal pluralists, they all agreed with the view expressed by van den Berghe: 'Social classes in the Marxian sense of the relationships to the means of production exist by definition, as they must in any capitalist county, but they are not meaningful social realities. Clearly, pigmentation, rather than ownership of land or capital, is the most significant criterion of status in South Africa.'[16]

There was a spectacular academic blind spot which made it impossible for any of these people to see, or even to consider as problematic, the complex origins of racism in South Africa. Subsequent scholarship[17] has demonstrated that, ironically, it was the founders of the liberal paradigm in South Africa who helped Smuts and Hertzog to create the systematic institutionalisation of racial discrimination in South African life which came to be called by the name of 'segregation' (and was later intensified under the name of apartheid). To the credit of many of them, it ought to be noted that once they realised that the political leadership of White South Africa were using the well-intentioned insights of their social anthropological and historical research in order to establish and consolidate an oppressive and potentially repressive regime, they resigned from the official parties and eventually formed or joined the Liberal Party. The reified notions of culture and of the dual economy in which they believed, made these scholars accept the idea of protecting the 'natives' from the inroads of 'modernity' by segregating them in town and country and letting them be subject to their own customary code, supervised, of course, by white magistrates or by some other local authority. With the benefit of hindsight, and allowing all of these analysts – with a large measure of generosity,[18] no doubt – complete moral-political integrity, it is clear that the processes of capitalist development as they unfolded in Africa generally and in southern Africa in particular were simply not questioned, much less understood, because they did not, and in many cases could not, have the appropriate analytical and theoretical tools with which to discern the movement of history. In Posel's precise formulation, the root of the problem was the fact that

> the liberal understanding of the economic underpinnings of South Africa's political system is confined within a methodologically individualist problematic; that is, the economic determinants of racial policy are characterised in terms of the intentions and volition of particular individuals or groups thereof. Class forces, on this view, represent merely the arithmetic sum of the power and influence of such groups … However sophisticated an interpretation we give to the liberal position, it still stops short of an understanding of the role of objective class forces which both constrain and enable individual intentions and actions, and which are not fully subject to conscious individual or group control.[19]

In trying to understand the origins and effects of racial ideology, the liberal pluralists followed two related lines of inquiry. In the first case, they tended to trace the origins of racist thinking to Calvinism and thus to the baneful influence of the Dutch Reformed Church and, after approximately 1870, of the Afrikaner nationalist movement.[20] Together with the dog-eat-dog modality of frontier life during the eighteenth and nineteenth centuries, Calvinist notions of predestination, later reinforced by Social Darwinist simplifications of evolutionary theory as applied to sub-specific human varieties, produced a potent cocktail which, in the theorisations of the later liberals assumed an independent causal significance, and at the very least co-determined the shape of political, social, and cultural development in South Africa. Scholarship, influenced by the perspectives of the radical revisionists after 1970, has shown, of course, that these views were extremely myopic and tendentious, and that the entire programme of what came to be known as segregation, and later apartheid, was formulated in the report of the South African Native Affairs Commission, set up by Lord Milner in his capacity as High Commissioner, in 1903–1905. Although the empirical details of how the report eventually came to be formulated were much more complex than this bald statement would imply, the fact remains that it was under the rule of the British Empire and not that of the Afrikaner, or *Boer*, nationalists that the political blueprint of segregation was originally proposed and, in part, actually implemented. To quote Worden's summary of the position:

Segregation needs to be distinguished from white supremacy. Although it was predicated on perceptions of racial difference and was developed in the aftermath of colonial conquest, South African segregation was not just racial subordination writ large. Its underlying principle was the enforced separation, not just subordination, of Blacks and whites in the spheres of work, residence and government ... [It] was only in the period between the end of the South African War in 1902 and the 1930s that a cogent ideology of segregation emerged and was implemented ... [It was the South African Native Affairs Commission that proposed] racial separation of land ownership, the establishment of 'Native locations' in towns, regulation of labour influx to the cities with pass laws, differential wage levels, mission-based schooling for Africans rather than state education, administration in separate Native Councils and no extension of the Cape's non-racial franchise to other parts of the Union.[21]

The second line of inquiry opened up by the liberal pluralists, which had a permanent influence on South African historiography and social science was the bringing of the African people on to the stage of 'History'.[22] You might think that this ought not to be worthy of comment but this attitude would betray considerable ignorance of the hegemony and the almost axiomatic status which white supremacist and Eurocentric views had in South Africa before approximately 1960. It is, therefore, noteworthy that both Macmillan[23] and De Kiewiet[24] mentioned African groups and even individuals in their writings. However, neither of them paid more than passing attention to the internal stratification and dynamics of the African 'tribes', chiefdoms, and kingdoms with which the white colonists and Boer republics came into conflict or with which they collaborated in pursuit of their particular social ends. In the final analysis, the indigenous African people were even for them an undifferentiated, relatively passive mass who had not yet become historical actors.

It was only in the late 1960s with the publication of the first volume of *Oxford History of South Africa*[25] that it became possible to speak of African agency becoming manifest in mainstream South African historiography. This work, indeed, marks the zenith of liberal-pluralist historical writing in South Africa and it had a profound influence on all subsequent social science scholarship in southern Africa. Nevertheless, even though it revealed many new sources and posed many new questions, it did not get beyond the liberal orthodoxy in terms of which South African history was perceived as the interaction between white people and Black people viewed as Manichaean entities. Like other liberal works, it condemned the irrationality of racial prejudice and underlined what the authors considered to be the deleterious economic and social effects of segregationist and apartheid policies. In addition, it made no serious effort to trace the manner in which race, class and other markers of social difference intersected and either reinforced or contradicted one another in the course of social action undertaken by large masses of people. As summarised by Saunders, this pathfinding work in a sense brought together in two volumes all the problematic aspects of the liberal-pluralist paradigm:

> Rejecting racism, the liberal Africanists did on occasion admit that race had not always been the dominant cleavage in South African history ... Yet some critics charged that they in fact disseminated the very ideology they professed to condemn. Their use of racial categories did not challenge, but served to buttress, the racial system, for racial groups were seen as fundamental givens. South African history was interpreted in terms of race and of racism ... Ethnic categories were inappropriately read back into the past, as if they had some primordial existence. The development of ethnic consciousness over time, among Afrikaners and Africans, was ignored. *The Oxford History* devoted little explicit attention to the growth of white racism, which was mostly taken for granted, as something that had been present since the eighteenth century and therefore did not require historical explanation.[26]

After World War II, the liberal pluralists arrived at the consensus that the Black people of South Africa would inevitably have to be integrated as equal citizens into the historically evolved South African state,[27] and that the segregationist and later apartheid strategies were going against the grain of history. As a result, much of their writing, including their historical writing, was intended to sound a warning to the Afrikaner political class – which, since Union, had effectively administered the country – against the danger of Bolshevik revolution. Indeed, as indicated earlier, the disaster of fascism and national socialism and the subsequent rush towards decolonisation in Asia and in Africa called into question all racist theories and practices. Consequently, White South Africa arrived at a fork in the historical road at the latest in 1946 when the Indian delegation to the UNO brought in a motion of censure against the Smuts government because of the way it treated people of Indian descent in South Africa.

In 1947, the Fagan Commission, which had been appointed by the very same Smuts government, recommended that the proletarianisation and urbanisation of the African people be accepted as a permanent phenomenon and that the racially discriminatory laws, such as the pass laws, the apprenticeship laws, job and residential segregation, among others, be gradually abolished.

The view was an acknowledgement by significant segments of the white population that the economic and social changes that had taken place between the two World Wars and during the Second World War had irrevocably changed the social and political realities in the country. However, the indoctrinated and privileged white community decided otherwise. In the 1948 'general' elections they gave a slight parliamentary majority to the 'Purified National Party' led by Dr D.F. Malan, who had broken away from the original National Party, led by General Hertzog, 15 years earlier because the latter had decided to form an alliance with the pro-British South African Party, led by General Smuts. The mandate given to Malan, which was at first considered to be a fluke of 'parliamentary democracy' by all liberal commentators and was not deemed to be sustainable,[28] in fact spelt the beginning of the end of the hegemony of the liberal paradigm in South African scholarship and rang in what O'Meara[29] refers to as the 'forty lost years' of South African development.

THE RADICAL REVISION OF SOUTH AFRICAN SOCIAL SCIENCE SCHOLARSHIP

It was the massacre at Sharpeville and the momentous events that it brought about in its wake that finally put an end to the hegemony of the liberal-pluralist paradigm. Before we briefly discuss the revisionist challenge to liberalism, I have to refer to two seminal texts which, though usually unacknowledged because they were virtually *samizdat* documents emanating from what was supposed to be a marginal political grouping, none the less exerted great influence on the thinking of all radical scholars during the 1960s and in the early 1970s. These were the works by Mnguni[30] and Majeke.[31] Both works were products of analyses and discussions that took place on a continuous basis within the milieu of the left socialist Unity Movement of South Africa (often misdescribed as a Trotskyite current within the broad liberation movement), rather than from the internationally better-known Stalinist Communist Party of South Africa.[32] Both works appeared in the year of the tercentenary celebrations

by White South Africa of the founding of Van Riebeeck's colony at the
Cape of Good Hope and were intended as a trenchant critique of those
celebrations. They took it as their point of departure that the history of
South Africa for the past 300 years was, in the words of Majeke, a story
'of continuous plunder of land and cattle by the European invaders, of
the devastation and decimation of people, followed by their economic
enslavement'.[33] What would now be called a vulgar Marxist analysis was
applied to the history of the country and both authors undertook exten-
sive research (mostly in printed primary sources) to substantiate their
interpretations. Saunders[34] points out that so-called professional historians ignored these works, or simply did not read them at the time because
of their anti-liberal and anti-capitalist 'bias', so that they did not find their
way into the historical works of the liberal pluralists. Elsewhere, Muller,[35]
one of the conservative Afrikaner nationalist historians, discusses these
works in a cryptic paragraph, surmising incidentally that the authors were
probably 'white' people who used 'African' pseudonyms. In fact, their significance as forerunners of the neo-Marxist critique undertaken by the
'revisionist' historians of the 1970s is now only being acknowledged.[36]

Although Majeke and Mnguni both used crude tools of class analysis,
there was no attempt to relate the 'underlying' economic class structures
to the political actions by different groups pursuing their ideologically
bounded interests on the ground. In this sense, these works were no more
than a blunt rebuttal of racist Eurocentric approaches, whether of the
settler or the liberal variety. As with Roux,[37] they left no doubt about the
decisive importance of African peasants and workers as historical subjects. However, it was only with the advent of the neo-Marxist radicals
from 1970 onwards that more refined conceptual and analytical tools
began to be used to revise South African historiography.

The impetus for this initiative came from exiled 'white' draft dodgers
and radical students mostly studying in Great Britain. These men and
women studied in the milieu produced by the 1968 revolts on European
campuses and by the anti-Vietnam-War demonstrations, under the influence of the extremely stimulating and creative historiographical works
of the left-wing socialist, communist, and ex-communist generation of
post-war scholars, among whom the names of Eric Hobsbawm, Barrington Moore, Christopher Hill, Raphael Simon, and E.P. Thompson in
Britain, as well as Eugene Genovese in the United States of America, are
central. Many of them were also influenced by the structuralist Marxism
of Nico Poulantzas. Although it is a complex and often contradictory

canvas which was punctuated by vicious polemics deriving from passionate disputes on strategy in the anti-apartheid political movement, notably with the ANC, it would be fair to say that the decisive role was played by the South African historian Harold Wolpe in the School of Sociology at Essex University, and by what came to be called the 'Sussex School' grouped around the 'Gang of Four' (Davies, Johnstone, Morris, and Kaplan) at Sussex University, as well as by Shula Marks, Anthony Atmore, Stanley Trapido and a few other South Africans at the Institute of Commonwealth Studies of the University of London. All of these scholars developed their original theses largely as a critical response to the analytical limitations of the *Oxford History of South Africa*, the first volume of which appeared in 1969, in terms of the exciting new perspectives which were opening up in this most scintillating of intellectual moments in the second half of the twentieth century.[38]

If we accept the judgement of Christopher Saunders, then Martin Legassick earns the title of 'the single most important figure in the radical challenge of the early 1970s'.[39] Saunders bestows this title on him because of the set of theoretical propositions he advanced in both published and unpublished papers in the early 1970s in which he stood most of the liberal-pluralist findings on their head, as it were:

> He ... argued that the essential features of segregation dated, not from the seventeenth- or eighteenth-century frontier, but from the early twentieth century, and that they were intimately related to the development of the modern economy ... [His] critique of 'the frontier tradition in South African historiography' questioned the use to which the notion of frontier had been put by liberal historians, and suggested that racism could not simply be explained on its own terms, as something carried intact from the eighteenth-century frontier into the twentieth century, but had to be related to the changing material base of society...That mature racism was intimately related to capitalism in its mining phase was a theme he explored in other papers.[40]

In one of the abovementioned papers, Legassick critiqued the liberal modernisation thesis according to which racism and similar 'atavistic' relics of the pre-modern era are dysfunctional to the development of capitalism. Basing himself on Barrington Moore's thesis as developed in his work on the *Social Origins of Dictatorship and Democracy*,[41] Legassick demonstrated persuasively that pre-capitalist conditions and relations,

unique to each social formation, always inform the specific development of capitalism in each such formation and that there is, therefore,
no general formula in terms of which the 'functionality' or otherwise of a
particular ideology can be checked off beforehand. In the South African
case, we were dealing not with a 'dual economy', as the liberal pluralists
would have it, but instead with a single 'forced labour economy of gold
and maize'.[42]

Taken together, the revisionist challenge amounted to a rout of the 'conventional wisdom' of the liberal orthodoxy. Their insistence on the need
to understand South African history primarily in terms of the economic
imperatives that drove events and individuals and their rejection of the
liberal idea and the historiographical practice of the separation between
the 'political' and the 'economic', led to a radical change in the ways of
seeing South Africa's past and, therefore, the present. It had been shown
at the very least that the structural conditions of deep-level mining as well
as the need for cheap Black labour on the part of the white farming class
were inescapable causes of the continuation and intensification of racial
discrimination and racial segregation. The overriding need of primary
(extractive) industry to keep the wage level of Black workers as low as
possible for the entire period before the gold price was allowed to be
determined freely according to the 'normal' laws of supply and demand
is the essential explanatory factor for our understanding of the institutional base and political-economic practices of segregation and of aspects
of its successor, apartheid.[43] The whole edifice of repressive laws and
bureaucratic structures, ranging from 'native reserves' and Bantustans at
the one end to the ludicrous details of 'petty apartheid', such as separate
post office queues and cemeteries, is explicable ultimately in terms of a
racist logic, the end of which was to guarantee cheap Black labour and the
continued profitability of 'maize and gold'. As long as the ceilings of the
labour-repressive economy had not been reached, that is, as long as shortages of skilled labour, market demand for the primary products and the
supply of investment capital had not been reached, racial ideology was
shown to be statistically and empirically functional to capitalist growth.

However, the functionality of racial ideology was put in question once
secondary (manufacturing) industry, in the wake of the World War I, and
then ever more rapidly, after World War II, became the dominant component of capital in South Africa. The actual implications of this development
were only realised much later, indeed, only once the negotiation process
for the dismantling of apartheid had gone some way. Although there were

numerous sectarian political and theoretical disagreements among the different 'schools' of revisionists, the general tendency of their historical and other social science work was to undermine thoroughly the long-held views of the liberal pluralists. And although there were different emphases among the individual scholars, most of them tended to adopt a dogmatic position in terms of which racial ideology was seen as a kind of 'false consciousness' originally, and a relationship of functional necessity was established between the development of capitalism and racism in South Africa.[44] This was related to the prevailing militant revolutionarism in the broad liberation movement at the time. It was to prove to be the analytical Achilles heel of the revisionist 'new history' since, ultimately, history itself was to indicate long before events themselves demonstrated the fact that the capitalist system is able to survive and even thrive in South Africa without recourse to racial ideology. Indeed, the changed circumstance in the global political economy would compel the system to slough off the integument of racially determined social relations. The 'power bloc' that constituted the base of white power, as it appeared on the surface, was identified as a class alliance between imperialist finance capital, the white capitalist class, and the white working class.[45]

Many important insights were gained for South African social science scholarship as a result of the academic and social research exertions of the men and women who initiated the critique of the liberal paradigm and of those who subsequently refined their tools. Besides a whole generation of Poulantzian and Althusserian sociological, anthropological, archaeological, and historical studies, as well as more down-to-earth empirical or field research conducted under the rubrics of economic, social, and local as well as oral history, all of which cleared up much of the nebulousness that enveloped the study of race relations, our understanding of the state and the refinement of the orthodox instrumentalist notions of the state was deepened. Together with these initiatives, discourse analysis, cultural studies, and the study of socio-linguistics, as well as profoundly influential gender studies set up a research agenda which will carry on well into the twenty-first century. The study of race and class inevitably triggered the transfer of the research methods and the conceptualisation of social inequality to the related fields of ethnic, gender, linguistic, and cultural studies. Much of this movement was a reflection of prior and similar developments in the United Kingdom and the United States of America, but in the context of a polarised South Africa where such revisionist scholarship was surrounded by the halo of revolutionary activist and working-class mobilisation, its pertinent effects were, to say the least, galvanising. History became one of the most popular school and university subjects even though in its various radical incarnations, it had to be conducted on the margins of the official curricula.

RECENT DEVELOPMENTS

The tendency towards dogmatic class reductionism or even towards a simplistic economic determinism, coupled, as it often was, with a claim to infallibility evinced by many of the practitioners and devotees of the new school, proved to be a serious weakness.[46] Because most of them had thrown in their political lot with the ANC and the SACP and because, until approximately 1988, they were encouraged in their belief that there would be a revolutionary overthrow of the apartheid state, they were totally unprepared – like most other people in the world, but with devastating intellectual and political consequences – for the earth-shaking events of 1989, that *annus mirabilis*, which led Fukuyama[47] to pronounce, prematurely, the end of history.

The quasi- often pseudo-revolutionary *Standort* of most of the revisionists had, naturally, informed their scholarship and their critique of the liberal school. When the leadership of the Congress Alliance decided that the time had come to make a deal with the Afrikaner nationalist and to restructure the power bloc that had been ruling South Africa since 1910, these scholars and activists were, in most cases, caught completely off guard. It was left to one of the moving spirits behind the new school to find the words and the conceptual tools with which to salvage some pride for those of that generation who did not capitulate to the neo-liberal hegemony in silence. Harold Wolpe,[48] in a slender volume that can be seen as a kind of limited self-criticism, put forward the thesis of the contingent relationship between racism and capitalist growth. In a nutshell, he condemned the liberal pluralists for their race-reductionist approach while at the same time accusing the neo-Marxists of the new school of South African history of crude class reductionism. Instead, he stated that

> the relationship between capitalism and white domination must be seen as an historically contingent, not a necessary one. Moreover, that relationship will be both functional and contradictory at the same time – functional for the reproduction of certain relations and class posi-

tions and contradictory for others. The contention is that the formation of structures and relations is always the outcome of struggles between contending groups or classes and that this outcome is Janus-faced, being always simultaneously functional and contradictory. Which pole of the relationship will be dominant depends on the historically specific conditions of the social formation ... It is precisely the analysis of the alteration of the conditions which is of central importance. This is not to suggest that each moment in history is to be treated as uniquely discrete. The point ... is to recognize the significance of diversity and discontinuity within a process of continuity.[49]

With these words, and in the rest of a jargon-loaded analysis of the mistakes of the new school, Wolpe prepared the intellectual terrain for coming to terms with the political compromise of 1993–1994, which had been casting its shadow ever since 1986 at the latest, when the rebellion of the urban youth was crushed in an orgy of total repression. Wolpe's 1998 *Race, Class and the Apartheid State* is one of the most sophisticated theoretical works to have come out of the period of anti-apartheid struggle after 1960. Unfortunately, it also contains some of the most overt apologetics for a South African political party other than the Afrikaner National Party, where this kind of thing was *de rigueur* right into the 1990s. For, while his treatment of the relationship between race, class, and capitalism in effect opens up conceptual and political space for more nuanced analysis and action, Wolpe also tries to salvage the dual-economy, liberal-pluralist notion of 'colonialism of a special type', which was supposed to be the paradigm within which the SACP analysed South African society but which, in reality, simply abdicated any pretensions to the political leadership of the mass movement and permitted the political allies of the party, that is, the aspiring Black middle-class leadership of the ANC, to lead the mass struggle. And lead it they did, as we now know, with single-minded clarity as to the ends of the African nationalist struggle.

Having said this, it is important to note that the basic thrust of Wolpe's argument which, if it is treated simplistically leads one into the swamps of empiricism, is methodologically unexceptionable and his insistence on bringing the focus of research (back) on to discontinuity, besides its political 'timeliness', corrects in a very useful manner the dogmatic, unilinear, and undialectical mode of analysis that had crept into the works of the new school. The relationship between what Marx called the class in itself and the class for itself is not a necessary but a contingent one. Classes in themselves may, in van den Berghe's words, never, or only seldom, be 'meaningful social realities',[50] but this does not mean that the groups that act against or with one another do not constitute classes for themselves, provided we scrutinise carefully the issue of class hegemony in any social movement. This kind of discussion rapidly becomes opaque and tedious and, in the final analysis, it is empirical research that is required to arrive at an approximation of the relationship between race (or gender, or ethnic group, etc.) and class, rather than reductionist formulae derived from abstract models of society.

And this is where the debate has landed today, even if it is being conducted *sotto voce*, no longer in the strident tones of even eight years ago. The two recent overviews by Saunders[51] and Worden[52] of the development of historiography in South Africa, even if somewhat wishfully, both arrive at the conclusion that a convergence between the liberal pluralist and the radical or revisionist approaches has been taking place. According to them, the liberals have for many years now quietly taken on board some of the critiques and findings of the new school and of the materialist approach to history, while the revisionists, for their part, have been jettisoning some of their reductionist and dogmatic positions. In words that remind me of a kind of historiographical truth and reconciliation commission, Saunders refers to Frederick Johnstone's self-criticism[53] (already in 1979) and continues as follows:

> For Johnstone class analysis remained essential, but it was not sufficient. Liberal pluralists, for their part, came to accept that class had been an important factor, along with race ... So the issue became the relative importance of, and the inter-relationship between, race and class, both fluid categories which changed over time, To assert the primacy of either race or class on *a priori* grounds was to be ahistorical; the nature of the relationship could only be determined by examining the evidence ...[54]

In my view, this amounts to a premature closure of a continuing debate, one which is being conducted at very different levels in quite different domains and disciplines under the general rubric of the implications and consequences of globalisation. In other words, it is a debate that will not lie down and die, because it continues to reflect the tenacious reality of class conflict mediated by historically contingent social, institutional, and mental structures, often harking back to remote pre-industrial times.[55] The dialectical relationship that exists between the global and the local, a social phenomenon that we are only now beginning to understand, and the ubiquity of xenophobic responses to mass migrations of peoples, especially from the economic South of the planet to the North and, recently, also from East to West, coupled with the phenomenon of mass tourism, have led to a resurgence of ethnic and racial studies, usually under the rubric of 'identity politics' within multicultural societies. For reasons connected with the destabilisation of the post-war order and the concomitant crisis of credibility of the socialist project, as well as the palpable difficulties experienced by those who attempt to project a coherent alternative to the capitalist 'free-market' system, discourse analysis, now associated with the portmanteau category of 'postmodernism', has become both a refuge for those who have withdrawn from the battlefields of the recent past, and a beacon of hope for those who in any case were seeking ways of getting away from the oversimplified, deterministic analytical frameworks which became associated with Marxism and with some variants of Weberian sociology.

This is a debate that is still in its infancy in most parts of the world. However, it has already led to us understanding that the verbalisation of discourse in such a way that everything can be perceived as changing and changeable is one of the main research and creative projects for the next period of human evolution. It is a matter of common sense that nominalisation or reification serves essentially the interests of dominant groups. They, rather than those who are in subaltern positions, stand to gain if people are conditioned to perceive their world as unchanging and unchangeable. In South Africa, where a liberal-democratic dispensation has been inaugurated and where the ruling elites are rapidly falling back into the ethnic ('tribal') and racial habitus of the period before the unifying impetus of the anti-apartheid struggle, such a verbalised discourse is one of an ensemble of academic-cum-political tasks which awaits us in the course of the struggles ahead for the deepening of democracy, the broadening of equality, and the revival of human solidarity.

'The Peculiarities of the Transition to Democracy in South Africa'[1]

South Africa's transition to a liberal-democratic dispensation is one of a generation of similar transitions which began in southern Europe in the last quarter of the twentieth century and which continues in Eastern Europe and in countries such as Northern Ireland and Burundi today. As such, it shares not only the global economic, technological, political, and ideological context but also a number of common process features with other similar transitions. Indeed, this general phenomenon is the basis of the new academic industry known as transitology, which already boasts many internationally recognised named – Huntington, Lijphart, Pzresworski, and Schmitter, among others – in the field of political studies. In our narrower South African arena, the names of scholars such as Friedman, Adam, and Giliomee come to mind. It is, therefore, not surprising that with regard to most aspects of the South African transition, we have available a fair number of competent comparative studies and chronicles of the process of transition. Among the most insightful, I would mention the studies of Giliomee and Schlemmer,[2] Horowits,[3] Lee and Schlemmer,[4] Adam and Moodley,[5] Friedman,[6] Friedman and Atkinson,[7] Murray,[8] Sparks,[9] O'Meara,[10] McKinley,[11] Adam, Moodley, and Slabbart,[12] Marais,[13] and Bond.[14]

All of these works stress the geopolitical and technological transformations which changed the face of the world in the period after the Second World War. Of these, the two most important factors were undoubtedly the ascendancy of what became the neoliberal orthodoxy in the theory and practice of economics, and the collapse of the Soviet Union and its satellite states. The rise to power of Gorbachev in the Union of Soviet Socialist Republics (USSR) inaugurated a new era in world politics since it heralded the end of the Cold War and, thus, of armed insurrection supported by a superpower as a viable method of revolutionary strategy.[15] Framed by these two parameters and by the necessary degree of internal contradictions and conflict, all the transitions to a liberal-democratic dispensation tended to manifest a similar political dramaturgy. In fact, the relative success or failure of earlier attempts at such transitions necessarily influenced subsequent initiatives and the academics as well as the political and economic consultants – mostly United States Americans – who were usually called upon to act as directors of the new order became increasingly expert at writing the appropriate scripts and choreographing the action. In one country after another, the same basic processes took place, beginning with stern and unconditional demands for submission by both sides in the conflict, leading on to informal contacts at quasi-governmental level, mediation by 'honest brokers', proximity talks, suspension of armed conflict, negotiations and pacting between the old and the new elites, various types of truth commissions, and culminating in the inauguration of the new leaders, usually in the presence of one of the highest representatives of the United States president.

South Africa, too, went through all of these, and many other, steps of the dance of the pacting elites. However, as in each of the other cases – ranging from Spain and Portugal in the 1970s to Burundi today – there were unique elements programmed into the process by the peculiarities of the history of each country. These features are important because they tend to account for both the continuities and the discontinuities between the 'old' and the 'new' situations. It is to these special features of the South African situation that I want to turn my attention in this chapter.

THE ROLE OF EXTERNAL CIRCUMSTANCES

It is clear that it was the overt and covert internal struggles of the oppressed people of South Africa against the economic and social deprivations of the system of racial capitalism coupled with international sanctions and diplomatic isolation which pushed the apartheid strategy of the ruling group up against its ceilings and forced Big Business to contemplate alternatives to the regimes of John Vorster and P.W. Botha. These developments, especially after the Soweto Uprising of 1976, foretold the inevitable demise of the apartheid delusion. However, the actual timing of the transition from apartheid to democratic rule was determined by the strategic shift in the politics of the former Soviet Union under Gorbachev. Once the ANC was no longer able to depend on that source of support for the strategy of armed propaganda and mass action, both it and the National Party were compelled to look at alternative strategies. The adoption of the policy of *perestroika* and *glasnost* by the ruling elite in the former Soviet Union ultimately implied the downgrading of post-war South African governments as guarantors of the strategic oil route around the Cape of Good Hope. It was illogical from the point of view of the governments of Western Europe and North America to continue their Machiavellian support for a white minority regime which espoused an internationally stigmatised policy of racial discrimination if, as proved to be the case, there was available a popular Black majority party which was willing to adopt the hegemonic neoliberal, free-market, multi-party formula of governance.

On the other side, as it were, the ANC, like similar movements and organisations in other Third-World countries, could no longer rely on the support of the Soviets for its military and training resources. As a result, the leverage in the Congress Alliance of the SACP generally and of its left wing in particular was reduced, so that the moderate centrist elements in the leadership of the ANC could rapidly become decisive in the determination of policy and strategy. These developments have been documented in all their contradictions in numerous journalistic and scholarly studies.[16] And, since the organisation was the recipient of assistance, especially for educational, training and administrative purposes, from many liberal and capitalist donors, the normal pressure from these quarters for more 'realistic' and peaceful tactics increased considerably.

If, therefore, the world-historical context affected the dynamics of South African society in the last quarter of the twentieth century in such a way that both the ruling elite and the primary challenger for state power were compelled to seek a compromise, it ought to be possible to discover the elements that facilitated the crafting of the 'miracle'. Why did the race war which everyone feared and predicted not occur in South Africa, that land which was the byword for racism among modern nations? Rather than satisfy ourselves with the mere proclamation of the 'miracle' as has been done by so many commentators on the South African transition, it is appropriate that we follow the method of the *Congregatio pro Causis Sanctorum*, that body charged by the Vatican with the task of checking on the claims about miraculous works performed by any person nominated for canonisation by the Roman Catholic Church.

THE ROLE OF THE ANC

Let us consider the question of the 'miracle' of South Africa's transition from the perspective of the ANC first. The essential points can be stated briefly even though this necessarily abstracts from the richness of the reality. In a nutshell, since its inception in 1912 and throughout its history, the ANC has never been a revolutionary organisation. Its leadership was not even rhetorically committed to the overthrow of the South African state, in spite of some talk in the mid-1980s about the fact that 'apartheid cannot be reformed'. At the height of the uprising of the youth in 1986, the president of the ANC, Oliver Tambo, made it clear that 'the ANC's main objective was "not a military victory but to force Pretoria to the negotiating table"'.[17] Besides spotlighting a fact which is mostly omitted from the hagiographic and sycophantic writings on contemporary South African history, this has another dimension which, in ethical terms, has a profound significance for the manner in which we, and posterity, do and should judge the leaders of the Congress Alliance. Whatever the individual hesitations and doubts of people such as Mandela, Sisulu, and others might have been from time to time, it is my view that they cannot be accused of having acted against their own moral principles or political objectives. Their essential aim, as it had been of virtually all ANC leaders since 1912, was to deracialise the South African polity and society, to create the conditions in which the classical liberal-democratic principle of 'equality of opportunity' for all citizens could be realised. This is very different from the case of many of those other people who actually were, or thought they were, on the 'left' in the Congress Alliance.[18] As I have stated, the ANC, like all similar ethnically- and racially-based organisations before the Second World War, did not question the international legality of the South African state. Rather, they rejected the legitimacy of all the white minority and white supremacist governments that ruled the territory between 1910 and 1993 on the grounds that they had not been elected by all eligible voters.

For this reason, therefore, the turn to arms after Sharpeville in 1960 represented for the leadership of the ANC a classical continuation of policy by other means. In spite of the exasperation caused by the Botha regime's obstinate arrogance born out of racial bigotry, which led the ANC underground media to speak of a Vietnam-style protracted, or people's war, it is doubtful whether the senior leadership of the organisation ever seriously contemplated anything beyond armed propaganda. This especially after the signing of the Nkomati Accord in 1984 between Samora Machel and P.W. Botha, as a result of which the ANC lost its most effective external bases. It is an undisputed fact that the armed incursions launched by the Umkhonto we Sizwe (MK) militants never transcended this phase of unconventional military operations. It is also clear that there were serious divisions with regard to the correct military strategy to be followed by the movement, especially as wave after wave of radicalised youth escaped into the ANC camps in exile and reinforced the more radical perspectives of the younger men and women in MK. However, as Marais states: '[It] was the patent failure of a strategy centred on an insurrectionary variant of armed struggle that probably tilted the ANC onto the negotiations path reconnoitred by Nelson Mandela since 1986'.[19]

He adds, 'The fact that Mandela opened a channel of communication with the regime – while his Lusaka colleagues were detecting the emergence of a "pre-revolutionary" climate in South Africa – suggests an acute awareness on his part of the foolhardiness of that strategy'.[20]

To this, I can only add that this was indeed the case, judging from a conversation Mandela and I had in prison as early as 1971. In the course of our discussion, he posed a leading (devil's advocate-type) question (one of his favourite tactics) along the lines that if we were dissatisfied with the manner in which the armed struggle was being waged 'outside', was it not time to consider using the existing constitutional channels, as flawed as they were (because of the regime's Bantustan policy, among other reasons)? In any case, the effectiveness of the apartheid regime's destabilisation strategy in the frontline states of southern Africa forced these states to lean on the South West African People's Organisation (Swapo) and the ANC to alter their strategy and to consider means other than guerrilla warfare in order to bring about a resolution of the conflict.

Between approximately 1969 and 1980, the ANC leadership had captured the organisation's strategy in the neat image of the 'four pillars', namely mass struggle at home, underground struggle, armed struggle, and the international isolation of the racist apartheid regime. The decade and a half from the mid-1970s until the end of the 1980s was, as is well known, a period of ever-intensifying mass struggle, one which began under the banner of the BCM and ended under the flag of the ANC and its allies. With the change in the geopolitical conditions after 1985, what little military success had been achieved as the result of incursions launched by MK became less and less relevant and the emphasis necessarily shifted to the fourth pillar (the international isolation of the apartheid regime). Gorbachev's move to the centre of the political spectrum was the one element that nobody could have foreseen but, in accordance with the insight of Louis Pasteur that 'chance favours those who are prepared', the ANC, by 1989 at the very latest, was ready to inherit the political kingdom. Among other things, this implied the demolition of the pillars labelled 'armed struggle' and 'underground operations' and imposing strict control over the mass movement.

Objectively, the ANC, in spite of its often militant rhetoric, was the ideal 'valid interlocutor' and ready to take over the reins of government, first as a kind of junior partner and then rapidly as 'the main player'. In Huntington's terms, the South African transition is a 'transplacement' since both the (previous) government and its opposition were crucial to initiating and sustaining it.[21] This came about because of the political stalemate that was reached in about mid-1985. It is, however, important to stress that the fact that the apartheid state was not overthrown by revolutionary means has had fundamental determining effects on the character of the post-apartheid state, where the continuities – in contrast with the discontinuities – with the apartheid state still tend to be dominant and, thus, to obstruct reform.

Although the ANC was, and is, a multi-class organisation, there is no doubt that for most of its existence as an organisation, its dominant, indeed hegemonic, ethos was represented by the interests of the upward-striving Black middle class, those people who, like the bourgeoisie in pre-1789 France, were most conscious of the unnecessary restrictions placed on their, and others', advancement by the *ancient régime*. Even a cursory perusal of the official manifestoes, programmes, and policy documents of the ANC amply confirms this. While the influence and the leverage of the SACP within the Congress Alliance were manifest, especially after 1961 when MK was formed, the SACP's theory of a 'two-stage' so-called socialist revolution in effect abdicated the leadership of the 'first' stage of 'national democratic revolution'; to the nationalist, that is, pro-democracy and pro-capitalist, forces in the alliance. While the SACP's embedment within the alliance may well have garnered for the party many individual members who were also by definition loyal members of the ANC, beyond rhetoric it had very little real influence on the macroeconomic conceptions and philosophical orientation of the popular leadership of the ANC.[22] The complete pragmatism of the ANC leaders in matters economic is now well-attested. Mandela's notorious somersault on the question of 'nationalisation' (of mines, monopoly companies, banks, etc.) is one of the more dramatic examples of this phenomenon. The ditching of the social-democratic Reconstruction and Development Programme (RDP) for the neoliberal Growth, Employment and Redistribution (GEAR) strategy was the logical outcome of this trajectory within the global context of the transition.[23] Every attempt by those who adhere to a more or less left-wing agenda within the Congress Alliance has been defeated hitherto. The Thatcherian argument that 'there is no alternative' (to the neoliberal macroeconomic strategy), popularly known as the TINA argument, wielded by the moderate leadership, and the failure of the left-wingers to come forward with a viable alternative strategy that would not alienate the national and the international bourgeoisie, have resulted in a situation where it can be said without any fear of contradiction that the ANC government, first and foremost, serves the interests of the capitalist class.

THE ROLE OF THE MINORITY WHITE REGIME

From the other side of the 'miracle' transition to democracy, we have a more complex perspective. The dilemma and the agony of the political representatives of the white minority in South Africa can be described as the problem of a blind spot, induced by racist ideology, having to be eliminated after the accident had already happened. It is the Gorbachev scenario where history punishes those who come late. The unreconstructed racism of a Vorster and a P.W. Botha led to a situation where the leadership of the white minority made their move ('across the Rubicon') too late to enable them to retain effective political power. Their real mistake was that they had misread the willingness and ability of the ANC leadership to 'accept' the neoliberal orthodoxy. To their, and most others', surprise, they found that their leverage vanished in front of their eyes as the real ANC stood up to be counted, as opposed to the mythologised 'communist' and 'terrorist' organisation which they had dressed it up as for the benefit of their various local and international constituencies for three decades. This misjudgement on the part of the leaders of the National Party after the ignominious departure of Botha from the scene explains the subsequent precipitous decline of that party. Nevertheless, it is more than obvious that their negotiators gave away nothing that had not already been taken away from them on the field of battle, in which I include all sites of struggle, not only the armed propaganda of the MK militants.[24] Even though men such as De Klerk took a calculated risk and knew that they would have to face extremely awkward situations involving former NP stalwarts who believed that they had sold them out, in the light of their understanding of the real relations of power in the country, they certainly expected that the outcome of the dance of the pacting elites would be no more than a pyrrhic victory for the ANC.

This provides us, however, with only a part of the explanation for the willingness of the white minority and their political representatives to 'transfer' power to the Black majority. Throughout the negotiation process, the NP saw itself as bargaining for a relatively long period of 'sharing' power but, in the end, it accepted that a five-year period of sharing, followed by a gradual transfer of political office to a democratically elected, effectively Black majority was a better option than risking a 'seizure' of power by violent means or a restructuring of the polity and the society by means of destabilising counter-revolutionary violence. While the larger electoral base of the NP would have been willing to contemplate this last option, the leadership and the bourgeoisified broad layer of white middle-class people knew that in the changed geopolitical conditions there would be hardly any support for such a move. Their wisdom was confirmed by the subsequent indifferent 'success' of General Constand Viljoen's quixotic attempt in Bophuthatswana, described in some detail by Sparks,[25] at salvaging some 'pride' for the armed forces of apartheid.

What made the mass base of the white minority give in to the moment of transition? Adam et al. venture the view that

[Given] all the external and internal factors conducive to negotiations, what made the critical difference from the dominant Afrikaner minority's side in the transition was an autocratic leadership style within the National Party, the personality of De Klerk that combined a newly experienced moral shift with political expediency and a strategic miscalculation as well as susceptible negotiators who were out manoeuvred in terms of the logic and assumptions of majoritarian democracy.[26]

This view is not incorrect, but it presents the factors as though they were dependent on a series of contingencies. It would be more correct, in my view, to state clearly that once the Afrikaner intelligentsia and the business community had come to realise that the 'game' of apartheid was up, the leadership would necessarily take the white tribe with it into the next 'trek', that is, into the new South Africa. They may have failed in not getting everything they said they wanted from the negotiation process, but they were very clear as to what they would not give up. The indigenous character of the Afrikaans-speaking white community as well as the racial caste system which had evolved in South Africa over a period of 350 years constitute the fundamental explanation for the willingness of the racist Pretoria regime to hand over office when the conditions of rule changed against them. The fact that they know no other home than South Africa in spite of all their 'European' pretensions and the fact of the economic interdependence of South Africa's diverse communities, derived from the unique distribution of skills and material resources which characterises the system of racial capitalism, meant that the leaders of Afrikaner nationalism could take the calculated risk of 'sharing' power with the leaders of African nationalism. Their position was categorically no different from that of Chief Buthelezi and the other leaders of the Inkatha Freedom party (IFP) with their social base in the rural home-land of Kwazulu and in some of the urban shacklands of Natal. They, too, were, and are, an indigenous group with nowhere else to go, faced with exactly the same kind of options: to fight a bloody war for ideological and continued economic dominance or to compromise in the belief that the moderate centre of the ANC would be able to push to the margins the left-wing 'adventurers' and other hangers-on in a new South Africa shaped to a very large degree by the cold reality of neoliberal hegemony.

My argument is, therefore, that the leadership of the white minor-ity, specifically of the Afrikaners, did not and could not hoodwink their followers. They merely did what, in the circumstances, any other non-communist, modernist leadership would have done.[27] That they failed to keep their core constituency together in the process has as much to do with the sectarian, factionalist traditions of Afrikaner nationalism as with the fact that a party as burdened with the stigma of racism as the NP was, had very little chance of survival in a 'non-racial' climate. This is the reason why most white supporters of the NP moved over *en bloc* into the Democratic Party (DP) – and the New National Party (NNP) and DP subsequently formed the Democratic Alliance (DA) – and some NP sup-porters even wandered off into the ANC itself. Subsequently, of course, at the end of 2001, the NNP reconstituted the 1994–1996 alliance with the ANC (for a Government of National Unity) after the DA was reduced to a shambolic 'alliance'. Only a tiny fraction of original NP supporters – which is none the less still capable of mounting destabilising actions – has remained in one or other right-wing funk hole.

Adam et al.[28] raise a significant point of difference between the South African transition and most others in drawing attention to the problem of 'the legitimate rights' of formerly privileged and dominant minorities. In this regard, the South African case is comparable to that of minority groups of Russians in some of the former states of the USSR such as the Baltic republics or of the Ulster Unionists in a united Ireland. While it is

true, as they maintain, that this would constitute an interesting addition
to the field of study of 'minority rights' viewed as a sub-set of 'human
rights', it is important to note that we cannot determine policy simply
from generalisations. Each case would still have to be examined and considered in terms of the relevant historical specificities. For example, in the
case of South Africa, besides the generally relevant point about whether
the guarantee of existing property rights does not perpetuate social inequality derived from colonial conquest and capitalist exploitation based
on 'race' (which it certainly does), the highly problematical issue (in
the South African context) of group rights with its implications for the
nation-building project and identity politics is immediately involved.

THE 'MADIBA FACTOR'

The role of certain individuals was, and is, extremely important in the
South African transition. The specifically South African style which
characterised the negotiations process, the oscillation between genteel
and brutal interventions, the transparency and the secrecy of the transition, was to a large extent the result of projections of the personalities
of 'the main players', especially, Mandela, Mbeki, Ramaphosa, Buthelezi,
De Klerk, Kobie Coetzee, Pik Botha, Constand Viljoen, and Roelf Meyer.
Like landscape artists, they fashioned the inherent but conflicting contours and trends of South African society to accord with their personal
perspectives which tended to converge precisely on an evolving consensus
in respect of the global socio-economic orthodoxy.[29] These predilections
are important because they have had an influence on the shape of institutions and processes in the new South Africa. To take a possibly fateful
example: the Commission for the Promotion and Protection of the Rights
of Cultural, Religious and Linguistic Communities, which straddles the
awkward divide between group rights and individual rights, is the direct
consequence of the interplay between the personalities and the ideological preoccupations and orientations of Mandela and Viljoen, respectively.
Similarly, the 'houses of traditional leaders' provided for in the Constitution[30] (see the Appendix to this book) are more than a mere sop to Chief
Buthelezi. It is an expression of deeply held convictions about the status
and the importance in African societies of traditional leadership by men
such as Mandela and Buthelezi.[31]

In its specificity, post-apartheid South Africa is inconceivable without
the personal contribution of Nelson Mandela. Indeed, his role has been

so decisive that, given the redemptive and millenarian climate of the time, the popular notion of a 'Madiba factor' was certainly justified. Nevertheless, as intimated throughout this book, the new South Africa had become inevitable and would have happened even without Mandela. It would, however, have been a very different place and it would have taken very much longer to come about. It was Mandela who gauged the moment to launch his initiative even without the knowledge and agreement of his comrades in prison and at ANC headquarters in Lusaka. As he writes in the authorised version of his autobiography:

> I chose to tell no one what I was about to do. Not my colleagues upstairs nor those in Lusaka. The ANC is a collective, but the government had made collectivity in this case impossible. I did not have the security or the time to discuss these issues with my organisation. I knew that my colleagues upstairs would condemn my proposal, and that would kill my initiative even before it was born There are times when a leader must move out ahead of the flock, go off in a new direction, confident that he is leading his people the right way ...[32]

Ironically, Mandela's reputation as a party person is legendary. It is well known that he will not make a move without consulting at least his peers in the leadership of the organisation. After 25 years in prison, during which he had been able to study his enemy in great detail both through the reading of South African history and through direct interaction with the prison and other government authorities, he had a shrewd idea that his initiative would meet with a positive response. This intuition was, naturally, reinforced by his approximate knowledge of the effects of financial sanctions on the ruling group and of the brutal repression of the mid-1980s on the Black youth of the country.

Because he had a keen sense of the real balance of forces, he put his stamp on the spirit in which the negotiations took place and on the accompanying rhetoric. In spite of the claims made around the defeat and enforced retreat of the South African Defence Force at Cuito Cuanavale in Angola in August 1998, Mandela saw to it that the impression was not given at any stage that the South Africans had been 'defeated' by the liberation forces. Militarily, of course, this was true, but in a holistically interpreted context, the very fact that the 'Boers' were willing to talk to the 'natives' represented a defeat of historic significance. It was a feat of the utmost importance for the successful conduct of negotiations that the less strategically minded younger people as well as other light-minded individuals in or close to the leadership did not upset the applecart with loud-mouthed and empty rhetoric. Mandela's normal approach of patient, reasonable, and rational dialogue, which amounts to a strategy of attrition, of wearing down his opponent, stood him and the ANC in good stead at this historical moment, and it came to symbolise the South African 'miracle', that is, the notion that with so-called good will and honest, transparent dialogue, even the most intractable of problems can be resolved.

The politics of reconciliation, which was the hallmark of the South African negotiations, is an excellent example of the interplay between personality and the force of objective circumstances.[33] For, it must be clear to anyone who has studied Mandela's utterances and his specific actions on occasion that 'non-racialism' is not his natural ambience. That is to say, his personal orientation is towards an understanding of South African society as consisting of four 'races', of whom 'the African people', that is, those who had to carry a pass under the previous white minority regimes, constitute the majority. These four categories of people – the 'Africans', the 'whites', the 'Coloureds', and the 'Indians' – are related to one another as 'national groups', of which the African group constitutes the 'nation' and the other three 'national', that is racial, minorities. I have no doubt that Mandela would not – today – recognise this particular description as the frame of reference with which he approaches South Africa's diverse population. It is, however, manifest in most of his utterances on the subject and examples are legion. In the present context, this observation is relevant only because the shape of the new Constitution could have been quite different if Mandela's personal view of the population had become decisive during the negotiations. It is not inconceivable that the ANC leadership might have gone into the negotiations with some notion of four coexisting national groups whose rights and duties might have been defined along the lines of some version of consociational democracy as in the examples of Lebanon, Switzerland, and other countries. For such an approach, the ANC would have found the ready support of the NP as well as other less important political formations at the table. Such a 'solution' was, however, impossible at the time of the negotiations.[34] Apartheid itself, which worked with precisely the same four categories, had been opposed, however inconsistently, and defeated under the banner of a 'non-racial, non-sexist, united, democratic South Africa'. Furthermore, most of the representatives of the ANC from the internal as

182 · AGAINST RACIAL CAPITALISM

well as the exile sectors could not and would not have supported anything other than the formulation which eventually prevailed. A new generation of Black youth had come into being for whom anything less was not even discussable. Moreover, besides matters of principle, the nation-building approach was politically expedient since it placed the white nationalists on the back foot by putting in question their cherished paradigm of an 'Afrikaner nation'. As the result of many long debates in prison on Robben Island during a period lasting about two years, I have personal ground for stating that for Mandela, 'nation-building' means no more and no less than ensuring the consolidation of the coherence of the South African state. As a socio-cultural construct, it might not mean for him what most people assume, that is, a people composed of individual citizens who are exploring and creating a new historical community. Naturally, if this view of the matter is correct, it speaks volumes for the leadership of the ANC generally, and for Mandela in particular, that they have helped to establish a framework within which such a voyage of exploration becomes possible. It is clear that the struggle around the content of 'nationhood', which involves the very meaning of the liberation of the oppressed social groups in the country, will continue in the twenty-first century as one of the defining moments of the new South Africa.

Another feature of the personality of Mandela which has become crystal clear to all who have observed him on the world stage is his genuine commitment to a classical British version of liberal democracy. In this, he is representative of his entire generation of political activists in the liberation movement with the possible exception of some revolutionary socialists. His political culture was influenced as much by Westminster as it was by the decorum and procedures of his chiefly background; it had almost nothing in common with Stalinist notions of 'democracy'. It would be wrong to put too fine a point on this, but I wonder whether the readiness with which the continuity of the Anglo-Afrikaner parliamentary trappings was accepted – all the nonsense about the honourable ministers and the honourable members of parliament, the tedious long introductory incantation of dignitaries' titles and status, and even the manner in which the state bureaucracy functions – would have happened if Mandela and his comrades had not shared the same colonial educational norms as their opponents on the white nationalist benches.

With regard to the other significant players, there is very little to be said. The personal contribution of De Klerk, in particular, has been written about by many scholars and journalists, most insightfully, I think, by Adam et al.[35] and more anecdotally by Sparks,[36] and Rosenthal.[37] As the night watchman of the apartheid regime, De Klerk, in a quite unintended way demonstrated the truth of the adage from a sexist era, 'cometh the time, cometh the man'. For the rest, he was very much his master's voice and served the bourgeois interests he represented as well as his background and the threadbare reputation of his party allowed him to. Even his famous speech of 2 February 1990 had been scripted four years earlier by the chairperson of Anglo-American Corporation, Gavin Relly. In an address given to the South African–British Trade Association on 26 August 1986, Relly spelt out the demands of Big Business for the inauguration of the process for a post-apartheid South Africa:

> Among ourselves ... we have reached agreement that statutory apartheid must go, that the political process be opened up by the release of prisoners of conscience, that political parties, currently banned, must be allowed to operate within the rule of law and that real attempts be made for constructive negotiation between all parties in South Africa.[38]

At one level, there is a measure of 'truth' in the woodcut image portrayed by Adam et al.[39] of two Machiavellian elites conning their respective constituencies and selling out on all the 'sacred' principles for the realisation of which they had led their people to war against each other. That there was a large measure of such consciously perpetrated chicanery is without any doubt. However, it is clear that once the process of negotiations had begun on a given basis, only those men and women who were not dogmatic about any of the things they preached from political platforms; those, in other words, for whom politics is the art of the possible, could come out of the process with 'a clear conscience'. This was true of most of the participants at Kempton Park, the site of the main negotiations meetings. Very few of these people would admit today that they brought about a series of unintended consequences, but they would, of course, not be 'politicians' if they did so.

At another level, however, because the only matter which had to be settled in order to bring about a 'successful' negotiations process was whether or not the liberation forces were willing to operate within a 'free-market, multi-party democratic system' – in short, within the prevailing capitalist system – without tampering in any fundamental way with the inherited property relations, the crucial battles had to be fought not between the ANC and the NP or between the ANC and the IFP. It was within the ANC itself that these battles had to be settled and although there are many works in which the democratic political traditions and the political culture of the ANC are extolled and reaffirmed as the victor in these bloodless battles, there can be little doubt that for endogenous as well as exogenous reasons, the radical forces suffered an almost irreversible defeat. The works of McKinley,[40] Marais,[41] and Bond,[42] among others, are eloquent references for the study of this transition within the transition. Marais, writing about the side-lining of the Reconstruction and Development Programme, with which the immediate post-apartheid government was supposed to be the transformation of South Africa, makes the salient point:

> The ANC has been *assimilated* into a web of institutional relations, systems and practices tailored to service the interests of (in the first instance) white privilege and (in the final instance) the capitalist class. Compared with its predecessor, the relative autonomy of the democratic state has perhaps *diminished*, furthering [sic] curtailing the ANC's ability to redistribute opportunity, infrastructural resources, access to productive activity and institutional power in favour of the popular classes.[43]

This is the crucial proposition, the one that tells us clearly what the defining outcome of the negotiations was. Because of the world-historical conjuncture within which the South African, like so many other, negotiations took place, it is clear that no other outcome was possible. Hence, the only issue to be settled is whether those people, mainly on the left of the political spectrum, who claim otherwise, are *disingenuously* covering their own backs and attempting to salve their own consciences for having been party to the 'revolutionary transformation' of their own political and personal beliefs.

Africa and the New World Order[1]

THE CONCEPT OF AFRICA

'Africa' is not simply a geographical expression. In this year when some people are celebrating the quincentenary of that fateful voyage by means of which Christopher Columbus inaugurated what the British historian, Lord Acton, euphemistically called 'the unification of the world', it is pertinent to remind ourselves that Africa is above all one of the many by-products of colonial-imperialist conquest and of world capitalist exploitation on the grand scale. To be precise: Africa is in the first instance the result of the resistance of the peoples of the continent to the inhuman process of 'the expansion of Europe'. It is particularly because of the Atlantic Slave Trade, which another British historian, Reginald Coupland, correctly labelled 'the greatest crime in history', and because of the fact that the peoples of Africa and of the African diaspora have been the main victims of racism in the world that a coherent sense of being African evolved. Today, with the generosity of spirit that is often the child of extreme suffering, the most far-seeing amongst us have widened the concept of African to embrace all those, regardless of their geographical provenance, who have a genuine commitment to the continent of Africa and who identify completely with the sufferings and the strivings of the people of the continent. Like Okelo in the recent film by Mira Nair, Mississippi Masala, we continue to maintain that Africa belongs to the Africans but unlike him, we do not qualify that claim by adding the phrase 'Black Africans'. It is indeed the 'message of this paper that it is out of Africa, by virtue of the depths of its suffering, that a new world order will be born, no matter how improbable that may appear at present'.

THE NEW WORLD ORDER

One of the reasons for this formally prophetic statement is that the much talked about New World Order of President George Bush, not unlike Columbus's 'New World', is not so new at all. It is no more than the old world order in a new jacket. It amounts to no more than the restructuring of the international division of labour to accord better with the economic and political interests of the three most powerful trading blocs in the world today. Of course, we have to add that the material basis for a new world order has been created through the new (micro-electronic and biochemical) technologies that have revolutionised production, distribution and communication processes in the post-war world.

After the ignominious collapse of the bureaucratic-centralist, so-called socialist states of Eastern Europe and of the Soviet Union itself, the kaleidoscope of the world economic system has stabilised to reveal that three trading blocs, viz., the American trading bloc, the European trading bloc, and the Asian trading bloc,[2] have during the past 30 years or so been re-dividing the world among themselves. For the moment, it appears as though the balance of power between these three is to be policed and maintained by the only remaining superpower, i.e. the United States of America. The recent war in the Persian Gulf gave us some idea of the shape of things to come. In the words of Noam Chomsky: 'The US has a virtual-monopoly of force, it is a tri-polar world economically, but it's a unipolar world militarily'.[3] Much of the common and the separate agendas of these trading blocs is going to be mediated by international agencies such as the United Nations (UNO), the World Bank (WB), and the International Monetary Fund (IMF). Accordingly, these agencies are going to appear to be much more independent of any particular political grouping than was the case in the past. In reality, however, the basic dilemmas of the restructured world economic system have not yet been resolved.

> Like empires that preceded them, the regional trading blocs of the new economic world order may divide into a handful of protectionist superstates. If by the new political world order we mean increased American hegemony disguised as international cooperation, we may come to know the new economic world order as regional hegemony disguised as free trade.[4]

Zbigniew Brzezinski[5] says bluntly that 'as of now', the phrase new world order is 'a slogan in search of substantive meaning'. According to him, the answer to this question will depend on 'the eventual resolution of the four large structural dilemmas'. These 'dilemmas' are (1) How will Europe define itself? (2) How will the Soviet Union be transformed? (3) How will the Pacific region organise itself? and (4) How will the Middle East be pacified?[6]

THE SECOND WAVE OF LIBERATION

At the time of writing, the answers to all four of these questions are still in the balance even though the Soviet Union has formally disappeared from the map of the world. At both the economic and the political levels, these questions continue to confront strategists and politicians as dilemmas. At the ideological level, however, there is widespread agreement among First World intellectuals that

> the philosophical tenor of our time is ... dominated by Western con-
> cepts of democracy and the free market ... [These] represent today's
> prevailing wisdom. The competing notions of Marxism, not to speak
> of its Leninist-Stalinist offshoot, once so intellectually dominant, are
> generally discredited.[7]

In Africa, indeed, the transition to democracy has become such a con-centrated and domino-like process that scholars and activists speak of a 'second wave of liberation'.[8] It is a fact that more than half of all the states on the continent 'have embarked on a fundamental transition from authoritarian governments, military and civilian, to more democratic systems'.[9] Among academics worldwide and Africanists in particular a veritable industry has been created around the complex of themes called 'transition to democracy' or the 'conditions of democracy debate'. This debate is not peculiarly African, indeed it is particularly conducted in the context of the dramatic changes being engineered in Eastern Europe.

Clearly, however, we Africans have to re-examine the basic theories of democracy in the context of our history and of the political-economic relations now existing in our respective countries. Detailed research as well as political moves towards a greater unity at the base should be inau-gurated. A pan-African unity of peoples rather than merely states should become the medium-term objective of those who wish to surf into a dem-ocratic future on this second wave of liberation. Democracy means power to the people. It is our task to concretise this concept at local, regional, and national levels, to find out organically, i.e. in consultation with those who will have to carry out whatever decisions are made at any of these levels, how this concept can be realised in practice. We have to find out which combinations of representative and direct democracy work in such a manner that the urban and the rural poor are empowered. It is neces-sary to stop the marginalisation of the poor, especially of the rural poor, and to resolve what Kühne[10] calls the 'democratisation dilemma of the urban middle classes' in Africa. He describes this dilemma as follows:

> On the one hand, their economic frustrations constitute the hard core of the 'second wave of liberation'. Unpaid salaries and stipends, threats to their survival because of difficulties on the supply side etc., push them in their millions towards resistance and into the streets against the existing regimes. After a short period of euphoria based on the attainment of the first signs of democratisation, precisely that happens which is to be expected in accordance with the literature on democratisation of processes, i.e. the same middle classes take to the streets again, even where the new regime in question has made considerable concessions, because their expectations of improvements in the material conditions of life have either not been fulfilled or only partially fulfilled.[11]

Incidentally, Kühne's 'urban middle classes' embrace, amongst others, teachers, civil servants, unionised workers, professionals, students, artisans, and traders. I am in agreement with his assessment that the manner in which this dilemma is resolved will influence decisively the direction of the present surge towards empowerment of the people.

In the African context, we have to re-examine at the continental level our understanding of pan-African unity. In a thought-provoking recent article on the subject, Horace Campbell raised all the relevant questions. He concluded, among other things, that

> political independence and the unity of states as inscribed in the Organisation of African Unity (OAU) cannot be the basis of African liberation. A federation of Africa based on the cultural diversity of the continent and the harnessing of the knowledge and skills developed over centuries are some of the challenges which face the African people in the next century.[12]

At the national state level, it has become a matter of life and death that we re-analyse honestly and relentlessly the myths that have been spun around the supposed links between the one-party state and so-called 'traditional African democracy'. Scholars like Peter Anyang'Nyong'o[13] have begun to sweep away some of the cobwebs. How basic this undertaking is can be read from the way in which Nyong'o[14] disentangles the problematic within which these fanciful claims used to be made. He shows, for example, that since

modern political parties did not exist in most pre-colonial African societies, it is a mere anachronism to use this concept, including derivatives such
as the one-party state, in order to analyse and understand these societies.

DEVELOPMENT, AID, AND SOVEREIGNTY

Africans, like the peoples of other continents, have the historic opportunity to give shape to the evolving new world order. This is obviously
an eccentric view if we look at the world from the vantage point of the
present centres of economic, political and military power. It is not for
nothing that the major analyses, with a few honourable exceptions, never
mention the African continent. If they do, it is usually as an extension
of Europe, one that is 'mediated' through the major economies of South
Africa and Nigeria. In one of his new world order scenarios, Brand[15]
writes quite unproblematically that

> the African nations, especially if joined together in the African
> Common Market (ACM), could present a problem or a prospect for
> the (European) Community. EC plus ACM equals two continents
> united in a trading bloc. The African nexus exists: Morocco has already
> applied to join the EC.

Similarly, he enumerates the usual devastating list of Africa's problems, to
wit water shortages, health problems, especially AIDS, one-party states,
falling GDP, etc., and concludes that 'the best hope for the (African)
common market would be leadership by Africa's two strongest economies, Nigeria and post-Apartheid South Africa'.[16]

Which brings us to the unavoidable question of the 'Bretton Wood
sisters'. There is general agreement among students on the question that
even though economic growth is not an essential condition for the initiation of the process of democratisation, it is such a condition for its
survival and consolidation. The parlous state of most African economies
is, therefore, an ill omen for the future of what little progress has been
made in the direction of a democratic dispensation on the continent. As
the base of the so-called Third World, the peoples of Africa are the main
victims of the post-war economic order of which the World Bank and the
International Monetary Fund are the twin pillars.[17] At the global level, the
Permanent Peoples' Tribunal (PPT) came to the following conclusion in
September 1988:

There is no doubt that the IMF and the World Bank, as international institutions for regulation and crisis management, have failed and that they are therefore responsible for the dramatic deterioration of the living conditions of peoples in many parts of the world. They serve the interests of the creditors rather than function for the benefit of the peoples of the world, particularly of the Third World.[18]

The assessment is substantiated by statistics that are, in general, incontrovertible. Thus, for example, the bank itself estimated that in the period 1984–1987, there was a net transfer of some $87.9 billion from South to North because of the imperatives of debt servicing. The OECD put this figure at $387 billion for the period 1982–1987.[19]

More than four decades of IMF/World Bank intervention in development programmes in Africa and a decade of Structural Adjustment Programmes (SAPs) have driven the continent over the edge of ruin. According to the Report of the United Nations Programme of Action for African Economic Recovery and Development, by 1990 Africa's debt had almost doubled its 1980 figure. At present, the debt stands at $280 billion and it is rising rapidly. For sub-Saharan Africa, the debt of $160 billion represents 112 per cent of GDP!

Servicing the mounting debt has become the main burden confronting the continent. Each year sub-Saharan African countries pay $12 billion. This is only one third of the interest due and about 30% of export earnings. Debt is costing Africa more than the continent is spending on the welfare of its people, including health education.[20]

This is not the place to examine the many reasons proffered as explanations for the shift that took place in the original developmental and stabilisation functions of the Bretton Wood sisters. More and more, objective scholars have come to agree with the PPT's view that today,

the IMF operates in the interests of private lending institutions. It is doing its best to extract debt service from Third World debtors in order to prevent defaults on private bank debts and their repercussions on the economies of the industrialised capitalist countries.[21]

Because of the ways in which the World Bank/IMF negotiators impose conditions, both economic and extra-economic, before making available new loans to countries in need, the whole question of sovereignty is raised. In the words of *The Economist*:[22]

> When the distinguished visitors from Washington, D.C. speak with one voice, they often become, in effect, a lobby with great clout in domestic politics. The government finds it harder than ever to keep up the appearance of being in control of events.

This brief reference to the economic dimension of the new world order as it affects the African continent has to suffice as an indication of the need to re-examine the post-colonial paradigm built up around concepts, such as 'modernisation', 'development', 'balanced growth', etc., African and non-African liberals see an approach to the solution in refinements of the instrument of 'conditionality' by, for example, linking aid to human rights 'performance' and to progress along the path of multi-party democracy.[23] At the economic level, the United States' Council of Economic Advisors (CEA)[24] recommends an infusion of humanitarian, financial, and technical aid to complement active policy reforms, especially in the first phases in the 'adjustment process' in order to avoid 'catastrophic declines in consumption and maintain support for reforms'. The longer-term agenda is stated unequivocally:

> Financial aid should be viewed as a transitional mechanism. Over the longer term, sustained growth depends on greater integration into the international trading system and increased access to private capital, both of which depend on comprehensive reforms.[25]

As against this recipe which, clearly, foresees a greater role for international agencies, including the Bretton Wood sisters, the radical agendas go in exactly the opposite direction. This includes the relatively moderate view of the Permanent Peoples' Tribunal that the dependency of the Third-World countries 'can only be overcome by a dissociation from the constraints of the monetary world market',[26] a view that explicitly denies the relevance and the possibility of autarchy for more regions but which insists that 'it has to mean a new form of political control of capital flows, nationally as well as internationally'.[27] They recommended a new Bretton Wood type conference in order to 'reshape the existing international institutions'.

At the furthest point on this spectrum stands the view that is associated with the name of Samir Amin and that has become known as the *theory of delinking.* In a nutshell, he maintains that democracy under capitalism is impossible in the periphery of the world system. This is the reason why capitalist expansion has brought about not the socialist revolutions expected by Marx and others to break out in the advanced capitalist countries but, rather, 'anti-capitalist' revolutions

> provoked by the polarisation inherent in worldwide capitalist expansion with socially intolerable consequences for the peoples of the peripheries and semi-peripheries of the system. The strategic aims of those revolutions entail delinking from the logic of worldwide capitalist expansion. The process of achieving these aims entails in turn gradual and continual progress of democratization of society through practical management of power and of the economy.[28]

PAN-AFRICAN UNITY

This important train of thought needs to be explored in detail. In particular, the link between radical democracy and delinking has to be demonstrated in both theory and practice. What has become crystal clear is that the nations of Africa will be unable to solve any of their major problems unless they tackle these on a continent-wide basis. From a totally different point of departure, for example, Martin Bangemann,[29] the Vice-President of the European Communities, concludes that Africa has to rely increasingly on its own strength. Classical development aid can never be more than the proverbial 'drop in the bucket' and private capital will not come in because 'national home markets in Africa are too small to attract investors'. His recommendation, not surprisingly, is strong regional blocs in order to make these areas more attractive to investors.

Whether or not this happens and because of the problem of conditionality, our longer-term goal must needs be a genuine pan-African unity of the peoples of the continent. An important starting point would be for all the African states to agree that the whole continent shall be a nuclear-free zone and that all 'offensive' weapons be destroyed throughout the length and breadth of the continent. Besides the putative economic and security gains that would flow from such a move, its demonstration effect would be massive in the USA and elsewhere. This is a case of turning a weakness into a strength. By outlawing war and using diplomacy and negotiations for the settlement of disputes among African nations or states, we would

be tackling one of the fundamentals of our epoch under the most favour-
able conditions imaginable. Because Africa is an area where, with the
exception of South Africa, no large-scale war industry exists, we would
be tackling a manageable problem in the most practical possible way; we
would promote the unity of African people, who are the victims of sense-
less and avoidable wars, and we would be putting a stop to the insane
waste of valuable foreign exchange on weaponry and munitions.

Once such a social movement for peace among the Africans gets off
the ground, it will become possible, indeed imperative, to tackle other
fundamentals of the continent today. I refer here to the questions of ecological preservation, especially the fight against desertification, health
provision, especially the fight against AIDS and other forms of plague
and, last but not least, we would expose those regimes that are no more
than an African mask behind which malign foreign interests hide their
rule.

It is essential that the search for pan-African unity in the course of this
second wave of liberation be based upon the struggle against those material conditions that hold the people of the continent in bondage. In this
way, the people themselves, the urban and especially the rural poor, will
become involved directly in their own liberation. Unity cannot simply
be forged in the drawing rooms of conference halls or in the corridors
of power more generally. It has to be built from below. And unity of the
people of Africa is the precondition for the liberation of the continent
from the divide-and-rule strategies that have subjugated our people ever
since 1416, when the first dot of African territory was conquered by a
European army.

If this generation succeeds in promoting the realistic programme of
action I have sketched here, a new world order will indeed be initiated
from out of Africa. The apparently unbreakable chain of a world system
of exploitation and oppression that began quite literally with the chains
that enslaved so many millions of our people and forced them out into the
diaspora will be broken at its weakest link.

I have used or referred to the notion of 'dilemma' repeatedly in this
address. In the period we are living in and for the next few years, this
is as it should be. For many of the certainties and the verities of yesterday have been blown away by the stormy events of this last decade of
the twentieth century. We are exploring new ways of solving the riddle
of constructing a just society. In this voyage of discovery, Africa is no
longer the *Maison des Esclaves* of the world, no longer the heart of dark-

ness. Just as our continent was the cradle of humanity and one of the main sources of world civilisation, so it can and will become a source of renewal, a bridge to the rediscovery of the oneness of the human species. The ancient Roman saying can acquire a quite unanticipated meaning: *ex Africa semper aliquid novi.*

Foreword to the isiZulu Translation of the Communist Manifesto[1]

The appearance of the first isiZulu edition of the Communist Manifesto reminds us of the fact that after the Christian Bible, this famous founding document of international socialism is one of the most translated and the most widely printed works in the world. According to Eric Hobsbawm, the diffusion via translation of the Manifesto was a slow process at first. However, after 1868 and even more so, after 1917, translations came thick and fast. The list of translations reads like the history of industrialisation and the accompanying emergence of a working class in one country after another. Significantly, Hobsbawm makes no mention of translation into any African language even though we know that it was in fact translated into Afrikaans in the early 1930s and distributed widely throughout the then predominantly white trade union leadership in the Union of South Africa. This omission may be the result of ignorance, of course. It does show, however, that no translation into any African language 'caught the eye of history', if we define an African language in the context of print languages as one that attained its written form on the continent of Africa. It shows, further, that the political education of the emerging leadership of the working class in colonial and post-colonial Africa took place in the languages of the colonial masters, i.e. in French and English.

Seen in this light, Comrade Ramadiro's translation of the Manifesto into isiZulu is itself a benchmark in the modern history of the continent. It marks one of the defining features of any so-called African Renaissance, i.e. the use of the languages of the peoples of Africa in all the important domains of life, specifically also as print languages. It is a commitment on the part of WOSA to workers' democracy since we insist that 'democracy' is only possible if people are able to use the languages they know best in order to conduct all the transactions of their daily lives. For us, the regeneration of Africa is not some rhetorical device used to blindfold the masses. We are committed to the position that it is only through the Socialist Renaissance that the peoples of the African continent will rise up out of the trench of despair in which imperialism and neo-colonialism have kept them stagnating and decomposing. In issuing this translation of the Manifesto at this juncture, therefore, we are saying very clearly to the working people of the continent of Africa and of the rest of the world that far from accepting the triumph of the capitalist classes, we are going back to the sources in order to revive the belief in and the passion for the radical transformation of this brave new capitalist world in which the poor are pushed down the evolutionary scale back into the animal kingdom. We are reminding the working people and their leadership that the alternative to a post-capitalist, socialist, world is the global barbarism that we are beginning to see the shape of in almost every country on the planet.

For us, in spite of its shortcomings, the Manifesto of the Communist Party, as it was named by its authors, remains a truly visionary document, one which has total relevance to the situation in which we find ourselves today. The world that Marx and Engels sketched in 1848 has become an eerie reality a little more than 150 years later. The uncanny sharpness of the vision which they derived from the basic tenets of the historical materialism they had together arrived at during five years of collaborative study, debate and episodic brushes with the outmoded feudal authorities of their native Germany, continues to baffle even the most critical of readers of this axial document. It's essential theme, which is simply that the epoch of capitalist production, like all other epochs of production, is historical, renders it most relevant to the current period of the crisis of credibility of socialism in the aftermath of the collapse of the Soviet bloc.

Re-reading the Manifesto has become an essential task of Marxist regeneration. The revolutionary optimism that informs the pamphlet, stripped of some of its unrealistic expectations of immediate permanent revolution (in Europe), is exactly what socialist activists and revolutionaries need to recover in today's arid environment where an increasing number of yesterday's 'revolutionary socialists' hum the same dismal tune as the Thatchers, the Blairs, the Reagans, and the Bush's, i.e. 'there is no alternative' (to the capitalist system). Instead, the Manifesto shows, there is always an alternative and another world will come about through the political action of the oppressed and exploited classes.

It follows that in the present conjuncture, the crucial flaw from the point of view of initiating the socialist alternative is the absence of revolutionary leadership. It is precisely for this reason that the literary accomplishment of the translation of the Manifesto into one of the major languages of Africa is so important. For, it is through the committed study of core documents of Marxism and of the international socialist movement generally as part and parcel of the class struggles that are once again shaking the world that a new leadership will arise to take the struggle forward from where a previous generation had been forced to reconsider their positions. And there is no better guarantee that such leadership will emerge from the ranks of the working people and from other strata of the oppressed than having this treasury of theoretical and strategic wisdom accessible in all the languages of the people.

Marx and Engels were certainly wrong in predicting the imminent end of the capitalist world system. They were followed in this erroneous prediction by one generation of revolutionary socialists after another for the next 150 years. Today, it is very obvious that the eradication of the capitalist system will require the convergence of many different local, national, and regional struggles, all of which are impelled by quite different, often even by contradictory, motives and visions. The working class alone does not in the real world of the twenty-first century constitute the gravediggers of the system that exploits them, an insight that the authors of the Manifesto would undoubtedly uphold as a matter of political strategy.

It is also obvious today that the socialist revolution or the radical transformation of our societies is a process and not some cataclysmic one-off event. Feminist and other women's, trade unionists', students', peasants', and even religion-based struggles against the ravages of neoliberal globalisation and against the fundamental injustices of the capitalist system are all necessary aspects of that process. This is why there is no contradiction at all in us reviving the optimistic, permanent revolutionary vision of Marx and Engels which, in the prevailing conditions at the dawn of a new era of world history is in tune with the insight of another great Marxist scholar who advises that we cultivate pessimism of the intellect but optimism of the will.

Let this little book herald the beginning of a new period of revolutionary class struggle in South and southern Africa. Let the workers, men and women, employed and unemployed, young and old, as well as all the other layers of the oppressed and exploited millions study and struggle. Let us link up our struggles with those of people in all the corners of the African continent and let us join forces with the exploited and oppressed billions throughout the rest of the world in the full knowledge that another world is possible and that the price of failure is barbarism and the destruction of all life on earth. Let us repeat the slogan of the international workers' movement:

WE HAVE NOTHING TO LOSE BUT OUR CHAINS,
WE HAVE A WORLD TO GAIN!

Foreword to *Racism Explained to my Daughter*[1]

The World Conference Against Racism took place in Durban, South Africa, in August and September 2001. Tens of thousands of people came together from almost every country in the world to consider how and why, at the beginning of the twenty-first century, most people in the world are still suffering under racial and other forms of discrimination. Above all, they wanted to find out what we should do in order to put an end to the inhuman practices and beliefs which we associate with ideas of 'race' and racism. Speaking at the conference, former President Nelson Mandela said,

> We hope that you will go home with a sense that you are part of a much larger family of humankind whose members need each other and must work to help and protect each other. We hope that you will find concrete ways to help combat racism, sexism, discrimination and other conditions and practices that rob human beings of their dignity and a decent quality of life.

This book comes at exactly the right moment, therefore. It's authors, Tahar Ben Jelloun and, his daughter, Mérième, discuss – in the most natural possible manner, as parents and their children sometimes do – the question which the conference examined:

- What is racism?
- How do we recognise it in practice?
- Why do racist beliefs and practices exist?
- What can we do to fight against racism?

Talking about these difficult questions reminds us of the simple but important fact that children are naturally curious: they are full of questions because they are trying to come to grips with a world that is often confusing and very threatening. Because they are less inhibited than their parents, they ask any question, even questions that are considered to be taboo by their elders. This little book shows how very important it is that we should not silence our children. We should allow them to speak out and to ask all the questions they want. We have to find the most appropriate and effective forms of conversation, analysis and discussion to help them find some of the answers. Today, after so many centuries of human endeavour, the universal ideal of a dignified existence for all people living as citizens in societies based on freedom, equality, and solidarity is called into question by many frightening threats: nuclear arms, the destruction of the biosphere, famine, AIDS, the abuse of children and women, genocide and racist behaviour generally, among many other horrors. Indeed, as more and more people are beginning to understand, these developments and conditions cast doubt on the very possibility of sustaining life on planet earth.

The conversations between Ben Jelloun and his daughter show us one of the places where we have to start in our struggles to combat racism. We have to create the conditions in our homes and in our schools, as well as in other important institutions of our different societies, in which children will be able to learn the truth about racism, conditions in which they will learn how to prevent it, and how to eradicate it wherever it happens. There are other important things we have to do, of course. We have to ensure that people are legally protected against racist practices, that all people have equal political voices, even if they see themselves as a minority in a given society and that economic goods and social benefits are equitably available to all. In the absence of such a framework, racism will thrive no matter how much we speak out against it. On the other hand, racist behaviour is a matter of attitudes and perceptions, and human beings are not simply mindless machines. Our behaviour towards each other is powerfully influenced by our understanding of what causes the problems in our society. Consequently, it is vital that conversations such as those contained in this book take place everywhere in the world and in every language that is spoken on earth.

We have a long way to go before we will see that other world in which racism will be a thing of the past. In South Africa, the country that became a byword among the nations for racist beliefs and practices under the label of apartheid, we have a special reason for paying careful attention to the struggle against racist beliefs and practices. The terrible legacy of 500 years of colonial and racial oppression did not disappear on 27 April 1994, the day when the first democratic elections took place in our country. As I write these words, there are news reports about South African workers in a community in one of the northern provinces setting alight the humble shacks of migrant workers from Zimbabwe, a neighbouring country which, during the struggle against apartheid, did everything possible to help the oppressed people here to free themselves. This news item demonstrates a point that Ben Jelloun stresses, namely, that anyone can be racist, even those who have themselves been victims of racist abuse.

Not only do we still have to deal with our own feelings of inferiority or superiority and the feelings of insecurity and worthlessness that go with that, which grew out of the apartheid system of legalised racism, but we are now faced with the racism of the poor, who, like dogs fighting over a bone, kill one another because they believe that people who are suffering the same poverty as they themselves, want to 'take the bread out of our mouths'. This is a dark legacy indeed.

This little book is a first step on that very long journey on which we have embarked to create conditions in which racism, hatred of foreigners, sexism, the abuse of women and children, caste beliefs and practices and all other forms of discrimination will be unable to take root and to thrive. It was written in France and some of the questions that Ben Jelloun's daughter asks deal directly with issues that relate to racism in France and other European countries and to former French colonies in Africa and Asia. It is, however, important that our children understand that racism is universal and that we can learn from the experience of other people in other countries to deal with similar problems in the country where we live.

Our thanks go to all the publishers and the translators that have made this book possible. Above all, we thank Tahar Ben Jelloun's young daughter for having asked the question: 'Daddy, what is racism?' and Tahar Ben Jelloun himself for considering the question worthy of a response.

Foreword to *Taking South African Education out of the Ghetto*[1]

During the next three or four years, South Africa will undergo gradual but none the less visible socio-economic and socio-political change. The present government, because of the compromise on which it is based will be able to undertake few if any fundamental or radical changes in any sphere of life. At best, it will be able to initiate patterns and rhythms that will eventually give rise to quite a different quality of life in South Africa. This is a common cause.

On the other hand, this transitional period affords all would-be reformers, whether radical or moderate, the opportunity and the space to test in practice whether their conceptions are feasible and what the financial and social implications of these are. In this sense, the next period may turn out to be the most creative in the twentieth-century history of our country. The research on which this publication is based should be viewed in this light. Its point of departure is the commitment of the new regime to a non-racial, non-sexist, democratic system of education in a democratic South Africa. In the Project for the Study of Alternative Education in South Africa (PRAESA), one of the questions we posed to ourselves was what should be done in order to realise the goal of a non-racial system of education in the peculiar historical conditions of this country. While there are obviously many answers to this question, we realised that in the longer term, certain structural elements of the system would have to be changed radically if all the different 'superstructural' changes were not to be set at nought. In other words, mere changes in syllabus content and in the philosophy of education would not be sufficient.

One of the most sensitive areas was, clearly, that of where schools are located. The colonial-apartheid heritage of ghettos (physical and 'mental') would have to be addressed if planned changes were not to be rendered nugatory or cosmetic. In this connection, the commitment of the new regime to nation-building is an important spur to the kind of reasoning on which this research was/is based. It was this line of inquiry that led us to consider what to do with all future schools and other educational institutions in terms of their physical location. We were convinced that the

United States 'solution' of bussing would lead to disaster in the context of South Africa and that far from breaking down ethnic consciousness and ethnic prejudice, it could lead to the strengthening thereof, something which in our context could have devastating consequences. The tentative answer we advanced was the concept of 'educational zoning' in terms of which learners would all come out of their respective ghettos in order to do their learning just as workers have to do in order to do their work in the economy.

It was clear to us from the beginning that there would be very high transport costs attached to the implementation of this concept but we assumed that compensatory economies of scale would derive from the clustering of the schools in the educational zones. Once we were led into the consideration of the economics of this conception, it became clear that this aspect of the project would be the most attractive to the politicians, who normally have to demonstrate that their ideas do not entail higher taxes. The socio-cultural integration effects that would derive from this approach, despite their importance at the level of principle, seemed more and more like ideological perfume sprayed on the sweaty body of economic necessity.

Since the urban-planning implications of our thinking were going to be pivotal to the acceptability or otherwise of our proposals, it was decided to commission research by qualified urban planners and we were exceptionally fortunate to be able to recruit for this purpose the two authors of this study. Their thoroughness and diligence are manifest in the document published here. Through their research, the complexity as well as the great potential of this idea became clear to us and as a result of the many discussions we conducted subsequently with urban planners and educationists committed to the dismantling of the apartheid city, it became obvious that the idea had come at the right time. The political authorities, including two of the ministers in the present cabinet, with whom we discussed the proposal were extremely supportive of it and a series of presentations and workshops is due to be held in the next few months in order to take the process a few steps further along the path of becoming a recognised criterion for the planning of the urban environment in a new South Africa.

It is also significant that different individuals and groups of educationists with very different points of departure and moving along independent paths are arriving at similar suggestions to that proposed here. At a recent primary school teachers' conference I addressed in George, a group of teachers from the Riversdale area explained that because of the well-known problems of farm schools and because of the space that had been opened up in the new dispensation, they had proposed that an empty formerly white school in the town be used as a central gathering place for children from the surrounding farms. Since transport did not appear to be a problem, it meant that the children would be able to be home every day, thus obviating the more expensive option of boarding schools. On similar lines, the Marico-Lehurutshe case study argues that:

> In the past, decisions taken with regard to placing of schools have not led to the efficient use of resources because of apartheid ideologies that severely influenced the physical location and access of children to schools.[2]

From the point of view of the building of the new nation in South Africa, it seems particularly important to us that the concept involves potentially the redefinition of 'community' in South Africa. We assume that parents of school children as well as other learners will tend to move closer to the places of learning and that the present ghettos will over a longer or shorter period tend to disappear 'naturally' or at the very least change their complexion in important ways. A further innovative effect of the school cluster concept is the contribution it makes to the redefinition of the 'school' itself. It leads to the concrete understanding that all kinds of public buildings can be and often are even now 'learning spaces' so that the education process becomes a much more embracing one in which parents, students, business, teachers and other professionals all play their dynamic parts.

At the end of the day, of course, it is the economic side of the proposal that influences the decisions of the power people most decisively. The fact that the school cluster concept makes possible in principle the maximum sharing of resources among all the educational institutions in a particular locality is undoubtedly its immediately attractive feature. In this regard, the preliminary character of the research will be obvious to the informed reader. Detailed empirical research sensitive to the local needs, interests and problems will have to be undertaken in specific cases in order to determine the cost-effectiveness of any particular cluster project. It is therefore important that the basic principles, advantages and disadvantages of the school cluster concept be thoroughly considered and debated

against the background of the historical period in which we find ourselves today. This is the reason why this publication has been undertaken.

For the interest of those who are not aware of all the dynamics involved
in this research, it is appropriate to mention that the other side of taking
education out of the ghetto is taking the ghetto out of education. At
PRAESA, the staff have concentrated on what is undoubtedly the most
important aspect of this enterprise, *viz.*, the realisation of multilingual
educational programmes. A volume devoted to the exploration of the
available options in South African schools is due to be published soon.

PART IV

Post-1994 Essays, Talks, and Op-Eds

Introduction to Part IV

The first article is a lecture in commemoration of the life of Strini Moodley, a founding member of the Black Consciousness Movement and a comrade of Steve Biko. Moodley had spent six years imprisoned on Robben Island. In this article, Alexander begins by venturing into a brief but thoughtful exploration about the provenance and development of the concepts of 'revolution', 'social revolution', 'political revolution', and 'cultural revolution' to distinguish especially the difference between 'political revolutions' (or 'regime change' as he sees it) and the wider and more compelling approaches to social change implied in social and cultural revolutions largely to 'put behind us the barbaric and vulgar universe in which we are forced to try to survive with dignity today'. This explanation was important for understanding the variety of conceptions of 'transformation' that were adopted by the differing orientations in the liberation movement and how that has played out in the trajectory of the post-apartheid state under the dominant leadership of the ANC, leading to its abandonment of the 'pro-poor' stance set out in its Freedom Charter of 1955.

He sets out to show how many of the principles in the Charter have been whittled down or recast by successive governments of the ANC and the 'somersaults' this necessitated amongst its most prominent leaders including Mandela. He argues that the purpose of this was, whatever the rhetoric about it, to stabilise the conditions for continued capitalist accumulation under the leadership of the ANC and its political allies, especially the South African Communist Party. His analysis provides an insight into the causal factors that led inevitably to the political compromise of 1994, the interests served by it, the evolution of a Black political elite, and the cynicism against not only the very ideas which inspired the Freedom Charter but also the socialist alternatives to the ANC's approach. He describes the enormity of the challenges faced by the post-apartheid government because of its reneging on the very ideas it had itself espoused, making it impossible for its leaders to reconcile their contradictory positions as they ascended to positions of political power. He discusses how the concept of a 'national democratic revolution' has been used as a justification of this political turn. But, as Alexander argues, these developments are not the end of the matter given the developing discord and opposition around them by the socio-political necessity to 'find the ideological and organisational means to build the counter-society that insulates the oppressed and exploited from the undermining and disempowering values and practices of bourgeois society'.

In *South Africa Today – The Moral Responsibility of Intellectuals*, Alexander, speaking on the tenth anniversary of the South African Foundation for Human Rights, explains the importance of human rights, especially for the lives of the urban and rural poor and the role of intellectuals in the struggle for entrenching such rights. This issue is particularly important to him in the context of what he regards as the betrayal perpetrated by an elite (including the intelligentsia) against the working class, despite the provisions of the South African Constitution, regarded by so many as an outstanding expression of the protection of human rights. He argues that there are real possibilities for the creation of a radical counter-culture in which the intelligentsia have a significant role to play. Such a counter-culture would require a thoughtful examination of the abiding contradiction that faced South African society including questions about the role of the ANC and of the liberation movement more generally, together with an examination of the role of capital and the alternatives to the neoliberal global paradigm. This is required to overcome the compromises made by the state and the violent socio-psychological effects of the betrayal of working-class and rural communities. Alexander stresses the importance of building a 'new historical community' towards the achievement of social cohesion and national unity built on appropriate concepts and practices for their achievement.

In the third brief article, Alexander makes the case for 'a humanism of the twenty-first century', speaking at the Sipho Maseko Memorial lecture. He discusses the erosion of the values of solidarity, freedom, democracy and the like and the ascendancy of a 'narcissistic, dog-eat-dog virus in the current era of the hegemony of neo-liberal capitalism'. Referring to the writings of Cabral, Biko, and others he calls for a return to a commitment to the values of a 'non-racial democratic republic' associated with the ideas of the Black Consciousness Movement and other less acknowledged parts of the liberation movement. Yet he reminds us of the necessity to transcend the limitations of concepts of psychological liberation which must be understood together with 'a combination of ideas, organisation and political-economic developments' as necessary to a fundamental reconstituting of society. This must be done while developing a 'culture of positive values', building communities of solidarity, voluntarism and struggle in support of the many democratic initiatives inspired by the ideas and practices of *ubuntu* that already exist to oppose the developing vulgarities that have emerged in post-apartheid society.

'The Elephant in the Room' was written against the background of the dystopic conditions that have emerged in South Africa in the post-apartheid-era, characterised by 'blatant examples of greed and corruption involving public figures ... the smug dishonesty, indiscipline and slothfulness' and of the violence perpetrated on working-class communities by those charged with public office. These characteristics are exacerbated not only by the false promises of equality and freedom but by the reality of the growing chasm between the new elite and the majority of the people fostered by a deliberate set of policies and their effects. He points to the consequent social and cultural differences and alienation that has emerged between the elite and the people as responsible for the emergence of an unbridgeable rift within society making the promise of post-apartheid reconciliation and nationhood inconceivable. And he warns those in power against the inevitable consequences of these developments. The essay proffers alternatives best summarised as follows: 'The world is changing rapidly, and we should not get stuck in the time warp of real capitalism as though there is no alternative. Another world is possible, indeed probable. The barbarism of real capitalism as we know it on the continent of Africa is not the only way'.

Alexander must rank amongst the most committed and knowledgeable intellectuals active in the debates about the socio-cultural, political, and economic meaning of language and its uses in society – especially in societies wracked by conflict over the very issue of language as the 1976 Uprising had shown. His approach reflected his radical views about the relationship between language, nationhood, and culture. In examining this issue, he raises a number of foundational questions about what has been taken for granted, such as whether it is true that a language group is synonymous with the concept of nation or a cultural group and whether constituting a nation requires all its inhabitants to speak 'one and the same language'. These issues are important especially in the light of the inability of the leadership elites of post-colonial states to develop policies in support of their struggles for independence. This inability in part has led to these countries continued political and socio-economic dependence and the failure to achieve national unification.

Alexander's approach expresses his view of building a nation and a dynamic evolving culture in the process of doing so, by facilitating communications between its language groups. He examines specific proposals beginning with a discussion of a lingua franca and a discussion of the implications of an approach to policy planning to counteract the effects of the Verwoerdian apartheid language policy.

'South Africa:
An Unfinished Revolution?'[1]

1. In her historical novel, *A Place of Greater Safety*, which is played out against the backdrop of the Great French Revolution through an illuminating character analysis and synthesis of three of that revolution's most prominent personalities, *viz.*, Maximilien Robespierre, Georges-Jacques Danton, and Camile Desmoulins, Hilary Mantel imagines the following conversation between Lucile Desmoulins and Danton:

> So has the revolution a philosophy, Lucile wanted to know, has it a future? She dared not ask Robespierre, or he would lecture her for the afternoon on the General Will: or Camile, for fear of a thoughtful and coherent two hours on the development of the Roman republic.
> So she asked Danton.
> 'Oh, I think it has a philosophy', he said seriously. 'Grab what you can, and get out while the going's good'.

This sentiment, I make bold to say, puts in the bluntest possible way the dominant sense of disillusionment and disbelief that most middle-class South Africans have when they feel compelled to 'whine' and complain about where we appear to have landed in post-apartheid South Africa. All the heady hopes which even those who were not in or of the Congress Alliance had in 1994–1995 seem to have turned into ash. There are few thinking South Africans today who would be prepared to say that they are happy with how things have turned out.

Because the title of my talk is bound to raise all kinds of expectations about its content, it is essential that I state clearly at the outset that I shall not wander off again into the well-trodden paths that are supposed to bring the excited novice to an understanding of the relationship between the 'bourgeois-democratic' and the 'socialist' revolutions or, even more superiorly to the realisation that 'the revolution' is permanent and that the first necessarily 'grows over' into the second under the conditions that obtain in semi-industrialised or newly industrialising countries. These debates are as relevant today as they were at the beginning of the last century. I do not for one second wish to deny the importance of getting conceptual and strategic clarity in this domain. For, without such clarity, we do no more than tap about in the dark in the hope of finding by chance a route out of the suffocating maze of the world capitalist system. I shall, however, have occasion to refer to this subject briefly when I discuss the illusion of the 'National Democratic Revolution'.

In the Marxist paradigm, the word 'revolution' has very precise meanings. Most often, it is used to refer to a 'social revolution', i.e. the displacement of the rule of one class by that of another, usually by violent means, i.e. in the course of a civil war or an armed struggle.[2] Thus, for example, the Great French Revolution formally put an end to the rule of the feudal nobility and the clergy in France and, later, in the rest of Western Europe, and the Great October Revolution ended the rule of the Tsarist aristocracy and of the incipient Russian bourgeoisie. It ought to be clear to everyone here tonight that, in South Africa, we have not, in this very precise sense, experienced a social revolution. If anything, the post-apartheid state is more capitalist than its apartheid parent. To deny the continuity between the apartheid capitalist state and the post-apartheid capitalist state, as some people actually do, is a futile and quixotic exercise.

A 'political revolution', in this context, refers to what we would nowadays term 'regime change'. That is to say, certain fundamental changes in the form of rule and of the institutions of the state machine are brought about without, however, a concomitant change in the fundamental power relations at the level of the economy and of the management of the repressive apparatuses of the state. In my view, what we have experienced in South Africa during the past two decades is precisely such a political revolution. For reasons of focus, I shall refer only briefly to the third social dimension, i.e. the 'cultural revolution', important though it is to grasp the integral but intricate relationship between these three aspects of any revolution.

Why and how the regime change came about is not the focus of my address this evening either. There have been many scholarly analyses, biographies of significant actors as well as insightful journalistic articles and documentaries on the transition from apartheid to post-apartheid South Africa. Read together, these provide us with a range of perspectives, which help us to make sense of the often bewildering events of the period. Instead, I want to talk about the fact that most South Africans, certainly most oppressed and exploited South Africans, feel that they have been, if not betrayed, then certainly misled. And, because I do not believe that political action is a monopoly of so-called politicians, I want to talk about what we can do in order to get out of the state of shock into which we have been driven. I want to talk about what we can do to find again that vision of a different South Africa that inspired all of us in one way or another regardless of what political tendency we belonged to at the time. For, I believe that if, through discussion and practical action, we can again visualise that other South Africa, we will very soon put behind us the barbaric and vulgar universe in which we are forced to try to survive with dignity today.

Let me also make it clear that in spite of the implication in its title, I have no idea what 'the finished revolution' would have looked like or what it will look like. Revolutions, I think, are never completed. Radical social transformation, even when it is imperceptible in the here and now, is a continuous and complex process. But, even though this is an essential part of the meaning of revolution, this objective process has to be articulated in concrete programmes and strategies for any kind of revolution to eventuate. The success or failure, the 'completeness' or otherwise of the revolution we speak of in South Africa can only be measured against the extent to which, roughly, the set of ideas and programmatic demands that have guided all sections of the National Liberation Movement since the axial period, 1928–1945 approximately, and which were refined and differentiated according to the ideological predispositions and class position of the different tendencies within the broad movement,[3] were realised in the course of the 80 years that have elapsed since then. Without reducing the complexity of contemporary South African history to some simplistic formula, I believe one can say without any distortion that the discourses of the National Liberation Movement were characterised by the intersection of nationalist, liberal-democratic, and broadly socialist paradigms and that the particularity of one or other political tendency was determined by the ways in which its exponents blended or interpreted these three discursive strategies, each of which, of course, derived from and reinforced specific class interests, whether or not the social actors involved were conscious of these.

2. Since the main burden of my talk concerns the developments after 1994, it seems to me most realistic and, in an important sense, also fair, to take as the point of departure for my analysis the general demands of the Freedom Charter, which guided the political strategy and tactics of the Congress Movement since 1955. Given the decision to negotiate a deal

with the apartheid regime rather than getting entangled in a 100-year war, such as that raging in Palestine,[4] the leadership of the Congress Alliance had to make definite decisions about which of the demands of the Charter could be put on the back burner, as it were, in order to make a deal acceptable to the economic and political elites of the old regime. Today, it is obvious to all who wish to look, that the fundamental concession was made with the agreement not to touch the existing property relations except for the virtually unimplementable provisions about land restitution and the clauses referring to affirmative action. To put it differently, these agreements deliberately restricted the horizon of the 'revolution' to the conditions that prevail in any bourgeois democracy. This means that the middle-class leadership of the Congress Movement were albeit 'temporarily' in effect abandoning their pro-poor and pro-proletarian comrades and the mass of its working-class members and supporters. This is where the theory of the 'National Democratic Revolution' was called upon to play a useful mediating role. At the crucial moment, i.e. when the actual concessions were being made, the NDR found its programmatic expression in the now-forgotten 'Reconstruction and Development Programme' (RDP). The simple, clear language of former President Mandela's version of it is how most of the oppressed and exploited masses understood the promises made by the leadership in the early 1990s:

> The ANC drafted a 150-page document known as the Reconstruction and Development Programme, which outlined our plan to create jobs through public works; to build a million new houses with electricity and flush toilets; to extend primary health care and provide ten years of free education to all South Africans; to redistribute land through a land claims court; and to end the value-added tax on basic foodstuffs. We were also committed to extensive affirmative action measures in both the private and public sectors. This document was translated into a simpler manifesto called 'A Better Life for All', which in turn became the ANC's campaign slogan.[5]

Mandela goes on to emphasise that he regularly reminded his audiences that 'freedom' would not translate into some kind of Cinderella-like overnight change into prosperity. In essence, he was truthfully warning his people that now the class struggle would become brutal and unrelenting.

Unlike some of his left-wing comrades, he did not try to sell this straight-forward fact as a so-called 'National Democratic Revolution'.

But, before I expand on this matter, let me say a few words about indi-vidual psychology and shifts of social or class positions. I should like to phrase this as simply and authentically as possible, since it is at this level that resentment and hostility are engendered when one criticises a move-ment, such as the Congress Movement, that has become so powerful and hegemonic in South Africa. I do not doubt for one minute that most, if not all, members of that movement sincerely believed in the ringing trumpet tones of the Freedom Charter: The people shall govern; there shall be houses, security, and comfort, and so forth. It is probable even that many, but certainly not the majority, of the leaders considered that the devia-tions from the trajectory which the Freedom Charter seemed to suggest, i.e. away from the race-based capitalism of more than 100 years towards some kind of African socialist or at least social-democratic future were no more than tactical adjustments necessitated by the realities of the political terrain at the end of the twentieth century after the collapse of the Soviet Union. It is impossible to guess at how each of the prominent individu-als actually came to terms with the psychological dissonance caused by the need, as they saw it, to carry out one or more ideological somersaults. Not all of them were as public and as forthright as Mandela himself, espe-cially in his famous U-turn with respect to nationalisation as the policy of the ANC. The biographies of many of the actors undoubtedly provide some insight into this matter. All I wish to stress here is that any blanket statement about 'sell-out' and 'betrayal' could only be made at the most general and abstract level against the background of the avowed previ-ous ideological or programmatic positions of the individuals or groups of people concerned.[6]

I want to say as clearly as possible that apart from incorrigible revo-lutionary socialists, such as myself and many others who were routinely maligned as 'ultra-leftists' or even more anachronistically, as 'Trotskyites', the bourgeoisie and a few of the leaders of the Congress Alliance were clear that the 1993–1994 agreements were in essence about stabilising the capitalist state and system in South Africa and creating the conditions for its expansion as a profitable venture. Examples of this understand-ing are today easily accessible even though they are, for obvious reasons, condemned as prejudiced, false, malignant, and even 'unpatriotic' by those who are now the powers that be. A few of the more significant statements will suffice to make the point. As early as 24 April 1991, almost 20 years ago, John Carlin, the South Africa correspondent of The Independent wrote:

> Mr. Mandela and the other 'moderates' in the ANC leadership ... believed that the government and the ANC would be equal partners in the voyage to the 'New South Africa', that apartheid would go and they, as the natural majority party, would glide into power ... In one sense [that] trust was not misplaced. Mr. de Klerk will remove apart- heid from the statute books ... But this was never the issue; he knew from the day he came to power that this was what had to be done. The real issue was to retain power, to perpetuate white privilege and the economic status quo after apartheid had gone.[7]

Of course, De Klerk also miscalculated on the dynamics of the negoti- ations but the essential point remains true. Today, thanks particularly to Professor Terreblanche's summary of the hidden negotiations about the economic aspects of the negotiated settlement, in his *A History of Inequality in South Africa 1652–2002*, we know that there was no inno- cence on the side of the leadership of the ANC and of prominent leaders of COSATU and the SACP, in spite of disagreements on policy, which fact became evident most dramatically with the eventual imposition of the macroeconomic policy [known as the Growth, Employment and Redistribution] GEAR. Chapters 3 and 4 of Terreblanche's book ought to be compulsory reading for any remaining 'doubting Thomases' in the former liberation movement. We cannot here thread our way through the intricacies of the debates and the manoeuvres that led to the shifts in the approach of the ANC leadership. The following statement gives a crystal clear picture of what actually happened.

At stake was not only the economic policy of a democratically elected government but also the nature of South Africa's future economic system. Given that South Africa was the most developed country in Africa, the stakes were extremely high, and the negotiations were strategically hugely important for the corporate sector. For almost 20 years all the joint attempts of the corporate sector and the NP [National Party] government to find a new accumulation strategy had been unsuccessful. After almost 20 years of prolonged stagflation, the latter was desperate to convince the core leaders of the democratic movement what the economic ideology and economic system in a democratic South Africa should be.

The strategy on which the corporate sector and the ANC agreed during the informal negotiations in 1993 can be described as the fourth phase of the AAC-led [Anglo-American Corporation] search for a new accumulation strategy ... The main characteristic of every phase of the AAC-led search for a new accumulation strategy was that the supreme goal of economic policy should be to attain a high economic growth rate, and that all other objectives should be subordinated to this. By convincing ANC leaders to accept the AAC's approach, the corporate sector in effect persuaded – or forced – the ANC to move away from its traditional priority, namely to uplift the impoverished Black majority socially and economically.[8]

Although it is tempting to dwell on the details of this shift, I think the essentials are clear enough. There ought to be no doubt in anyone's mind after a close reading of this text that, and why, the bourgeoisie, the self-same capitalist class of yesterday, is in command of all the strategic positions, no matter what the 'democratic' posturing of the politicians might be. And, although it would be an oversimplification to maintain that the ANC at the beginning of the twenty-first century has become a party of the capitalist class, it ought to be equally clear that the bloodletting and the cruel battles that are currently tearing the organisation apart are precisely about how soon it will become such a party rather than the supposed broad church it continues to be marketed as by the bureaucratic leadership. The sketch I have given, without any attempt on my part to join all the dots, does, I think, explain to a large extent why we have been catapulted into the ugly world of modern-day capitalist barbarism with its devastating features of high and growing unemployment, increasing social inequality, horrific violent crime, racist and xenophobic dog-eat-dog conflicts, among many other things. This is very far from the almost utopian revolutionary euphoria with which most South Africans, unaware of what had been agreed upon in the devilish details of the negotiation process, had so proudly cast their votes on 27–28 April 1994.

I cannot resist the temptation to cite one of my favourite texts in order to illuminate the dilemma of the governing party. President Zuma and his team are reaping the bitter fruits of the negotiated settlement. They find themselves in the tragic situation described by Friedrich Engels in the memorable paragraph in the *Peasant War in Germany*:

The worst thing that can befall a leader of an extreme party is to be compelled to take over a government in an epoch when the movement is not yet ripe for the domination of the class which he represents, and for the realization of the measures which that domination implies. ... Thus he necessarily finds himself in an unsolvable dilemma. What he can do contradicts all his previous actions, principles, and the immediate interests of his party, and what he ought to do cannot be done. In a word, he is compelled to represent not his party or his class, but the class for whose domination the movement is then ripe. In the interests of the movement he is compelled to advance the interests of an alien class, and to feed his own class with phrases and promises, and with the asseveration [solemn assertion] that the interests of that alien class are its own interests. Whoever is put into this awkward position is irrevocably lost.

3. Enter the National Democratic Revolution, i.e. the smoke and mirrors of the so-called left in the Congress Alliance. Let me say it very clearly: the new South Africa has brought about fundamental changes in the form of rule and in the institutional furniture of the capitalist state. The realm of freedom has been expanded beyond anything that most people imagined in the 1960s, and millions of people have been lifted out of abject pauperism to some level of human dignity. The struggle has not been in vain in any sense of the term. But, the struggle continues. After 1994, and especially after 1996, it is no longer a struggle for national liberation. It is a class struggle 'pure and simple' or, in good South African English: *finish en klaar*. The inverted commas are necessary because one cannot discard overnight the birthmarks that are imprinted on the new body politic by the old order. Social inequality continues to be reproduced objectively largely as racial inequality in spite of the continued growth of the 'Black' middle class. Racial prejudice, inequalities justified on alleged cultural, linguistic, ethnic or nationality differences, all the things that defaced colonial-apartheid South Africa, persist even if in attenuated forms. They will require decades, perhaps centuries, to become completely irrelevant.

The attempt to frame the class struggles in which we are now engaged in terms of the so-called NDR is no more than tilting at windmills. To put it bluntly: for the leadership of this NDR to be an integral part of a bourgeois government while pretending to conduct a revolutionary struggle against the capitalist system is the merest political buffoonery. Workers and other poor people can be seduced to mouth and repeat all the heroic

phrases that are supposed to give expression to the demands and aspirations of this 'revolution' but at some point, they will realise that they
are being sold a dummy. What is at issue here is not the value or the
socio-historical impact of the day-to-day struggles being waged by the
working class and other strata of the urban and the rural poor. That does
not depend on the misleading discourses of the NDR that are supposed
to guide their struggles. The real danger is that the goal, the destination,
of these struggles is being described and presented in terms that necessarily limit the horizons of the class struggle to the bourgeois universe.
Strategically, this can only lead to the consolidation of the social democratisation of the workers' movement in South Africa, a process that began
with the tying of the main trade union federation to the goals and modalities of the Congress Alliance in the mid-1980s. In doing so, a vital part
of the workers' movement was agreeing to the leadership of the liberation
movement by the nationalists, as opposed to the socialists. The SACP had
gone even further by allowing, indeed compelling, its members to become
card-carrying members of the ANC. Things can change, of course, but,
as I see it, the SACP is currently not an independent political formation.

Theoretically, we are once again faced with a concept of the state that
makes any movement beyond capitalism inconceivable. I have neither the
time nor the inclination to enter into this particular debate in any detail
in this address. Suffice it to say that the question can be formulated quite
clearly in terms that Rosa Luxemburg first made famous in her essay on
Reform or Revolution, published in 1900, i.e. 110 years ago. In her own
words:

> [People] who pronounce themselves in favour of the method of leg-
> islative reform in place of and in contradistinction to the conquest
> of political power and social revolution, do not really choose a more
> tranquil, calmer and slower road to the same goal, but a different goal.
> Instead of taking a stand for the establishment of a new society they
> take a stand for surface modification of the old society. If we follow the
> political conceptions of revisionism, we arrive at the same conclusion
> that is reached when we follow the economic theories of revisionism.
> Our program becomes not the realization of socialism, but the reform
> of capitalism; not the suppression of the system of wage labour, but
> the diminution of exploitation, that is, the suppression of the abuses of
> capitalism instead of the suppression of capitalism itself.[9]

Another way of putting this is the proposition that, in Gramscian terms, the class struggle gets stuck, as it were, in a war of position in the belief that these manoeuvres in themselves constitute a transformation of the capitalist state and society into a socialist society and a workers' state.[10] This, as I see it, is the tendency of much that is put forward as the programme of the NDR, quite apart from the fundamental sleight of hand perpetrated by those who are busy stabilising the capitalist system in South Africa while they pontificate at the same time about the 'fundamental transformation' of our society. By way of example, I refer to the resolutions of the 1997 COSATU national conference, all of which remain on the agenda in 2010.

- building a robust anti-capitalism, which means a relentless criticism of capitalism; building working-class hegemony in many areas such as sport, culture, values, the media, and most importantly [sic], in politics; and tirelessly upholding a vision of full equality (and not just constitutional equality), including gender equality;
- rolling back the market – water, education, shelter, healthcare are basic human rights, not commodities. Everyone should have a right to these things, regardless of whether they can afford them. We should not allow the market to dominate in meeting the basic needs of people;
- transforming the state – a powerful public sector is a crucial component of socialism, but should not be big for its own sake. Our vision is that it should be developmental and facilitate participation and consultation; it should be more responsive and accountable, and the higher, bureaucratic echelons should be reduced;
- advancing and experimenting with other, non-capitalist forms of ownership such as cooperatives and 'social capital' (e.g. Workers' pension and provident funds);
- transforming how work is organised and managed – toward worker control and worker self- management. The actual conditions of the workplace should change, so as to empower working people;
- strengthening worker organisation – in addition to trade unions, there are other organisations in which workers are active, and these should be part of a socialist programme.[11]

While few left-wing people will disagree with any of this, except for the give-away phrase about 'transforming the state', it is clear that these objectives are put forward in the mode of Bernsteinian revisionism and that, as a consequence, they can at best lead to what I have already referred to as the consolidation of social democracy in the workers' movement. The entire strategy depends on a notion of the state as being essentially neutral.[12] The final disillusionment will come, of course, when the repressive apparatuses of the state, instead of supporting the exploited classes and other oppressed strata, turn their weapons on the masses to protect the interests of the capitalist class. The response of police personnel to many of the so-called service delivery protests prefigures what I am saying here.

4. On the other hand, this is not an inevitable outcome, as the history of every successful revolution attests and we are probably decades away from any such scenario at this moment. However, not to postulate consistently and as a matter of daily practical political education the need to end the rule of the local and international capitalist class, as eccentric as that may appear to be at present, is to disarm the working class and its allies ideologically before the decisive battles are fought.[13]

So, what should we be doing, those of us who consider ourselves to be on the left and as being committed to bringing about that other world which socialists across the globe and across the centuries have envisaged? I want to address this question briefly at a general, rather than at an operational level, since this is not a forum for the discussion of tactical issues.

In a sentence, I would say that we have to find the ideological and organisational means to build the counter-society that insulates the oppressed and exploited from the undermining and disempowering values and practices of bourgeois society. This goal must once again become an integral part of the class struggle against exploitation and oppression. Today, because of the massive pollution of the popular consciousness by means of (mostly) US consumerist culture, this is a much more difficult task than it was for those who fashioned – in struggle – the mass social-democratic parties and workers' movements of Europe towards the end of the nineteenth century, or of some of the mass parties of the newly industrialising countries, including, incipiently, the Black Consciousness Movement in South Africa during the 1970s and 1980s.

In order to get to the orientation I wish to suggest, I want to put forward a number of propositions that have to be borne in mind.

First, for reasons that I assume need not be spelt out, the collapse of the USSR and of its satellite states in Eastern Europe catapulted the pro-socialism forces in the world into one of their most deep-going and enduring crises. In particular, I think, there can be no doubt that the credibility of the socialist project as the only viable alternative to capitalism as a world system has been called into question. The very fact that the majority of human beings in the second half of the last century equated socialism with what had come into existence in the Soviet Union has once again raised the question of what we mean by the concept. This is not new, of course. At the end of the nineteenth century, similar debates were conducted among, especially, socialists in Europe, notably in the German Social Democratic Party. However, we live in an entirely different world today and the question has, therefore, to be approached with the new technological and ideological environment in mind. I realise, of course, that most of us have ready answers to this question but I believe it is essential that we find a different language in which to articulate these answers. Otherwise, our cliché-ridden formulae will continue to alienate the popular consciousness. We have to use traditional as well as modern media in order to disseminate these answers in diverse and innovative forms among all of humanity. Stories, utopias, novels, plays, songs, rapping, even 'soapies', we need to experiment with all of these forms, and more, in order to get our message across more effectively.

Second, the caving in of layer after layer of former so-called socialists to the pressures and enticements of neoliberal bourgeois norms and aspirations, which has been one of the most melodramatic political developments of the late twentieth century, has temporarily weakened the socialist forces numerically and intellectually but, in the longer term, has also laid the foundation for a much more solid political edifice built with the will and the knowledge of many dedicated men and women. Clearly, the question that we have to consider here is something along these lines: how do we, among other things, maximise the acceptance of the need by the majority of people in our societies to base their lives and their aspirations on the principle of sufficiency? The question implies an understanding of the moral economy in an industrial environment, a countering of the capitalist myth of 'economic rationality' and a reintegration of the, if you wish, pre-industrial, pre-capitalist values based on the notion that 'enough is as good as a feast'.[14] This approach has obviously been reinforced by the insights derived from the research of ecological science and activism. It is from this ideological mindset, formulated in political programmes of principle and practical action plans, that the motivation and the passion will be generated to oppose, and, therefore, not to emulate, the acquisitive and status-seeking desiderata which are the stock-in-trade of the capitalist system.

We need as a corollary to this to spell out what we mean in practice when we proclaim that socialism is a process, not an event. For example, in the educational domain, should we not place the spotlight firmly on pre-school education and, consequently, universalise this phase of education as a defining component of any modern democracy? (It goes without saying that we have to work out all the curricular and training implications of this proposal).

Third, there is very little doubt in the mind of any serious revolutionary socialist protagonist that the form of organisation, the party, for short, that will lead or guide the struggle for socialism in the world has once again become a point of debate. This is so because of the elitist pretensions, authoritarian ethos and undemocratic practices that have often come to be associated with so-called vanguard parties of the working class. It ought not to be necessary to say that this is a fundamental question, one that requires from all of us total honesty and intellectual integrity, since the fact that socialist activists are – ideally – people who have specialised in the study of society and of history, necessarily equips them with a certain kind of knowledge that others either don't have or do not consider to be essential to their 'happiness'. Because of the social power that this knowledge endows us with, which, incidentally, is not very different from the power that technocrats such as civil engineers or nuclear scientists have, we are called upon to display higher levels of social responsibility than most 'ordinary' people, something that recent history has taught us not to take for granted at all.

Fourth, we find ourselves in a strategic impasse. Both theory and history tell us that socialism in one country is impossible. Yet, the domino effect of socialist revolutions seems always to be interrupted by imperialist machinations and direct intervention. Hence, at the international level, where one always has to begin any analysis, the strategic question today is: what do we have to do in order to prevent the isolation of any socialist revolution such as that which is underway in Latin America? This question is not about 'not fighting against your own bourgeoisie', as some wiseacre tried to tell me at a recent conference; it is about ensuring that your own efforts at the national level can be sustainable once they eventuate in successful overthrow of the existing system. It is also about the most effective practical manner of countering the paralysing sectarianism of the left. It is only when all revolutionary socialists in the world act together (in international brigades, large-scale boycotts and sanctions campaigns against aggressor nations, etc.) that some of the edges that make it impossible for left-wing people to act in concert will begin to be rubbed off.

5. Let me add a few points with respect to political economy issues at the beginning of the twenty-first century. The centrality and dominance of the USA in the world economic landscape, though it continues to shape events and political economy processes, is beginning to become less taken for granted than even five years ago. This situation is most visibly manifest in the decline of the dollar and the zigzag rise of the euro. Besides the ever more obvious inter-imperialist rivalry between North America and the European Union, we are witnessing the appearance on the world stage of the Asian capitalist giants of China, India, and Indonesia, as well as of the more established capitalist regimes of Japan, South Korea, Malaysia–Singapore, and an assertive Russia. The new dynamic that these relations have inserted into the world capitalist system has been exhaustively analysed by many Marxist and other progressive scholars. It will suffice, therefore, if I highlight a few issues that appear to me to be relevant to our present context.

First, the dominance of finance capital is clearly a high-risk situation as far as the system as a whole is concerned. The latest series of crises triggered by the collapse of the so-called sub-prime market in the USA demonstrates this most clearly. Not only the banking system of the USA but those of all countries have been put in jeopardy and are relying on their central banks (i.e. their taxpayers) to bail them out.

Second, and related to the first point, the bull markets of the past decade or more have been demand-driven, i.e. based on consumption that is itself the result of the expansion (over-expansion) of credit. This situation is unsustainable and the continued creation of ever more sophisticated credit-creating instruments (especially the plethora of loyalty cards and smart cards for their not-so-smart 'owners') is a recipe for the deepest possible recession and, ultimately, depression. This predictable fact has produced the usual oracular pronouncements about the collapse of capitalism from all manner of Marxist and other socialist analysts. It is my view that we should avoid this eschatological tendency, since it really does not enrich our understanding of how the system actually works. We cannot at one and the same time say that the system will not collapse of its own accord and, without any reference to whether or not the subjective factor, i.e. the leadership, the party and all that that implies, is adequately prepared to deliver the final blows, predict its 'inevitable' fall. The so-called resilience of the capitalist system, as we know from especially the world and other wars of the last century, is based on its 'creative destruction' of resources through, among other things, primarily investment in the military-industrial complex and the conduct of war on the most threadbare of 'justifications'. If any person on earth still doubts the truth of this proposition after the exposure of the official lies about the so-called weapons of mass destruction in Saddam's Iraq, nothing will convince them. Not even two years ago, George Bush was embarrassingly stopped from publicly pushing in the direction of preparing for a similar war scenario in Iran by his own 'intelligence service' releasing a report that shows clearly that Iran had given up any notion of producing nuclear arms as far back as 2003!

Of course, a realistic assessment of the prospects for successful anti-capitalist-imperialist actions by large masses of exploited and oppressed people in many different parts of the world does not mean that one is suggesting that socialist revolution is not on the immediate agenda. In Latin America, as I have pointed out, the conditions for such a leap across the ideological and political hurdles that have been placed so very deliberately and effectively in the path of the workers of the world has become decidedly possible, even probable.

Third, from the point of view of the economic South of the globe, the entrance of China and India as major investors in infrastructure and consumers of raw materials and other commodities has the potential of re-establishing a 'neutral' space for the elites that is not dissimilar from that which made it possible during the Cold War for a Nehru, a Nasser, an Nkrumah, and others to strut large on the world stage, whatever their nationalist and personal attributes might have contributed to their stature. Bloc formation such as that manifest in the EU, African Union, Association of South-East Asian Nations, Bolivarian Alternative for Our Americas (ALBA), and other similar entities, is, in Manuel Castell's terms, initially a form of resistance to 'globalisation' by the elites. It implies the manifest rejection of the new international division of labour imposed by the international financial institutions on behalf of the USA hegemon on the rest of humanity.[15] It can, however, only succeed in the long run if it manages to create what he calls 'project identities', i.e. if the generality of the population identifies with the newly created block. This is the reason for the discussion about a European identity and for the ongoing discussion in South Africa of the question: Who Is an African? For the left, it poses the question (in Africa, for example) whether we can and should give new meaning to the pan-African project, i.e. as a left project that is implacably opposed to the capitalist- imperialist basis and the elitist ethos of NEPAD [New Partnership for Africa's Development] and all its ancillary formations. I believe that this is a fundamental question for socialists in Africa, one the consideration of which we can no longer defer.

Fourth, the increasingly coordinated strategies of the world capitalist class via entities such as the World Economic Forum as well as the yawning gaps between the rich and the poor that are the direct consequence of the neoliberal economic orthodoxy and its barbaric practical instantiations in most countries of the world, especially in the economic South, have given rise to a worldwide protest movement that has come to be associated in the main with the World Social Forum and its geographical offshoots with the catchy motto/slogan to the effect that 'Another world is possible', reminiscent of Schiller's *Ode to Joy* eternalised in the Chorale of Beethoven's *Ninth Symphony*. Now, whatever else the WSF might be, it is universally acknowledged that it is not, and should not try to be, a new International. It does, however, by implication raise many questions about the international coordination of revolutionary socialist and other working-class activities.

6. Any illusions individual socialists or groups of socialists may have had about the class nature of most co-opted regimes, especially in Africa, have been dispelled by the blatant and abject subordination of the South African liberation struggle to the dictates of international and domestic capital. Africa's position in the international division of labour has been very firmly defined as supplier of certain raw materials, especially oil, gas, precious metals, and plantation goods such as sisal and cotton. Only South Africa itself has a sufficiently diversified economic structure to withstand to some extent the devastating consequences of essentially monocultural economies. As has been pointed out by authors such as John Saul and Colin Leys in numerous publications, the situation of the urban and especially the rural poor in most of Africa is exacerbated by the fact that all previous populist notions of 'African' socialism have been discredited, most of them even before the implosion of the USSR. In spite of this, of course, the sporadic and sometimes sustained protests and uprisings against the International Monetary Fund and World Bank imposed austerity regimes, most prominently in Zimbabwe in recent years, but equally so in Zambia, in Uganda, Senegal, and elsewhere, are a sign of the latent force of anti-neo-colonial and anti-capitalist resistance, of the

potential of the second chimurenga. These actions have highlighted the need for ... nation-wide movements and/or parties through which such local groups and initiatives can ultimately unite to confront the political and economic power of the transnationals and the states that back them.[16]

For this reason, as well as others, the direction that the class struggle takes in South Africa during the next few years will be crucial to the rest of the continent. Currently, because of all the smoke that is being projected by SACP sleight of hand as a raging fire of revolutionary 'transformation' of the ANC into a quasi-socialist party, there appears to be much confusion. However, the position can be stated clearly and simply. The working and unemployed masses are voting with their feet. Whatever their lingering loyalties and ever more feeble hopes in the myth that 'the ANC will deliver', however big the gap between political consciousness and material practice, the thousands of township uprisings, countrywide strikes and serial metropolitan protest actions have one simple meaning: we reject your policies and your practices as anti-worker and anti-poor. It is, in my view, a misnomer to refer to these stirrings of self-organisation of the working class as an expression of 'collective insubordination',[17] even though their immediate impulse is usually reactive rather than proactive. They are saying very clearly and very loudly that the appeal to nationalist, blood and soil rhetoric has lost its power and that we are standing on the threshold of a politics that will be shaped by a heightened sense of class struggle. It is this understanding that should inform our analysis and our estimation of the prospects for a more principled socialist-orientated direction of the struggle in South Africa.

The Biko generation inculcated positive values of self-respect, self-esteem, and self-consciousness into the young people at schools and at higher education institutions as well as older people in communities and in workplaces. They did so because they understood that the slave mentality is the proximate source of the sense of disempowerment, despair, and political apathy that keeps the oppressed in thrall. Above all, they understood intuitively that power is not simply the control of armed force, legitimate or otherwise. Hence, they undertook community development programmes and mobilised people at the grassroots in order that they might survive in the menacing environments of apartheid South Africa. Under the banner of the slogan: You are your own liberators! the Black Community Programmes empowered whole communities across the entire country. Together with the evolving modern labour movement inside the country, it was this war of position that eventually put an end to the apparently linear curve on which the apartheid regime thought itself to be proceeding ever upwards. There is no doubt, of course, that the struggle against racial oppression in all its reprehensible forms compelled everyone to focus on the overriding objective of throwing off the yoke of racism. The mistake that many made, was to assume that the end of apartheid would bring about the end of class exploitation.

Let us try, however briefly, to sketch some of the consequences of applying the principle of sufficiency as the major moral force shaping post-apartheid South Africa, a principle that can create the kind of unifying vision, based on the paramountcy of working-class interests. To begin with, in the domain of education, where the state and other public institutions can legitimately intervene, the content, orientation and delivery of the curriculum at all levels of the system would be changed fundamentally. The psychological, pedagogical, ideological, and emotional revolution implied by an approach that does not glorify individual or group domination while allowing for the full development and flowering of the potential inherent in each and every human being can be imagined and extrapolated very easily. Individual brilliance expressed and deployed on behalf and for the benefit of democratically legitimated groups at different levels of society will continue to be one of the drivers of all social progress, including economic development. In the domain of the media and especially advertising, we would be rid of the brutalities and socially disreputable messages which subject us to the domination of capital. Adverts like one that is currently popular in South Africa which claims that everyone wants to be a 'winner' and in the 'first team', rather than a 'deputy chairperson' or a 'benchwarmer' – or words to that effect – would become as absurd and counterproductive as they are from the point of view of a more humane social order. The glorification of the ostentatious consumption and high life of so-called celebrities in politics, culture, sport, and even religion would cease to be the supposedly inspiring models of 'the good life' that they are marketed as being in television programmes such as Top Billing and others. All domains of life would be affected in the most profound possible way.

What a drab and boring vision, I hear the privileged strata exclaiming. On the absolute contrary, I should like to respond to my imagined detractors. Artists, designers, architects, urban planners, in fact all creative individuals and agencies will be faced with the challenge of finding the optimal ways of expressing and realising the entire range of possibilities in every domain of life. This will be the terrain of competition, not for individual glory and unequal reward but precisely for the common good, the old-fashioned commonwealth!

Is this no more than John Lennon or Vladimir Lenin's dream? How do we begin to initiate and incrementally realise this vision and this set of values? Besides the ongoing political and economic class struggles, in which we are willy-nilly involved and by means of which we attempt to create and to consolidate more democratic space in the short to medium term, we have to go back to the community development tasks that the Black Consciousness Movement initiated so successfully, if not always sustainably, owing to the ravages of the apartheid system.

We have to rebuild our communities and our neighbourhoods by means of establishing, as far as possible on a voluntary basis, all manner of community projects which bring visible short-term benefit to the people and which initiate at the same time the trajectories of fundamental social transformation, which I have been referring to. These could range from relatively simple programmes such as keeping the streets and the public toilets clean, preferably in liaison with the local authority, whether or not it is 'delivering' at this level, to more complex programmes such as bulk buying clubs, community reading clubs, enrichment programmes for students preparing for exams, teachers' resource groups at local level, and, of course, sports activities on a more convivial basis. It is important that I stress that wherever possible, the relevant democratic authority should be asked to support the initiative. On the other hand, the community and its community-based organisations must remain in control of what they are doing. This is the difference between South Africa today and South Africa yesterday. As long as, and to the extent that, we have a democratic system, there is no reason why any of these programmes have to be initiated as anti-government initiatives. Any representative democratic government would welcome and vigorously support such initiatives, since they are pro-people and, in the current context, pro-poor initiatives.

There are already many of these initiatives and programmes in existence. They will, if they are conducted with integrity and not for party-political gain, inevitably gravitate towards one another, converge and network. In this way, the fabric of civil society non-government organisations that was the real matrix of the anti-apartheid movement will be refreshed and we will once again have that sense of a safety net of communities inspired by the spirit and the real practices of *ubuntu*, the 'counter-society' I referred to earlier, that saved so many of us from being destroyed by the racist system. Today, the struggle is much more obviously being conducted as a class struggle against exploitation and unconscionable as well as totally unnecessary and unjustifiable social inequality, manifest in the miserable lives of the vast majority and the vulgar parading of wealth and comfort of the few.

7. Viewed from a different angle, the question we are confronted with is whether the revolutionary left cadres will be able to find the requisite solution to the organisational question so that the debilitating and paralysing fragmentation that has marginalised them can be overcome before this passionate resistance of the workers is transformed into the kind of passive resistance we associate with most other post-colonial African states or the nightmare scenario of race war and ethnic cleansing that we saw in Kenya not so long ago, finally overwhelms us. The strategic and tactical implications of this proposition are numerous and radical; among other things, we shall have to find practical answers to old questions in a new context, questions such as:

- What kind of party or organisation should be created out of the confluence of all our political tendencies and traditions in order for the socialist alternative to be firmly rooted within this evolving social base?
- What are the core issues around which a programme of transitional demands and an action plan can be formulated in a democratic process?
- How can such a programme be connected to and informed by the essential task of rebuilding our communities and our neighbourhoods on the basis of cooperativist and collectivist values of *ubuntu*, of sharing and caring?
- How do we align ourselves politically with COSATU and with the other union federations or with individual unions?
- How do we work with the rest of the African working class, especially in southern Africa? What position do we take with regard to the World Social Forum?
- How do we relate to other left-wing international formations without getting encoiled in the sectarian knots or getting side-tracked and lost in the maze of largely irrelevant apologetics that constitutes the stuff of the debates among these sects?

There are, as we speak, a few serious national initiatives underway, all of which are posing these and other relevant questions from slightly different perspectives. I think I have spoken, and speak, in the spirit of Strini Moodley and his comrades when I express the hope that we will find unity in action even as we try to find new ways of seeing the struggle for another world and another South Africa.

South Africa Today – The Moral Responsibility of Intellectuals[1]

> It is the role of the Arab intellectual today to articulate and defend the principles of liberation and democracy at all costs, and to do so by impressing the leadership of the Arab nation with these realities and values. Otherwise, our future – if we are to have one at all – is extremely grim, and in a sense not worth defending.[2]
>
> – Edward Said

1. On the occasion of the tenth anniversary of the Foundation for Human Rights, it is appropriate to remind ourselves of the historic significance of the negotiated settlement that brought a formal end to the rule of the apartheid regime. Elsewhere, I have referred to this as the last act in the very gradual abolition of slavery. Above all, however, in constitutional terms, the settlement initiated the establishment of a liberal democracy in which civic, social and economic rights were entrenched. As one who has spent my entire adult life in the cause of the urban and rural poor of this country and beyond, I am, naturally, especially interested in the realisation and entrenchment of those rights that are relevant to them, such as the right to work, the right to form trade unions, the right to strike, the right to maternity leave, the right to use the language of one's choice, in short, all those rights that potentially improve and secure the well-being of the oppressed and exploited majority. This is, to repeat the point, a momentous achievement of the new South Africa. However, as Edward Said's words, cited in the epigraph, make abundantly clear, we would be failing in our duty as organic intellectuals of the working classes, were we to keep quiet about the very real dangers that are engulfing us in South Africa today.

2. The moral crisis of the elite in the new South Africa has been the subject of much recent media attention, and deservedly so. All of a sudden, examples of corruption, profligate spending of public money for the personal edification of political and other prominent public figures, incredible sexism, outright theft and fraud, and even murder and assassination, apparently linked to somehow shady business deals, among many

other things, are reaching the headlines and front pages of electronic and print media on a daily basis. In this connection, the goings-on around the person of Mr Jacob Zuma are, not to put too fine a point on it, the tip of a melting iceberg. Within the circles of the elite itself, the question about the kinds of role models that a society that is supposedly committed to democracy, equality, freedom, and, as incongruous as it already sounds today, to solidarity, should be projecting and preferring. The tidal wave of violent crime and abuse, which is the direct consequence of the structural inequality and the mental structures that characterise post-apartheid South Africa, demands of the radical intelligentsia that we go into emergency mode. And, while we have to consider seriously the pertinent effects of the legacy of colonialism and apartheid in this context, it is time that we stop justifying our intellectual timidity and lack of historical imagination with this threadbare mantra.

3. Ever more frequently, those of us who fought consciously and often at great personal cost for the liberation of South Africa from the shackles of apartheid and capitalism are left asking ourselves whether this is the kind of society we had in mind when, like Faust in Scene 2 of Goethe's enduring drama, we dreamt of a country where we would be able to exclaim triumphantly: *Hier bin ich Mensch, hier darf ich's sein!*

4. In the context of this celebration of ten years of the Foundation for Human Rights, I am tempted to pose the question slightly differently: Why is it that in spite of a constitution that was arrived at in a twentieth-century model of democratic bargaining and consensus building and in which are enshrined some of the noblest sentiments and insights concerning human rights, we are living in a situation where very few of those rights appear to be realised, or even realisable, in practice?

5. Why single out the elite, and the intellectuals in particular, for special scrutiny? Is it not true that a people get the government it deserves? Did the vast majority of the people not choose this government in a free and fair election? Are we not all to blame? The short answer to these questions is the simple word: leadership. Because it is impossible to analyse this issue adequately in the space of a short talk, I shall present no more than the outline of what I consider to be essential social research.

6. I wish to emphasise that this is not a critique of the government. That would be a different kind of exercise. It is, instead, a critique of and a challenge to South Africa's elite, specifically the intelligentsia.

7. Elites are the inevitable result of asymmetrical power relations which are themselves the consequence of historically evolved class societies. Elites are not necessarily elitist. University students, for example, who in all societies continue to be among the privileged few hence an elite don't have to behave in an elitist manner. Elitism is an aspect of the ideology of a ruling class that has become a class for itself, i.e. one that consciously acts on the assumption that if all people did as its members do, they would be doing the right thing. In the era of capitalism, it is an ideology that justifies privilege and inequality in terms of merit based on individual competition, regardless of how and why some of the individuals are endowed with a head-start while others are hobbled by handicaps at the starting blocks. Because capitalism is an integrated world system, this phenomenon is global in scope. It shapes the consciousness of all modern elites. Oscar Lafontaine, one of the leaders of the German party of the left, in a recent critique of the dominant neoliberal ideology,[3] cites a statement by the German Chancellor, Angela Merkel, to the effect that the efficiency and productivity of the strong and powerful is the driving force of democracy and freedom. According to her, more freedom is dependent on us having many more strong and powerful people so that they can pull everyone else along with them and, thus, make available more to the weaker ones. We need a country where performance is the heart of the system and if we have the stomach for performance, then we should also have the stomach for more and ever more performance. To this, the left social democrat, Lafontaine responds with words that capture exactly the point I wish to make:

> The fact that the weak and the strong ones go to the starting blocks endowed with very unequal skills, wealth and social capital is not mentioned in this way of seeing the matter. To take account of this would entail recognition of the right to freedom and to equality of opportunity of every individual. We see, therefore, that the neoliberal idea of freedom represents a regression to the prevailing ethos before the era of the French Enlightenment when it was already clear that it is law that establishes equality between the weak and the strong and that freedom without law is tantamount to oppression. Neoliberalism does not believe in strengthening the weak and promoting equality of opportunity. Their wellbeing is, instead, supposed to depend on the generosity and the uplifting example of the stronger ones. The weak are social ballast, able to relate to the strong only as dependants and beggars.

8. There are too many issues to be dealt with in the time at our disposal. Hence, I shall discuss a few of those I consider to be crucial to understanding and, more importantly, to acting towards the creation of a counter-current to that which seems to be prevalent at the moment.

(a) The discussion about whether or not the ANC has become an ordinary political party as opposed to a nationalist or even a quasi-socialist movement should be conducted in terms of whether the driving force of that organisation and of the millions it represents is constituted by passion or by interests. Edward Said, taking up a strand of social analysis originally suggested by Albert Hirschman in an attempt to explain why the Renaissance curiosity and the imaginative exploratory prowess of the Early Modern Europeans degenerated into the cynical expansion of capitalism that it became, concluded that it boiled down to the argument that human passion should give way to interests as a method of governing the world.[4] Once this pattern is established, the mindset of those who have to coordinate and manage the system changes fundamentally and the continuities with the past weigh much more heavily than the discontinuities. To put it differently, in our specific case, the fact that there was no social revolution in the early 1990s means that the capitalist class continues to hold all the strategic positions and the new cohort of managers of the system (to use a traditional Marxist postulate) have had to adapt their ways of seeing and thinking about things. There is no doubt about this. Only vested interest prevents one from registering this phenomenon as fact.

(b) Capital is amoral. Ardent as well as reluctant racists of yesteryear have all become convinced non-racialists bound to all South Africans under the united colours of capitalism[5] in an egregious atmosphere of Rainbow nationalism. The same class of people, often the very same individuals, who funded Verwoerd, Vorster and Botha are funding the present regime. The latter has facilitated the expansion of South African capital into the African hinterland in ways of which the likes of Cecil John Rhodes or Ernest Oppenheimer could only dream. Be that as it may: it is simply foolish to think that it could have been otherwise. In this connection, it is pertinent to point out that the strategy of Black Economic Empowerment broad-based or narrow is immaterial and is no more than smoke and mirrors, political theatre on the stage of the national economy. The only way that erstwhile Marxist revolutionaries in the liberation movement can justify their support and even enthusiastic promotion of these developments is by chanting the no longer convincing mantra: There is no alternative! Hence, we need to examine this particular mystification and abdication of intellectual responsibility.

(c) To begin with, this was never true. Human beings always have alternatives. Otherwise, they would not be human beings. In the extreme case, the alternative is death. But, it is unnecessary to be melodramatic. In our case, as in the case of so many other countries in the South, the alternative to the neoliberal hegemony of the past three decades has been, and continues to be, the long march. The very nature of the capitalist system guarantees not that it will collapse of its own accord, since wars and other forms of wanton destruction ensure that it can always be resilient hence the success in the Middle East of Bush and of the military-industrial complex behind him, but that it will reach the point where the wretched of the earth, under the leadership of organised masses of productive workers will bring it to a dead halt in one country after another. This is identifiably the master narrative of classical Marxism and of other brands of socialist thought. Whether or not it is still feasible after the collapse of the USSR and other state socialist entities after 1989 is irrelevant. The alliance of historical agents that will initiate the collapse of the system will in all likelihood look very different from that which we had in mind even a few years ago. The important point is that the alternative to promoting the neoliberal hegemony is to undermine the capitalist system by strengthening democracy. In other words, there is a profound truth in Marx's aphorism that democracy as we know it is nothing else than the dictatorship of the bourgeoisie. I refer you again to the quote from Lafontaine. It is the inadequacy and the inconsistency inherent in bourgeois notions of freedom and democracy that have to be exposed by the intelligentsia. This is our continuing revolutionary task and our challenge, one that is particularly relevant to organisations such as the Foundation for Human Rights.

(d) I will not waste our time by discussing the vulgarity and the philistinism that characterise the behaviour of so many of the new elite as described in media reports and as one can observe at any gathering of these people. Bishop Tutu and other professional custodians of our moral well-being have albeit with very little success done this eloquently enough. More important are questions such as whether even

in the context of a liberal democracy for example, it is necessary to perpetuate racial identities, the cynical, almost psychopathic disregard for
ordinary human fellow-feeling that is supposed to lie at the heart of our
vaunted African humanism of *ubuntu*, or, at a more mundane level,
the utterly stupid custom of continuing to dress ourselves in the inap-
propriate garments that evolved in a remote European climate. (I am
particularly irritated by the gowns and hoods that South African universities and even preschools think to be *de rigueur!*).

(e) Given the global paradigms within which we are willy-nilly operating and the imperatives of historical redress, it is one of the most
tragic facts of post-apartheid South Africa that we have comprehensively fooled ourselves into believing that because we have Black skins,
we are automatically good people. This is the reason why all too often
we have incompetent, inexperienced people appointed to positions
that are way above their actual capacity at the time. This is a wrong
and thoughtless, short-term response to the legacy of colonial and
apartheid racism. There are other ways of dealing with this issue and
with related issues of education and training. To fool ourselves, as we
have also done in respect of the AIDS challenge, is the worst possible
redress. We are going to pay bitterly in terms of socio-psychological
and economic damage for this unnecessary strategy. Most instructive
in this regard is the story of Khanya College, which was founded on,
among other things, the fact that Bantu and other forms of apartheid
education for Black people, had to be recognised as having actually
disadvantaged our children, the young activists of the 1980s, given the
hegemonic educational mindsets at the time. Denialism in all dimensions of our society, including, devastatingly – until very recently – that
of crime, is the beginning of a disaster waiting to happen.

(f) The quality of all our lives has been ruined by the understandable paranoia that the ubiquity of violent crime in a thousand different
forms has brought with it. This crime wave, as we see in comparable situations in countries like Russia, is one of the results of the democratic
opening up of the apartheid society, where it had been confined to the
Black locations and the Bantustans, unseen by the inhabitants of the
largely white leafy suburbs. It is none the less difficult to believe that a
party that had prided itself for some five years in the early 1990s that
it was preparing to govern had somehow not realised that this would
be one of the immediate challenges to continuing bourgeois stability

in the new South Africa. Now, it is imperative, for all the best imaginable reasons, including especially the protection and realisation in practice of our constitutional and natural rights to dignity and safety, that decisive action be taken, regardless of how such action will affect the popularity and the voting profile in future elections of any parliamentary party. Otherwise, the future of our children will be mortgaged to a kind of Bacchic dystopia as portrayed in Euripides's ancient play. Already, we are witness to the brazen and systematic disregard for the law and for the orderly behaviour that is the hallmark and the precondition of a civilised society. And, this is the real point, it is not just the crazed taxi drivers who are possessed by this Bacchanalian spirit.

(g) We are building a new historical community in South Africa. The Truth and Reconciliation Commission, whatever its virtues and positive legacies – I have referred to these in my book *An Ordinary Country* – could not establish the social basis for this new community. Reconciliation and forgiveness between two individuals or even small groups of people, such as families, is possible and often happens. Social reconciliation under conditions of cruel inequality such as we have in South Africa is not only impossible, but it is also a lie that has to be exposed. We will have to work very hard at bringing about social cohesion and national unity. How and for what purposes such a project should be undertaken is too big a subject to enter into here. Suffice it to say that unless the Gini coefficient is tackled seriously, all talk of social cohesion and national unity is so much nonsense. The implications of this apparently simple and apodeictic statement are profound. As profound, I am bold enough to say, as the Benedictine demolition of limbo as a site of sterile happiness for the luckless many that were consigned to it until a few weeks ago.

(h) What should we do? Is there a more or less clear road map to a different destination than the one on which we seem to be hell-bent at the moment? The short answer is YES! There is, as this statement implies, a very long answer, almost as long as the long march, but that is precisely what I meant at the beginning of this talk when I referred to the social research that awaits those of us who are not satisfied to be towed along by the Bacchanalian drivers of the neoliberal tow-trucks currently controlled and deployed by President Mbeki and his colleagues. It has always been the task of the intelligentsia to speak out and to indicate what the alternatives are. In sum, I believe that we have to transform our uhuru into *ubuntu*.[6] We have to find our way back to the passion and the values of freedom, equality, and solidarity that drove us to struggle against the apartheid system. We have to get back to the modesty and the generosity of spirit that inspired most of us then. Besides ensuring that democratic legislation in favour of the poor and the oppressed strata of our new South Africa is put on the statute book and implemented efficiently, we have to go back to the communities and to the grassroots in all their different forms. We have to rebuild our neighbourhoods on the basis of mutual trust and mutual aid, sharing our resources and our skills, by gradually establishing cooperative forms of production, distribution and exchange until these reach all levels of the economy. It is not true that human beings, including Black-skinned human beings, are necessarily good or necessarily bad. We have to insist that we want to create the kind of society where, as the late Ernest Mandel said in a memorable speech on the campus of the University of the Western Cape in Cape Town in 1992, the Biblical simplicity of the injunction of the Sermon on the Mount becomes the practical programme of socialism:

FEED THE HUNGRY/CLOTHE THE NAKED/HOUSE THE HOMELESS/VISIT THE SICK/CARE FOR THE OLD, THE YOUNG AND THE WEAK.

Can we do this in South Africa today?

'Let Us Return to the Source! In Quest of a Humanism of the 21st Century'[1]

1. It was with much pleasure that I accepted the invitation of the organisers of this memorial event to speak in honour of the late Sipho Maseko, whom I knew for most of his life as an activist operating within the paradigms of Black Consciousness. I accepted the invitation with a sense of gratitude, especially because I believe that this is the kind of occasion where we should reflect with care and seriousness on the paths we have travelled during our short post-apartheid journey. Sipho, whose widow, Pam, worked with me in the National Language Project and in other contexts for many years, was one of those young people of the 1980s, who were totally committed to the total liberation of South Africa and of the continent as a whole. The sincere, indeed the naïve, belief in the values of freedom, equality, solidarity, and democracy, which drove all of us at the time, has been systematically eroded by the irruption of the narcissistic, dog-eat-dog virus that is spreading across the globe in the current era of the hegemony of neoliberal capitalism.

2. It is against this backdrop, that I want to put the spotlight on the question of whether it is possible for us to 'return to the source' – to borrow an exhortation from Amílcar Cabral – to once again place at the centre of our vision, our plans and our behaviour the values on the basis of which we hoped to build the non-racial, democratic republic after the demise of apartheid-capitalism. Because of time constraints, I shall not analyse the many important writings of the Black Consciousness generation, in which they grappled, among other things, with questions of identity and social structure. Allow me to highlight two central issues only. The first is the vision that actually illuminated the path of struggle chosen by that entire generation, whether or not they belonged to formal organisations of the Black Consciousness Movement. In the words of Steve Biko in one of his very last interviews shortly before he was murdered:

> We are of the view that we should operate as one united whole toward attainment of an egalitarian society for the whole of Azania. Therefore,

entrenchment of tribalistic, racialistic or any form of sectional outlook is abhorred by us. We hate it and we seek to destroy it.[2]

Elsewhere,[3] I have written about the dynamics of the Black Consciousness Movement. All I wish to stress here is that the Biko generation set out on that long march implicit in the Gramscian notion of the war of position. Through the University Christian Movement and other sources, they came into contact with the pedagogical and social conceptions of Paulo Freire and the theology of liberation, among others, and all of these influences, besides the ideas current in the different organisations involved in the national liberation struggle, in the context of the repression and against the background of the mixture of Christian philanthropy and African communal life that all of us who were adults in those days had experienced in the countryside, undoubtedly contributed to their formulation and conscious promotion of this strategy. The promotion of the Black Community Programmes, together with the development of a modern labour movement, which had a more differentiated but related source and a sometimes converging, sometimes diverging, trajectory, was no less than such a war of position, one which eventually brought about a change in the balance of forces and helped to reshape the political space in the worst years of the repression.

While bearing this in mind, let me refer you to the other issue that I consider as having been central to the strategic path of the BCM, i.e. the idea of 'psychological liberation'.

In dealing with this concept critically, we have, in philosophical terms, to navigate carefully between the Scylla of voluntarism and the Charybdis of political paralysis. Today, we would deal with the question in terms of the relationship between structure and agency. However, let us keep the discourse at a manageable level by stating quite simply that the question we are faced with is whether, and if so, how it is possible in the era of neoliberal barbarism to implant a different set of values among especially the younger people in South Africa and elsewhere, in spite of the many structural constraints that determine their individual existential projects and the massive bombardment of negative and self-destructive ethical messages emanating from the media and other ideological state and non-state apparatuses. It is clear, certainly to me, that this is the challenge that faces all thinking South Africans, and people on the left specifically, if we are to have any hope of turning our society to head once again in a direction that can lead to the post-apartheid and even post-capitalist situation we had envisaged before 1996, more or less.

We know, of course, that it is a combination of ideas, organisation, and political-economic developments at the macro-level that brings about fundamental social shifts at any given time and place. It would, therefore, be a mistake to think that by harking back to a concept such as psychological liberation, I want to suggest that we focus all our energies on moral education of the youth, as important as that activity is. The real question behind these reflections is how we can tap back into the power that actually exists in many different social spaces and instantiations but which we have made ourselves believe is vested only in and, indeed, *belongs to*, 'the government'. If the BCM and other movements, especially in the 1970s and 1980s, taught us anything, it is that we always have access to power, as long as we know how it is distributed.

The Biko generation inculcated positive values of self-respect, self-esteem, and self-consciousness into the young people at schools and at higher education institutions as well as older people in communities and in workplaces. They did so because they understood that the slave mentality is the proximate source of the sense of disempowerment, despair and political apathy that keeps the oppressed in thrall. Above all, they understood intuitively that power is not simply the control of armed force, legitimate or otherwise. Hence, they undertook community development programmes and mobilised people at the grassroots in order that they might survive in the menacing environments of apartheid South Africa. Sipho Maseko himself and others in accordance with the injunction *Education for Liberation*, organised in Cape Town the Black Students Project that undertook political education as well as enrichment programmes that sought to help students understand their schoolwork properly and pass their examinations, among many other things. Under the banner of the slogan, *You are your own liberators!* the Black Community Programmes empowered whole communities across the entire country. As indicated earlier, together with the evolving modern labour movement inside the country, it was this war of position that eventually put an end to the apparently linear curve on which the apartheid regime thought itself to be proceeding ever upwards. Again, I do not have to go into details; many articles and reports are available for those who have a more serious interest in what was done by the young people of the 1970s and the 1980s. There is no doubt, of course, that the struggle against racial oppression in all its reprehensible forms compelled everyone to focus on the overriding objective of throwing off the yoke of racism. The mistake that many made, as we shall see, was to assume that the end of apartheid would bring about the end of class exploitation which, in this country because of the peculiar historical dynamics, continues to perpetuate racial inequality.

3. What does the picture look like today? Let me begin to answer this question by referring to the fact that when Evo Morales became President of Bolivia not so long ago, one of his first official acts was to get a law passed that reduced his presidential salary by 57 per cent. In post-apartheid South Africa, the very opposite occurred. The recommendations of the Melamet Commission of 1994 and of the subsequent annual increases recommended by the Independent Commission for the Remuneration of Public Office Bearers, based on the principles of remuneration of the apartheid dispensation, were accepted without much soul-searching among the new elite. This, in my view, was the first signal that we were headed in the wrong direction. It sent entirely the wrong message to the youth of a poor, 'Third-World' country, South Africa, to the effect that successful Black people are people who earn in these brackets and who own fancy cars and houses. The role model effect of this kind of lifestyle and value system which, today, 15 years later, has become the accepted thing, will take many years and many alternative models of success to turn around. I cite the effect of the acceptance of the salary packages recommended by the Melamet Commission in its different instantiations as the first of a series of lifestyle signposts for the youth. Add to this the fact that during the struggle against the apartheid regime, everyone, including your 'Comtsotsi',[4] was seen to be and treated as an equal, whereas after 1994 there was this sudden and very visible divide between those who were deemed to have been 'successful', on the one side, and the Great Unwashed, on the other side, the veritable underclass, victims of apartheid before 1996 and of neoliberalism thereafter. One does not need a degree in philosophy to work out the socio-psychological results of this situation.

The thousands of 'service delivery protests' – a euphemism for localised mini-uprisings – the vandalism that accompanies them as well as 'ordinary' crimes such as hijackings, cash heists, kidnappings, armed robberies, etc.: all of these horrendous manifestations of barbarism induced by the logic of capitalism in the twenty-first century, are payback acts of entitlement. '*If you who, yesterday, were in the trenches with us or with our parents can now drive around in a Mercedes Benz or a BMW, live in a mansion, or even a palace in the leafy suburbs, and generally live it up, why should I continue to be mired in poverty and filth in so-called informal settlements with pit latrines, no garbage removal and no proper educational and health facilities?'* This is the logic that is playing itself out on our streets. The simple fact is that if young people in the townships and in the rural areas are unemployed, hungry, frustrated, and angry, they will, under these circumstances, resort to theft and even murder in order to live like those few others who, by grace of birth or because of political patronage, belong to the new elite. Given the retreat of all the moral and political censors that kept things 'looking good' during the post-War years, one can hardly 'blame' this youth for behaving in such a reactionary manner. Drugs and Americanised TV are increasingly added to this lethal syndrome of social pathologies.

There have been many more or less sophisticated attempts at explaining the sociology of the current disaster and it is unnecessary to add another such attempt to this list. What is clear, however, is that if we fail to address the question of values with even a modicum of success, we will inevitably arrive at the edge of the abyss, pushed there by this logic of capitalism. The intelligentsia in particular have a moral obligation to help the entire nation to find and accept the alternative. Today, when we are witnessing the collapse of the global financial system which reflects the terminal condition of the system of capitalism as a whole, the Thatcherite mantra: 'there is no alternative', which in any case never had any basis in fact, is no more and no less than an expression of social dementia and denialism of the most self-destructive kind. For, not only are there alternatives, they are staring us in the face if we have the boldness and the imagination to explore them and, like the generation of Sipho Maseko, begin to make a difference on the ground.

4. How do we re-establish a culture of positive values, one that is socially critical but not destructive in its modalities? What is the foundational value that should inform everything else we believe in and do? I am here referring to the kind of value system that can inspire an entire generation of young people to take on to themselves the task and to forge the instruments of social mobilisation on a large scale and for decades, rather than just a few years, knowing full well that the realisation of their 'dream' will change everything from the bottom up and shape social structures and processes that will be very different in form and effect from those of the

neoliberal imperialist agencies that now disfigure their lives and ruin our societies. In the previous dispensation, anti-racism and anti-apartheid for most, as well as anti-capitalism for some, were such a set of beliefs that not only fostered solidarity and unity but also charged the imagination of young people with a vision of the 'non-racial, non-sexist, and democratic' alternative to apartheid.

The answer has been lurking in, among other places, the ecological economics of scholars such as Andre Gorz[5] for many years, but it has taken global climatic disasters and the collapse of the tyrannical political structures in Africa, Latin America, Asia, Eastern Europe, and elsewhere to make us understand the full significance of the present stage of bourgeois rule. Today, we know that political diversity is as important for a humane society as are bio- and cultural diversity. For some years now, it has dawned on me that a humanism of the twenty-first century will have to be based on what Gorz calls the *principle of sufficiency* which, for the sake of a broader understanding of what this concept entails, I have transliterated as 'Enough is as good as a feast'.[6]

It ought to be obvious that if the structures and processes of modern industrial societies were informed and shaped by this view of life, most of the currently existing social modalities and human desires and activities in most contemporary states would forthwith become antiquated and counterproductive. The hegemony of the world view that proclaims, among many other things, that 'more is better', that in terms of the much-vaunted 'intellectual property rights', I deserve all the fruits of what I have initiated, and that the ideal is to be the 'world champion' in all spheres of life: in short, that the good life is to be had by competing and fighting against other human beings who, in the extreme case, have to be dehumanised so that I am not constrained by any fellow-feeling from killing them.

5. I am all too aware of the fact that this has turned out to be a kind of secular sermon. It would have been easier, and it was probably expected by most of my audience, for me to have formulated yet another analysis of 'the global crisis of the capitalist system'. There are more than enough of these, I think. Here, too, enough is as good as a feast. It has been more difficult and challenging for me to return to the source, to reflect on the first principles that motivate us in our struggle for a humane world order, one where every child and every person has more than an outside chance of fulfilling his or her human potential. Today, we have to formulate these

principles in a new language, one that will find readier access among the youth, to whom, as we say so beautifully but so ineffectually, the future belongs. I have probably not succeeded in finding those words but I hope that my attempt to do so will inspire others to take up the challenge. I also know that I have spoken very much in the spirit of the late Sipho Maseko and his generation of revolutionaries.

"'Race" is Skin Deep, Humanity is Not'[1]

The furore about the racist remarks attributed to Jimmy Manyi[2] and to a few other would-be pacesetters in the aspiring leadership cadre of the new South Africa is without any doubt one of the defining moments of our country's history.

Enough has been written and more than enough said in 'jest' or otherwise about what these people actually said or wrote, about why solidarity, with its not-so-hidden agenda, suddenly sprang this revelation on an 'unsuspecting' South African middle-class public, and about the positions taken by various professional politicians, especially those in and around the ANC.

I shall therefore spare myself the agony and the embarrassment of commenting on the disgusting crassness and the latent brutality of the utterances and passages attributed to Manyi, Kuli Roberts, and the others.

This is all the more justified because the general sense of outrage, cathartic as it might be, is not the real point. Whether some, or all, of the critics and commentators are more or less 'racist' than Roberts, Manyi and Co is not worthy of serious discussion.

The very fact that 'race' and racial labels can become a point of contestation in what is no more than a rather childish name-calling exercise is indicative of the profound ironies of the 'new' South Africa. Indeed, I intervene in this matter with a sense of shame.

Shame, because all of us who have advocated and fought for so many decades and even generations for the goal of a non-racial South Africa have so patently failed in our mission. Shame, but not defeat! This 'debate' merely underlines the fact that the struggle for the total liberation of the people of South Africa continues.

In my view, we need to restate the underlying issues involved in 'the race debate' and stop making things worse by dwelling on what are no more than superficial features of actual and potential conflict deriving from vested economic and political interests.

Let me begin by saying again, as I have done a thousand times in many articles and speeches on this issue: race thinking is real and it has real consequences, which will not disappear overnight.

248 · AGAINST RACIAL CAPITALISM

Most South Africans will continue for a very long time to see themselves, and see one another, as 'Africans', 'Indians', 'Coloureds', and 'whites', simply because these identities were constructed in terms of ruling-class agendas and interests over decades and centuries.

These people have a right to see themselves as such but, given the history of racial conflict and inequality, it is the duty of those who have the power to do so to create conditions in which the need to identify in this way becomes unnecessary and undesirable.

Although there are many things we can do in the short to medium term to create a more tolerant and tolerable social climate, it will take generations of consistent and patient work to alter the underlying structures that cause and entrench racial prejudice and all the awful expressions of hatred and ignorance that inevitably go with racial stereotyping.

I want to deal briefly with three fundamental issues involved in this debate. Many South African scholars, starting from different points of view, have written on these issues and anyone who is seriously concerned about understanding the complexities of the racial order could do worse than to go back to these sources.

First and foremost, we have to confront the question: is a raceless society possible? Should such a society be our desired destination? Is this what we all mean when we speak about a 'non-racial South Africa'? If, when using these and related terms, we mean minimally the kind of society in which the colour of one's skin, the texture of one's hair, etc. are irrelevant in terms of one's human dignity and life chances, we have to face a few stubborn facts not only of South African society but also of all racist societies.

Given the tenacity and the apparent solidity of the colonial-apartheid social and economic structures and their ideological underpinnings that have shaped all our lives, how realistic or feasible is a non-racial South Africa? Is it not an even more utopian notion than the 'classless society' that many of us continue to carry around with us as our political GPS?

The short answer to this question is that, if you can believe in heaven and other notions of a life of perfect harmony after death, it ought not to be difficult to conceive of the possibility of a raceless or a classless society here on earth.

If you cannot envision such a society, you are saying to all of us, among other things, that biology is fate and that there is nothing much we can do about improving our conditions of life, depending on which 'race' or 'class' is on top.

Such fatalism is antithetical to any society that is bent on social transformation.

The longer answer to the question is that because we are human beings, we create meaning for ourselves, and a social goal such as a 'non-racial South Africa' is not only conceivable but also eminently feasible.

To make it happen, we have to do many things in the short, medium and very long term.

What Roberts, Manyi and Co seem to have done, or seem to be doing, as far as I am concerned, points in the opposite direction, i.e. the kind of South Africa from which we thought we were ready to escape in 1994.

The second issue we have to confront is that of human worth or dignity. If Manyi has been quoted correctly, he has done no more than take to its logical conclusion the implications of any human capital theory, i.e. a way of seeing people as assets and in terms of their exchange value.

Once you are on that road – and most capitalist business ideologues are on that road – it is very easy to fall into the kind of discourse where one or other group of people is considered to be 'superfluous', 'over-concentrated', etc.

The Hitlers and the Fronemans of the world eventually forced these people into railway trucks or lorries and transported them to their deaths in the gas chambers or to their last graves in the many Dimbazas of our beloved country (Frank Froneman was the former Deputy Minister of Bantu Administration who referred to the wives and children of Black workers as 'superfluous appendages').

The dehumanisation of language and discourse corresponds to the dehumanisation of stigmatised persons. Once the commodity value of people displaces their intrinsic human worth or dignity, we are well on the way to a state of barbarism.

Unless and until we bring back into our paradigms, and thus into our social analyses, the entire human being and the ways in which human beings can live fulfilled lives beyond their mere economic needs, we will continue to promote anti-human philosophies and policies that ultimately tend to work to the benefit of those who have, and to the detriment of those who do not have.

Thirdly, and finally, it is time that we admit publicly and without any qualification that you cannot fight racial inequality, racial prejudice and race thinking by using racial categories as a 'site of redress'.

Among many others, I have written about alternatives to affirmative action policies, so I shall not repeat those points here. Suffice it to say that fighting race with race is bad social science and even worse practical politics.

Besides tackling the structural economic and social inequalities that we took over without much modification from the apartheid state, we have to do the hard work of exploring, researching and piloting alternative approaches to those based on the apartheid racial categories to counter the perpetuation of white and other social privilege.

It is a fundamental theoretical and strategic error to try to do so by perpetuating racial identities in the nonsensical belief that this will not have any negative or destructive social consequences. The Employment Equity Act and all related legislation should be reviewed, not in the direction that the department of labour seems to want to do but in a totally different direction, one that moves away decisively from any notion of 'race' and looks specifically at 'disadvantage'.

Seventeen years into the new South Africa, we can afford to interrogate even our most dearly held views about things. In South Africa, because we do live in a liberal democracy, we can actually ask these questions without fear of losing our limbs or even our lives.

The Manyi affair is much larger than the few individuals involved. It is a matter that, unless we look beneath the verbiage, may ruin any future of peace and prosperity our children may hope for.

'The Elephant in the Room'[1]

Only an inveterate denialist or a fool will maintain that the new South Africa as a political and social entity is not facing one of its deepest crises. The electricity as well as the political power crisis has ripped away the threadbare mask of infallibility from the faces of those in leading positions in the ruling party who would have us believe that they know it all. But the exposure of the poseurs behind these masks to reveal their naivety is hardly worth writing about. Our real concerns are the palpable signs of social breakdown all around us: the ever more blatant examples of greed and corruption involving public figures, who are expected to be the role models for our youth; the unspeakable abuse of children, of the aged, and of women; the smug dishonesty, indiscipline, slothfulness of those who are paid to render public services; the lack of respect for life-preserving rules, such as those of the road; the unthinkable violence in so many communities, unknown even in conditions of conventional warfare; the boundary-crossing abuse of all manner of drugs in all layers of society; the massive number of deaths caused by AIDS, the trashing of the public health system; in short, the general mayhem and apparently suicidal chaos that ordinary people experience in their daily lives. These things are our everyday reality.

Against this bleak picture, the signs of real progress pale into insignificance and hardly feature in the media. The fact that many of our children and young people, especially in the middle class, are beginning to get on with one another without any serious hang-ups, live together, enjoy themselves together as children and youth do across the globe, this most remarkable negation of the pet prejudices the apartheid ideologues and of racists elsewhere in the world is seldom taken notice of. Yet this is one of a few things that make it possible to continue to hope and to build for a better future. Another such correction of the grey men of yesterday can be found in the many examples of successful Black professionals, managers, scientists, sportspersons, artists and the thousands of Black workers, men and women, who have emerged out of virtual slavery and illiteracy to occupy with great distinction the most responsible of jobs.

THE NATURE OF THE PRESENT CRISIS

There are many such 'good news stories' in the new South Africa. And yet, the crisis is undeniable. It is very obviously a crisis of leadership, one that derives from certain historical and structural facts. In the following paragraphs, I can do no more than point to a few of the issues that I consider to be of critical importance in this regard.

In my youth, one of the organisations that inspired me to political consciousness and activism was the Cape African Teachers' Association. It produced a regular newsletter called *The Vision* after the wisdom formulated in the King James version of the Bible: 'Where there is no vision, the people perish.'[2] With this in mind, I want to put forward a controversial but, in my view, profoundly true set of propositions by way of challenging those who are willing to think carefully and constructively about where we are headed.

To begin with, the demise of apartheid as a political-ideological system with all its attendant rigmarole of Bantustans, 'Bush Colleges', separate schools for separate 'races' and 'nations', among all its other tragic absurdities, did not lead to the kind of society that many of us, including many in the present government, had imagined a post-apartheid South Africa would be. The collapse of the Soviet Union and the end of the Cold War, among a few other historic events, for very complex reasons, put all socialists and would-be revolutionaries on the back foot, at least in the short to medium term. It allowed genuine moderates and former 'leftists' in many parts of the world to seize the opportunity and – genuinely and not so genuinely – to try to refashion the national capitalist systems they came to manage. This is what happened in South Africa as well. Instead of the socialist Azania of our dreams not even 16 years ago, apartheid-capitalism was succeeded by post-apartheid-capitalism. There was no revolution, at best what we got was no more than regime change, to use a blunt Americanism.

This stubborn fact had fundamental and undeniable consequences for all of us. In brackets, let it be said that we can argue until the cows come home about whether or not any other outcome was possible. The equally stubborn fact is that the ANC-led government was placed in charge of an unchanged, unreformed, unreconstructed capitalist state and system which had just been forced to put an end to its symbiotic relationship with the racist Pretoria regime. Suddenly, as though by some sleight of hand, our role models changed. Far from the cooperative, street committee, shop-steward, comradely ethos that had made the country both ungovernable and irreversibly democratic, we were, and are, enjoined to be 'like them', like the entrepreneurial, individualistic whiz-kids of the neoliberal epoch. In short, we, especially our young people, were, and are, encouraged to become rich without being ashamed or feeling guilty. We were led to believe that in the confines of the capitalist system where – necessarily – a small minority of very rich people dominate society in all its dimensions and serve as the never-to-be-equalled role models for the countless numbers of the poor and the very poor, all of us, if we would only make use of all the wonderful new 'opportunities', could become like 'the best of them'.

What utter nonsense! Yet, this lie is the place where the dog lies buried. It is the real source of the ruthless and barbaric behaviour that has come to define so much of South African life: it is the explanation for the taxi drivers who murder one another and kill their customers and themselves over 'ownership' of routes; it explains the syndicated hijackings of vehicles sold over the border by the faceless landlord-Mafiosi which lead to innocent citizens being violated and killed in case they get their killers caught and gaoled; it is the explanation for all the savagery I mentioned at the beginning of this chapter and of many other social illnesses besides.

Let's face it, if the capitalist system has produced anything like *ubuntu* in some European countries, in Japan and in a few other places in the world, this is largely because of the super-dividends that have accrued from colonialism, slavery, and centuries of exploitation of the labouring poor of Europe and of other places. By these means, capitalism in those countries created a very strong middle class and an upper working class that together often constitute the majority of the national population. I will not in this context discuss the relatively recent phenomenon of migrants in these same countries. These conditions will never be reproduced anywhere else in the world without planet earth imploding; it is a well-known fact that if all the people on earth were to live at the average standard of the people of the USA today, we would have to 'discover' or invent two or three more planets such as this one to generate the natural resources required.

So, this vision of individual enrichment for all South Africans is a fraudulent one. Those who kill, steal, commit fraud, want to be like 'the Americans', are either living or chasing after a lie. In the process, they have lost us the moral high ground, even the bit of it that we seemed to occupy for a few brief moments after Madiba's release from prison.

How are we to recover this ground? Can we do so?

I would not be writing these notes if I did not believe it to be possible. The worst thing we can do is to run away from the problem, either into ourselves by denying its existence, or to the UK, New Zealand, Australia, Canada, or other English-speaking parts of the Old Colonial Empire, where the aboriginal inhabitants were all but exterminated through 'the expansion of Europe'. No! We must face it head-on. We must go to the people, tell them why they are poor. We must point out to them that it is simply untrue when our Minister of Finance tells us annually in all eleven official languages in his budget speech that 'the economic fundamentals are sound'. Once they understand the basic truth about the economic fundamentals, especially about the Gini coefficient, we can together rebuild our communities and our neighbourhoods, since they will come to know the simple truth that *uhuru* without *ubuntu* is a mirage intended to blind the poor to the stark reality of the yawning gap between themselves and the rich, including the BEEs and the wannaBEEs.

We have to mobilise our people on the basis of the cooperative values of *ubuntu*, defined as sharing and caring based on the principle of sufficiency, among others. Our youth have to learn that excellence is completely compatible with the old saying that 'enough is as good as a feast'. To excel in any domain simply means that you have more than most others to share with them in that domain, just as they may have more in other domains. To excel does not have to imply that you appropriate everything to the exclusion of others in some kind of 'beggar my neighbour' spirit.

We have to go and live among the poor and undertake the essential literacy and micro-economic projects that will rekindle the flame of hope and compel government to reconsider its priorities, to abandon its GEAR strategy even if it means a drying up of foreign direct investment of 'Western' provenance and put a stop to the 'hit-and-run' investment that turns the Rand into a yo-yo and makes a mockery of 'our' national sovereignty. We will find other sympathetic but sovereign partners in Africa, Asia and Latin America. And, especially in the short term, we must hold government accountable in terms of the Constitution of the country and insist on delivery in respect of the political, social, economic and cultural rights that are enshrined in it.

The world is changing rapidly and we should not get stuck in the time warp of real capitalism as though there is no alternative. Another world *is* possible, indeed probable. The barbarism of real capitalism as we know it on the continent of Africa is not the only way.

THE WIDENING GAP BETWEEN THE ELITE AND THE MASSES

There are numerous scholarly studies of the origins and development of social inequality in what is now the Republic of South Africa. The most recent of these, Professor Terreblanche's *apologia pro via sua* is the most immediately relevant to this discussion, in that it demonstrates with unanswerable clarity the continuities as well as the minor discontinuities at the economic level between apartheid and post-apartheid South Africa.[3] Stated in a few words, his argument is that the adoption in 1996 of the neoliberal GEAR strategy by the democratically elected government under pressure from what he calls 'the corporate sector and global financial institutions', far from realising the mirage of rapid economic growth and the promised cascade of wealth and prosperity down to the urban and rural poor, has in fact led to the gap between the rich and the poor, especially between the supposedly increasing number of Black rich and the poor, becoming ever wider.

The finding is not in itself remarkable. Virtually all economic and sociological studies undertaken after 1996 confirm it, however different their points of departure, their definitions, and conceptual givens. Among many other studies, I refer to those by Terreblanche himself, Adam, Slabbert and Moodley, Seekings, Leibbrandt and Nattrass, and Simkins and Patterson.[4] Taking the changing Gini coefficient as a guide to whether economic inequality has improved or worsened, Seekings and colleagues conclude: 'The census data suggests that overall levels of inequality changed little through the second half of the twentieth century. The Gini Coefficient for gross income inequality hovered in the high 0.6s. IES [Income and Expenditure Survey] data suggests that inequality worsened between 1995 and 2000, with the Gini coefficient for *per capita* incomes rising from 0.65 to 0.69 ... or 0.70 ...'[5]

These are obviously crude impressions, but they are indicative of socio-economic trends and they are confirmed by all the studies referred to above, as well as by others. Because of the affirmative action-driven salience of 'race' in post-apartheid South Africa, and the continuing large overlap between colour and class, one of the new focuses of sociological and economic studies is what is called the narrowing of the 'inter-racial gap' between 'Black' and 'white' and between other shades of these two social 'groups', on the one hand, and the widening or deepening 'intra-racial gap' (especially within the 'Black' group), on the other. This continuing racialisation of economic and social statistics is caused by the alleged need to measure whether 'we' in the 'new' South Africa are progressing towards the deracialisation of the bourgeoisie and other ruling strata. In the present context, I shall not comment further on the implications of this deplorable practice for the future of this country.[6] Suffice it to say that all the relevant studies are agreed that the 'middle classes' and a few Black people in the 'upper class' are the real beneficiaries of the post-apartheid dispensation, and that the plight of the 'lower classes' and of the 'underclass' has deteriorated considerably, although Professor Lawrence Schlemmer found that what he called 'deep poverty' has not increased because 'the extension of social grants has indeed stopped the socio-economic rot at the lower levels of livelihoods'.[7]

There is no doubt that since 1994, and even before that decisive date, the ruling strata have been gradually deracialising. However, the impression created in many media that there is a sudden burgeoning of Black millionaires, and even Black billionaires, is a myth.[8] Schlemmer came to the conclusion that the 'Black' persons who fit into this category are no more than 'a few dozen individuals'.[9] He also exposed as a myth the notion of the 'exploding Black middle class', which has been one of the fashionable topics of the print and electronic media for some time now. Lack of space precludes a detailed analysis of his approach and of his findings. However, his conclusions warrant serious consideration if we are to arrive at a sensible assessment of the situation and of the prospective social dynamics of the next decade in South Africa. In a nutshell:

[Most] of the stereotypes and loose impressions about a burgeoning new middle class floating around in popular debate are generally gross exaggerations. Class breakdowns and associated trends are far more complex than the media hype allows for. The reality is rather bad news for those who are committed to rapid or quick fix transformation. Africans are making progress but it is slower than most people think.[10]

The crucial propositions in respect of changing class and racial stratification come from Terreblanche, who, perhaps somewhat mechanically, relates the proportionate size of the elite to the dominant economic sectors in different periods of capitalist development.[11] The dominance of 'maize and gold' until the mid-1930s, according to free-market capitalist strategists, implied a sustainable, mainly English-speaking, elite of not more than 10 per cent of the population as a whole, whereas the 'long boom' of 1934–1974 could sustain a larger elite of between 10 and 15 per cent that included some Afrikaners. Closer to our own focus here, he makes what I consider to be the decisive judgement:

> [Although] the economy grew at an unsatisfactory rate after 1974, socio-political events required the further expansion of the elite to 15 to 20 per cent of the population, incorporating some 3.5 million members of the Black bourgeoisie and a further 6 million members of the Black petit bourgeoisie.[12] Although the protagonists of free-market capitalism do not acknowledge this explicitly, this argument implies that it was only possible to include 33 per cent of the population in the upper classes by further impoverishing the lower classes.

CHIVAS AND VROTTES

This brings us to the focal issue of this chapter, that is, the social and cultural distance that has so obviously developed between the Black middle class and the Black working classes. In order not to be misunderstood, it is important that I state up-front that the caste-like distance between the white elites and the Black working class, although it ought to become integrated into social stratification studies, is significant in the present context only in so far as there is evidence of cultural osmosis at the top of the system. Indeed, working-class youth in the townships have already done so in practice. They often refer to an obviously wealthy Black person as *umlungu* (white man or white woman), thereby recognising the class shift that has taken place for a tiny section of the formerly oppressed people but expressing this in racial terms, the only discourse of social hierarchy that they know.

What I have in other essays referred to as the 'Garieb nation' is undergoing a period of change inasmuch as the African current is clearly flowing more strongly than in the past. However, the continuing relative strength of the 'European' current and its tendency towards eddying are undoubtedly the result of uncertainty among many of those labelled 'white' about the stability of the new dispensation.

Because of the significance of the culture of the Black elites, who serve willy-nilly, as models for the rest of the oppressed people, it is on this category that, albeit somewhat arbitrarily, I shall concentrate here. Personal observation, backed by numerous sociological and anthropological studies and reports, leads one to the incontrovertible conclusion that – to use a Bacchanalian comparison – the gap between those who drink *vrottes*[13] and those who have got used to drinking the best whiskies is becoming unbridgeable. South Africa, as I have said elsewhere, is becoming an ordinary country.[14] The class divide between the rich and the poor is taking on cultural features that are, necessarily, an amalgam of historical and contemporary influences. In the process, institutions such as the extended family, initiation ceremonies, *hlonipha* linguistic registers, virginity testing, and many others are being challenged or are falling into disuse. The issue is not whether this should be happening; it is an inevitable aspect of industrialisation and modernisation and has been going on in southern Africa since the mineral discoveries of the late nineteenth century. Technological advance and 'globalisation' have simply led to the acceleration of these processes. The real issue is whether it is possible to establish an African version of modernisation that is perceived by everybody as a natural outcome of capitalist development in Africa, rather than merely some bad photocopy of metropolitan European and North American 'culture'. Terreblanche speaks for all of us, and not merely those of us in South Africa, when he laments the fact that

> [on] top of the vast discrepancies in wealth [between the Black elite and the lower sixty per cent of the Black population] a thorough Americanisation [of ideological attitudes] has penetrated all segments. American habits and ostentatious consumption have become the desired yardstick by which South African progress is measured. An unashamedly elitist self-confidence pervades the new bourgeoisie. The emulation of Hollywood lifestyle by a new Ebony resembles the silly glorification of royal titles, quaint British county culture, or English dress codes by the old colonisers. It should have been no concern were it not for the squandering of public money amidst a sea of poverty.[15]

The metamorphosis of the Black elite, by which I refer to those individuals who occupy the top three deciles of the income graph, into what all such elites eventually become is a mystery and a surprise only to the naïve and to those who have a romantic notion of *ubuntu* as their hope against hope. Marx's dictum (borrowed from Horace) *de te fabula narrator* (the same story applies to you) is only too true in this anthropological puzzle. Many of us who fought in the trenches against apartheid-capitalism with many of the leading lights of this elite find it difficult to comprehend the mental structures that have made it possible for them to make such a fundamental shift in such a short period. Be that as it may, the fact is that in essence, the philosophical and economic stances these people take towards 'the masses', that is, the Great Unwashed, hardly differ from those that the *Herrenvolk* used to have towards Black people in general and towards the Black worker in particular. They, too, believe that people are differently 'endowed' and that those lucky few who are well endowed have to use their talents to the full and enrich themselves without apology to anyone. Sometimes they justify these crude expressions of their cupidity by suggesting that their actions are perfectly justifiable as long as they 'plough back' some of their spoils into the communities whence they come.

WHO'S AFRAID OF THE GINI?

Ongoing protests and even violent demonstrations against the lack of service delivery, especially by local government, are the most obvious signs of growing disillusionment and resentment on the part of the very masses who put the ANC government in office. However, the prestige of the ANC as the main instrument of liberation from apartheid, and the accumulated goodwill among all sectors of the oppressed people, are such that it would be a mistake to imagine that we have entered the oft-proclaimed pre-revolutionary situation. Even the vociferous quarrel between the components of the Tripartite Alliance, especially around the question of President Jacob Zuma's leadership, and the justified attacks on the corruption and private sector ambitions of the Black middle class, do not detract from the current stability of the government. The simple fact is that most Black people continue to believe that, given better economic conditions and more time, the present government will deliver. Those among the working and unemployed 'masses' who genuinely have lost confidence in the commitment to delivery on the part of the government are still, I have no doubt, a relatively small number of people. And the fact that there does not yet appear to be a credible alternative on the left of the political spectrum might do no more than to drive many more into a state of political apathy. On the other hand, these 'IMF riots' are the first sign of a government that could soon be placed on the defensive against social movements and even a Poor People's Party, and unless the ANC reconsiders its economic, social, and cultural policies, it might well become as embattled as is the government of President Mugabe in Zimbabwe. In short, the scissors-like movement of the Gini coefficient is something this government dare not ignore if it is to remain true even to the minimum programme of deracialisation and democratisation that brought it into office.

'The Language Question and Social Inequality'[1]

What is the language question? Why should we want to write a book on this question? Surely, we have enough 'questions' or problems to worry about without adding another one to the long list? Why don't we first try to find answers to the racial question, the land question, the housing question, the wages question, the constitutional question and to all the other important questions in our country? Why is the language question so terribly important?

The answer to this question is extremely simple and straightforward, as I hope to show. But it is as well to stress that all these different 'questions' are part and parcel of one overriding question, *viz.*, how do we abolish social inequality based on colour, class, religious beliefs, sex, language group, or on any other basis? The answer to every one of the many questions that complicate our lives in South Africa must in the final analysis help to find answers to that larger question.

Let us try to put down the answer to our question of why the issue of language is important in South Africa as clearly and logically as possible. Most people who are involved in the struggle against apartheid and racial discrimination believe that this struggle is one for national liberation or national democracy. In spite of the many differences that divide the anti-apartheid forces in South Africa, there is general agreement that in some sense we are building a nation by means of this struggle. Again, people have different ideas about what it means when we say we are building a nation. But on one thing all are agreed, *viz.*, that we are trying to bring about national unity; we are trying to encourage all our people to become conscious of the fact that they belong to one South African/Azanian nation.

In South Africa at this moment, building the nation means, among other things, fighting against racism and against ethnic divisions or ethnic consciousness. That is to say, the promotion of non-racialism, anti-racism, and anti-ethnicism or anti-tribalism is to a large extent the meaning of the phrase 'building the South African/Azanian nation'. For too many people unfortunately, words like non-racialism and anti-racism are no more than political slogans to be shouted at the top of one's voice in and out of season. This holier-than-thou attitude has made people forget that being non-racial or anti-racist is much more than not being this or being against that. Too few people realise that being non-racial or anti-racist means being *for* something. In our case in South Africa, even if it means more, it certainly means no less than being for a single nation and, therefore, for national unity.

Now, it is a fact that most people. have a rather vague but nonetheless particular idea of what a nation is. Probably most people in South Africa today believe that the people who are part of the nation have got to speak the same language. This idea that nations are groups of people who speak a particular language under particular historical and geographical circumstances has come down to us from the experience of European nationalist movements during the last 200 years or so. In Western Europe – we think of Portugal, Spain, Great Britain, France, Holland, and others – it is generally true that the vast majority of the people in the respective countries speak the national language, i.e. Portuguese, Spanish, English, French, Dutch, etc.

However, let us pause for a moment and consider the implications of accepting this point of view! Let us leave aside the difficult question of what 'a particular language' means.[2] As soon as we ask ourselves: does this mean that the people of most African states are not 'nations', since they speak many languages? it becomes clear that there is something wrong with this Eurocentric definition of 'a nation'. Surely, Zambians and Nigerians, Kenyans and Zaireans, Angolans and Algerians are nations and not just conglomerations of language groups?

Of course, there is a real basis for this widespread belief in the monolingualism or language exclusiveness of nations. The simple fact of the matter, after all, is that if people cannot speak to one another they cannot in fact constitute a nation. *The crucial question, however, is whether they have to speak to one another in one particular language in order to be a nation.* Is it not in fact a matter of communication rather than of this or that particular language? To put the matter differently: to be a nation, the individuals who make up that nation have got to be able, among other things, to communicate with one another. They need not, however, do so in any specific language. All that is necessary is that they are able to switch to the most appropriate language demanded by a particular situation.

There is more than enough evidence available that this is indeed what happens in most countries in the world today. Most of the nations of the modem world are in fact multilingual nations, i.e. the people who make up these nations have different home languages. In this regard, a very important book entitled *Imagined Communities* was published a few years ago by the English author Benedict Anderson. There, he shows very clearly that modem nations are usually not monolingual and that

> Language is not an instrument of exclusion: in principle, anyone can learn any language ... Print languages is what invents nationalism, not a particular language per se ... In a world in which the nation state is the overwhelming norm, all this means that nations can now be imagined without linguistic communality.

What we are saying, then, is that if we are serious about such ideas as non-racialism, anti-racism, anti-ethnicism, and others, we must, among other things, seek a democratic solution to the language question in our country. Racial prejudice and racism are without any doubt reinforced and maintained by language barriers (as well as by group areas, separate schools, separate amenities, etc!). If we want to fight against racial prejudice and racism then we have, among other things, to break down the language barriers. How to do this so as to bring about maximum unity among our people is the meaning of a democratic solution to the language question in South Africa.

The matter is urgent because the present government – like its predecessors – is pursuing a policy that goes in exactly the opposite direction. It is no exaggeration to say that in South Africa today a historic decision has to be made by the people. The choice, in a nutshell, which confronts us is whether we are going to solve our problems in a federation or confederation of ethnic states based on language and 'racial' groups or in a non-racial, non-ethnic unitary state. In the final chapter of this book, we shall return to this point. For the moment, it is necessary only to establish the fact that the National Party and all those to the right of it link 'race', language, and 'culture' in such a way that they inevitably and deliberately pursue the division. Language Policy and National Unity in South Africa/Azania not the unification, of the people of South Africa. As we shall see in the next chapter, their idea of a 'nation' is based on the experience of certain European peoples in the eighteenth and nineteenth centuries. Hence, language, nation, and culture are for them different aspects of one and the same group of people. Quite logically, they end up with the absurd idea that in South Africa today, there are some twelve nations as well as two nations-to-be. Since these ideas accord very well with the economic and political domination of the white minority in this country, it is a perfect ideological instrument to sow division among the oppressed and exploited people. It is a tried and tested weapon of the rulers against the majority of the people.

Clearly, the oppressed people have to forge weapons out of the same materials so that they can defend themselves and break the domination of the ruling group. It is against this background that the language question in South Africa has to be considered. There is a wealth of literature on this question in many parts of the world. The sociology of language has become an accepted branch of the social sciences and many insights have been gained that are helpful in understanding our own situation. Although I shall not, generally speaking, concern myself with points of theory in this essay, it is nonetheless informed by a serious attempt to understand the relationships between language, class, exploitation, domination, nationalism, education, culture, and ideology.[3]

Bibliography

Selected Publications of Neville Alexander

The repository for The Neville Alexander Archives is at the University of Cape Town Libraries: Special Collections (Manuscripts and Archives): https://atom.lib. uct.ac.za/index.php/neville-alexander-papers.

BOOKS

1979. *One Azania, One Nation: The National Question in South Africa*. London: Zed Press.

1983. *Three Essays on Namibian History*. Windhoek: Namibian Review Publications.

1985. *Sow the Wind: Contemporary Speeches*. Braamfontein: Skotaville Publishers.

1989. *Language Policy and National Unity in South Africa/Azania*. Cape Town: Buchu Books.

1990. *Education and the Struggle for National Liberation in South Africa*. Braamfontein: Skotaville Publishers.

1993. *Robben Island Dossier: 1964–1974. Report to the International Community*. Cape Town: UCT Press and Buchu Books.

1993. *Some Are More Equal Than Others. Essays on the Transition in South Africa*. Cape Town: Buchu Books.

1994. *South Africa: Which Road to Freedom?* San Francisco: Walnut Publishing Co, Inc.

2002. *An Ordinary Country. Issues in the Transition from Apartheid to Democracy in South Africa*. Pietermaritzburg: University of Natal Press.

2013. *Thoughts on the New South Africa*. Braamfontein: Jacana Media.

2014. (with Arnulf von Scheliha) *Language Policy and the Promotion of Peace; African and European Case Studies*. Pretoria: Unisa Press.

CHAPTERS, ARTICLES, ESSAYS, AND BOOKLETS

1958. 'The Universities'. *The Student*, May. Produced for the 1st Annual Conference of the Cape Peninsula Students' Union, Crawford, Cape Town. May 1958.

1958. 'Education in a Modern World'. *The Student*, November. Newsletter of the Cape Peninsula Student Union, Cape Town.

1964. *Studien zum Stilwandel in Dramatischen Werk Gerhart Hauptmanns*. Stuttgart: J. B. Metzlersche Verlagsbuchhandlung.

1986. 'Approaches to the National Question in South Africa'. *Transformation*, 1: 63–95.

1989. 'Liberation Pedagogy in the South African Context'. In C. Criticos (ed), *Experiential Learning in Formal and Non-Formal Education*. Durban: Media Resource Centre, Dept. of Education, University of Natal, Durban.

1989. *The Language Question*. Cape Town: Institute for Public Policy (UCT).

1990. 'Educational Strategies for a New South Africa'. In J. Samuel and B. Nasson (eds), *Education: From Poverty to Liberty*. (Vol 2 series of reports of the Second Carnegie Inquiry into Poverty in South Africa). Cape Town: David Philip.

1990. 'The Language Question'. In R. Schrire (ed), *Critical Choices for South African Society*. Cape Town: Oxford University Press.

1992. 'Robben Island: A Site of Struggle'. In N. Penn, H. Deacon, and N. Alexander, *Robben Island: The Politics of Rock and Sand*. Cape Town: Institute for Public Policy (UCT).

1992. 'Language Planning from Below'. In R. Herbert (ed), *Language and Society in Africa. The Theory and Practice of Sociolinguistics*. Johannesburg: Witwatersrand University Press.

1992. 'The National Political Situation. The Real South Africa'. Address delivered at the Third National Conference of the Workers' Organisation for Socialist Action, April 1993. Cape Town.

1992. 'Africa and the New World Order'. *Mitteilungen*, Heft 60.

1994. 'The National Forum'. In I. Liebenberg, B. Nel, F. Lortan, and G. Van der Westhuizen (eds), *The Long March: The Story of the Struggle For Liberation in South Africa*. Pretoria: HAUM, pp. 199–204.

1995. 'Race, Ethnicity and Nation in Post-Apartheid South Africa'. South Asia Bulletin. *Comparative Studies of South Asia, Africa and the Middle East*, XV (1): 5–11.

1995. 'Mainstreaming by Confluence: The Multilingual Context of Literature in South Africa'. *World Literature Today*, 70(1): 9–11.

1996. *Towards a National Language Plan for South Africa*. Final Report of the Language Plan Task Group (Langtag). Pretoria: State Language Services.

1998. 'Building a New Nation: Promoting Unity and Accommodating Diversity'. In M. Cross, Z. Mkwanazi-Twala, and G. Klein (eds), *Dealing with Diversity in South African Education. A Debate on the Politics of a National Curriculum*. Cape Town: Juta.

1996. 'No Need for the God Hypothesis'. In C. Villa-Vicencio (ed), *The Spirit of Freedom: South African Leaders on Religion and Politics*. Berkeley, Los Angeles, and Oxford: University of California.

1999. (with Karen Press) *Investigating Economics*. Grade 7 Learner's Book. Kenwyn: Juta.

2000. 'Human Rights in the African Context: A Cross-Cultural Perspective'. In W. Krull (ed) *Debates on Issues of Our Common Future*. Weilerswist: Velbrück Wissenschaft, pp. 13–29.

2000. 'Why the Nguni and Sotho Languages in South Africa Should be Harmonised'. In K. Deprez and T. Du Plessis (eds), *Multilingualism and Government. Studies in Language Policy in South Africa*. Pretoria: Van Schaik Publishers, pp. 171–175.

2000. *English Unassailable but Unattainable: The Dilemma of Language Policy in South African Education.* PRAESA Occasional Paper No. 3. Cape Town: PRAESA.

2000. 'Manuel Castells and the New South Africa'. *Social Dynamics*, 26(1): 18–36.

2000. (compiler) *Educational Innovation in Post-Colonial Africa.* Selected Papers from the Panafrican Colloquium, 1994. Cape Town: PRAESA.

2001. 'Prospects for a Nonracial Future in South Africa'. In Charles V. Hamilton, Lynn Huntley, Neville Alexander, Antonio Sérgio, Alfredo Guimarães, and Wilmot James (eds), *Beyond Racism: Race and Inequality in Brazil, South Africa, and the United States.* London: Lynne Rienner Publishers.

2003. 'The Moment of Manoeuvre: "Race", Ethnicity, and Nation in Post-Apartheid South Africa'. In Vasant Kaiwar and Sucheta Mazumdar (eds), *Antinomies of Modernity: Essays on Race, Orient, Nation:* 174–189. New York: Duke University Press.

2003. *The African Renaissance and the Use of African Languages in Tertiary Education.* PRAESA Occasional Papers No. 13. Cape Town: PRAESA.

2003. Foreword. In T. Jelloun, *Racism Explained to My Daughter.* Cape Town: New Africa Books and PRAESA.

2003. *Implications of Brown v Board of Education. A Post-Apartheid South African Perspective.* PRAESA Occasional Papers No. 20. Cape Town: PRAESA.

2003. *Language Educational Policy, National and Sub-National Identities in South Africa.* Strasbourg: Council of Europe.

2004. *Implications of Brown vs Board of Education: A Post-Apartheid South African Perspective.* PRAESA Occasional Papers, no. 20. Cape Town: Project for the Study of Alternative Education in South Africa.

2006. 'Language Policy, Symbolic Power and the Democratic Responsibility of the Post-Apartheid University'. In R. Pithouse (ed), *Asinamali: University Struggles in Post-Apartheid South Africa.* Trenton and Asmara: Africa World Press, Inc.

2006. *After Harare. Introduction to Unesco. Language Policies in Africa.* Final Report on the Intergovernmental Conference on Language Policies in Africa. Paris: Unesco.

2006. 'We Should Not Compare Ourselves With America'. Interview with Neville Alexander. Hu*mboldt Kosmos*, 87: 28–29.

2007. 'Ten Years after Apartheid: The State of Nation-Building in South Africa'. In S. Dorman, D. Hammett, and P. Nugent (eds), *Making Nations, Creating Strangers. States and Citizenship in Africa.* Leiden and Boston: Brill.

2008. 'An Illuminating Moment. Background to the Azanian Manifest'. In A. Mngxitama, and A. Alexander (eds), *Biko Lives: Contemporary Black History.* London: Palgrave Macmillan.

2008. 'An Illuminating Moment: Background to the Azanian Manifesto. In A. Mngxitama, A. Alexander, and N. Gibson (eds), *Biko Lives! Contesting the Legacies of Steve Biko.* New York: Palgrave Macmillan, 157–170.

2010. 'Schooling in and for the New South Africa'. *Focus*, 56: 7–13.

2011. (with S. Vally) *Racism and Education.* Johannesburg: Centre for Education Rights and Transformation.

2012. 'Let Us Return to the Source! In Quest of a Humanism of the 21st Century'. In H. Vally and M. Isaacson (eds), *Enough is A Feast: A Tribute to Dr. Neville Alexander*. Johannesburg: Foundation for Human Rights, pp. 53–60.

2012. 'The Unresolved National Question in South Africa'. In N. Jeenah (ed). *Pretending Democracy: Israel, an Ethnocratic State*. Craighall: Afro-Middle East Centre.

2014. 'Nation Building and Language in the New South Africa'. In M. Pütz (ed), *Discrimination Through Language in Africa? Perspectives on the Namibian Experience*. Berlin and Boston: De Gruyter Mouton, pp. 29–43.

Notes

THE LIFE AND TIMES OF NEVILLE ALEXANDER

1. The basis for the Union was established by a whites-only convention in Durban in 1908 and an act of the British Parliament in 1909. The Union assisted a developing relationship between Afrikaner politicians and mining capitalists. Black people were excluded from political power although they were taxed and policed more efficiently.

2. The miners were angered by the Chamber of Mines announcement in December 1921 that it planned to replace semi-skilled white workers with lower-paid Black workers.

3. Busch, B., Busch, L., and Press, K. 2014. Interviews with Neville Alexander: The Power of Languages against the Language of Power. Pietermaritzburg: University of KwaZulu-Natal Press, p. 16.

4. Villa-Vicencio, Charles. 1996. 'Neville Alexander: No Need for the God Hypothesis'. In The Spirit of Freedom: South African Leaders on Religion and Politics. Berkeley: University of California Press, p. 8.

5. Alexander intended to study Bertolt Brecht but was advised against this since the books by and about Brecht were either banned or not readily available. Alexander explains: 'So even though I wanted to work on Brecht, my professor in Cape Town, Professor Rosteutscher, partly for ideological reasons but also because of the banning said, "Look, it's not going to be fertile, it won't work because you won't have access to the material". The next "best" was Hauptmann, as a socialist. I wanted to work on a radical dramatist' (Busch, Busch, and Press, 2014, p. 59).

6. Czada, Roland. 2012. 'Sehnsucht nach Azania. Neville Alexander's Leben und Werk für ein anti-rassistisches Südafrika'. In Osnabrücker Jahrbuch Frieden und Wissenschaft 19. Göttingen: V&R Unipress, pp. 193–204.

7. Those arrested included Alexander's sister Dorothy Alexander, Dulcie September, Leslie van der Heyden, Elizabeth van der Heyden, Marcus Solomon, Fikile Bam, Lionel Davis, Doris van der Heyden, Don Davis, and Gordon Hendricks. They were all in their 20s, and their sentences ranged between five and ten years.

8. For his Honours essays, researched and written in prison, Alexander gains close to maximum marks on the philosophy of history. His essays are still used as a model by Unisa's history department (see Busch Lucijan, and Press, 2014, p. 83; Dollie, Na-iem. 2015. 'Dialogical Narratives: Reading Neville Alexander's Writings' (Phd thesis, UCT, pp. 50–53).

9. Dick, L. Archie. 2018. 'Learning from the Alexander Defence Committee Archives'. In Aziz Choudry and Salim Vally (eds), Reflections on Knowledge, Learning and Social Movements: History's Schools. Abingdon: Routledge.

10. Ibid., p. 48. Commenting on the campaigning work of Connie Kirby, Dick writes: 'In one instance, she attached a letter from C.L.R. James to the Times Literary Supplement about Neville's literary work that also mentions the Alexander Defence Committee in England', pp. 48–49.

11. Members of Black Consciousness groups, together with members of the National Liberation Front (see Alexander's essay in Part II ('Steve Biko's Last Attempt at Uniting the Liberation Forces') and members of the Transkei-based People's United Front for the Liberation of South Africa (PUFLSA) attempt to plan united actions against the Bantustans. Lungisile Ntsebeza, a key member of the PUFLSA mentions in his address at the tenth Alexander Commemorative Conference that, 'five of us, my brother Dumisa (accused 1), Meluxolo Silinga (accused 3), Matthew Goniwe (accused 4 – murdered in 1985 by the security police) and Michael Mgobozi (accused 5), with me as accused 2, were on trial in Mthatha under the Suppression of Communism Act … There is little doubt in my mind that Steve Biko knew about our activities prior to our arrest and followed our trial. In addition, the late Fikile Bam, who is reported to have made attempts to facilitate a meeting between Biko and Neville, was held in detention in the Mthatha prison towards the end of 1976, the same prison we were also held in. We spent most of our evenings talking to each other about our various experiences. Bam knew about us and our attempts to establish a United Front' (Ntsebeza, Lungisile. 2022. 'Back to the Basics: Reflections on the Politics of the 1960s and 1970s', tenth anniversary lecture on Neville Alexander at the UNISA Campus in Parow, Western Cape on Friday, 11 November 2022).

12. Villa-Vicencio, 1996; see also Alexander, 2008. 'Steve Biko's Last Attempt to Unite the Liberation Forces'. Unpublished Address. Rhodes University, September 2007; interview with Armien Abrahams (5 December 2022). Biko, Jones, and Bam stayed at Abraham's house in Athlone, Cape Town, and were ferried to Alexander's home by Bam.

13. The National Forum Committee included then Bishop Desmond Tutu, General Secretary of the South African Council of Churches; Lybon Mabasa, then President of the Azanian People's Organisation (AZAPO); and Saths Cooper, a close comrade of Steve Biko and former prominent member of the South African Students' Organisation (SASO) and the Black People's Convention (BPC).

14. An explanatory note on the terminology used in this book is important. The apartheid state marshalled a taxonomy of racial classifications besides the four main categories of the apartheid registrar's 'population registration groups' namely, 'African', 'white', 'Coloured', and 'Indian' (see Alexander's article 'Nation and Ethnicity in South Africa' in Part II of this collection). South Africans were separated and deemed to belong to one or another group often in an arbitrary manner. The present state continues using these categorisations. The Black Consciousness Movement in the 1970s rejected

and actively opposed these classifications as well as the collective phrase 'non-white' preferring instead the term 'Black' as a political term for all who were oppressed. Despite these efforts, the apartheid terms took on a salience and an acceptance, both under apartheid and after, amongst many people classified in this way by the apartheid regime. While we reject the discredited and debunked notion of 'race' as a biological entity, we use the apartheid categories for pragmatic explanatory purposes and use 'race' as a social construct. We signal our discomfort with the apartheid categories using quotes and embrace the term 'Black' when all oppressed groups are referred to.

15. Alexander, N. 2013. *Thoughts on the New South Africa*. Auckland Park: Jacana Media.

INTRODUCTION

1. Cabral, A. 1973. *Return to the Source: Selected Speeches of Amilcar Cabral*. New York: Monthly Review Press.
2. Alexander, N. 1985. 'Nation and Ethnicity in South Africa'. In *Sow the Wind*. Johannesburg: Skotaville, p. x.
3. He writes as follows about the veiled and sometimes explicit threats against him by his political detractors in the preface to *Sow the Wind* (Ibid.): 'In these times of "night and fog" when mysterious death or imprisonment can so suddenly remove one from the scene, it is perhaps an act of wisdom to publish and be damned. I have no doubt that what I have said and the way I have sometimes said it will give rise to much discussion and disagreement. That is as it should be, at least in my opinion, provided that those who disagree with me go for my ideas, criticise them and put forward feasible alternatives. The sectarian and totalitarian hubris that seduces some people who disagree with one's ideas to brand one immediately as "an enemy of South Africa" or as "an enemy of the people" is without any doubt the greatest danger to our liberation struggle. My appeal to such people is to allow history to decide the questions on which we disagree fundamentally. My appeal to them is to remember the words of the prophet, "For they have sown the wind, and they shall reap the whirlwind"'.
4. In an interview Alexander describes 'house arrest': 'Being under house arrest meant we could go out to work, but otherwise, from six in the evening to six in the morning we had to be at home. And also on Sundays and public holidays we couldn't leave the house. And then of course you could only be in the company of one person at a time other than the family ... so no meetings could take place' (Busch, B., Busch, L., and Press, K. 2014. *Interviews with Neville Alexander: The Power of Language Against the Language of Power*. Pietermaritzburg: University of Kwa-Zulu Natal Press).
5. Alexander, N. 1958. 'The Universities'. *The Student*, May. Produced for the 1st Annual Conference of the Cape Peninsula Students' Union, Crawford, Cape Town.
6. Alexander, N. 1958b. 'Education in a Modern World'. *The Student*, November. Newsletter of the Cape Peninsula Student Union, Cape Town, p. 12.

7. Alexander, N. 2013. *Thoughts on the New South Africa.* Johannesburg: Jacana Media, p. 40.
8. Alexander, N. 2012. 'Let Us Return to the Source! In Quest of a Humanism of the 21st Century'. In H. Vally and M. Isaacson (eds), *Enough is A Feast: A Tribute to Dr. Neville Alexander.* Johannesburg: Foundation for Human Rights, p. 60.
9. Alexander, N. 2013. *Thoughts on the New South Africa.* Johannesburg: Jacana Media, p. viii.
10. Ibid., viii–ix.
11. Ibid., p. viii.
12. Gramsci, A. 1977. *Antonio Gramsci: Selections from Political Writings (1910–1920).* Q. Hoare (ed). London: Lawrence and Wishart.
13. Alexander, 1985, p. viii.
14. Ibid.
15. No Sizwe (Neville Alexander). 1979. *One Azania, One Nation: The National Question in South Africa.* London: Zed Press.
16. Busch, Busch, and Press. 2014, pp. 103–104.
17. No Sizwe. 1979, p. viii.
18. Ibid., p. 4.
19. Alexander argues that 'bourgeois sociology' with its debilitating definitions, required a clarification of misused concepts such as 'race', 'nation', 'nationalism', 'ethnic group', 'color caste', and 'class' (No Sizwe, 1979, p. 7).
20. From the early 1950s, Alexander was profoundly influenced by the views of Ashley Montagu (Montagu, A. 1942. *Man's Most Dangerous Myth: The Fallacy of Race.* Lanham: Rowman & Littlefield). For a more contemporary analysis of the illusions of 'race' see Fields, K.E. and Fields B.J. 2022. *Racecraft: The Soul of Inequality in American Life.* London: Verso. They use a quote by Montagu in the epigram to their book, *'Race' is the Witchcraft of Our Time* (Ibid., p. 1).
21. Ibid., p. viii.
22. Alexander, 2013, p. vii.
23. Motala, E. and Vally, S. 2017. 'Neville Alexander and the National Question'. In E. Webster (ed), *The Unresolved National Question: Left Thought under Apartheid.* Johannesburg: Wits University Press.
24. Alexander, N. 1986. Approaches to the National Question in South Africa. *Transformation,* 1: 63–95. p. 67.
25. Anderson, B. 1983. *Imagined Communities.* London: Verso.
26. Alexander, 1986, 1: 63–95. p. 68.
27. Ibid., p. 69.
28. Anderson, 1983, p. 15.
29. 'Our struggle for national liberation is directed against the system of racial capitalism, which holds the people of Azania in bondage for the benefit of the small minority of white capitalists and their allies, the white workers and the reactionary sections of the black middle class. The struggle against apartheid is no more than the point of departure for our liberation efforts. Apartheid will be eradicated with the system of racial capitalism' (The Azanian Mani-

festo. 1983. Reprinted as Appendix A in Alexander, 2008. 'An Illuminating Moment. Background to the Azanian Manifest'. In A. Mngxitama and A. Alexander (eds), *Biko Lives: Contemporary Black History*. London: Palgrave Macmillan, pp. 168–169).

30. Alexander, 1986, p. 71.
31. Drew, A. and Binns, D. 1992. 'Prospects for Socialism in South Africa: An Interview with Neville Alexander'. *The Journal of Communist Studies and Transitional Politics*, 8(4): 251–274; Clarno, A. and Vally, S. 2022. 'The Context of Struggle: Racial Capitalism and Political Praxis'. *Ethnic and Racial Studies* 45(18).
32. The phrase 'racial capitalism' first emerged in the context of the anti-apartheid and southern African liberation struggles in the 1970s, used by activists largely aligned to groups ideologically to the left of the ANC/South African Communist Party (SACP) alliance. The SACP favoured an analysis and strategy based on the phrase 'colonialism of a special type' and promoted a 'two-stage struggle' – first against apartheid and then for socialism. The editors of the US-based *Black Agenda Report* write that those who supported the racial capitalism thesis 'rejected liberal analyses that believed the racial inequalities of Apartheid could be reformed through the organisation of a better capitalism, and they were critical of Marxist analyses that insufficiently attended to questions of race. At the same time, the use of racial capitalism became a way of bringing a stronger class analysis into the vocabularies of Black Consciousness. We see, then, powerful deployments of the term 'racial capitalism' in Martin Legassick and David Hemson's pamphlet *Foreign Investment and the Reproduction of Racial Capitalism in South Africa* (1976), in the work of Africana Studies professor James A. Turner's research on US investment in South Africa in the *Western Journal of Black Studies* (1976), in Bernard Magubane's attacks on liberal analysis of the South African situation in the *Review* of the Fernand Braudel Center (1977) ... Among the most important figures using the term racial capitalism in the South African context was Neville Alexander' (www.blackagendareport.com/racial-capitalism-black-liberation-and-south-africa)). See also Clarno and Vally, 2022.
33. Drew and Binns, 1992, p. 257.
34. Similarly, Kelley refers to it as 'a kind of manufactured debate over who owns racial capitalism, who coined it first, and what is the lineage of the term' Kelley, D. G. R. 2021. Keynote Address, 'The Struggle Against Racial Capitalism in the USA, SA, and Palestine' 9th Neville Alexander Commemorative Conference, held virtually and hosted by the Centre for Education Rights and Transformation and the Centre for Sociological Research and Practice, University of Johannesburg, 30 March 2021.
   Kelley notes that the term began to proliferate after Alexander's death and in the last few years of Cedric Robinson's life (he died in 2016) and that for 25 years after Robinson's Black Marxism was published 'there was nary a word about racial capitalism here in the US which makes sense since the term is only used four times in his book and once as a subtitle ... this is followed by

a kind of dramatic pivot after 2014 toward his use of racial capitalism which coincides with both new directions in black studies as well as the kind of sudden interest in the study of capitalism that is sort of the new capitalist studies and this led to a kind of explosion of scholarship, conferences symposia, debates, which elevated racial capitalism as an idea to be reckoned with. And yet, a lesson here is that neither man was trying to build a career on the discovery of racial capitalism and both paid a price for bucking conventional wisdom and hegemonic ideas. In fact, clearly Neville Alexander paid the greatest price for the positions that he took, becoming a target of the ruling party both before formal apartheid as we know it ended and after, so this leads me to the main point I wish to make in that Robinson and Alexander actually have much more in common than we might think especially on the way we think about National Liberation as a class question as historical context or framework for class struggle they both recognize national identities not as chimera but historical and they both reveal in their work exactly how racial capitalism deploys what Neville Alexander calls racial fundamentalism, that is racism, ethnocentrism and tribalism to exploit the working class to extract surplus and to arrest national development' (Ibid.).

35. Alexander, N. 1990. *Education and the Struggle for National Liberation in South Africa*. Johannesburg: Skotaville.
36. Alexander, N. 1985. *Sow the Wind: Contemporary Speeches*. Braamfontein: Skotaville Publishers, p. vii.
37. Alexander, 1990, p. 6.
38. Ibid., p. 7.
39. Ibid., p. 12.
40. Ibid., p. 13 (emphasis in original).
41. Ibid., p. 24.
42. Alexander, N. 2010. 'Schooling in and for the New South Africa'. *Focus* 56: 7–13. p. 7.
43. Ibid., p. 7.
44. Zinn, A. (ed). 2016. *Non-Racialism in South Africa: The Life and Times of Neville Alexander*. Stellenbosch & Port Elizabeth: African Sun Media & Centre for the Advancement of Non-Racialism and Democracy.
45. Porteus, K. A. 2016. 'Neville Alexander: Being Human (and Enough) is Enough'. Keynote Address at the Conference on 'Education for a New Humanism in the 21st Century'. In A. Zinn (ed), *Non-Racialism in South Africa: The Life and Times of Neville Alexander*. Stellenbosch & Port Elizabeth: African Sun Media & Centre for the Advancement of Non-Racialism and Democracy, p. 44.
46. Busch, B. 2014. 'Introduction'. In B. Busch, L. Busch, and K. Press, *Interviews with Neville Alexander: The Power of Language Against the Language of Power*. Pietermaritzburg: University of Kwa-Zulu Natal Press.
47. Ibid., p. 3.
48. Ramadiro, B. 2018. 'The Influence of Alexander on the South African Language Debate'. In T. Kamusella and F. Ndhlovu (eds), The Social and

Political History of Southern Africa's Languages. London: Palgrave Macmillan, pp. xxi–xxxiv, xxvii.

49. Busch, 2014, p. 3.
50. Ibid., p. 4.
51. Ibid., p. 5.
52. Ramadiro, B. 2016. 'Language, Culture and National Consciousness: The Thoughts of Neville Alexander'. In A. Zinn (ed), *Non-Racialism in South Africa: The Life and Times of Neville Alexander*. Stellenbosch & Port Elizabeth: African Sun Media & Centre for the Advancement of Non-Racialism and Democracy.
53. Alexander, 2013, p. 74.
54. Ibid., p. 125.
55. Motala, E. and Vally, S. 2021. 'Neville Alexander's Warning'. *New Frame*, 21 July. www.newframe.com/neville-alexanders-warning/.
56. Alexander, N. 2004. *Implications of Brown vs Board of Education: A Post-Apartheid South African Perspective*. PRAESA Occasional Papers, no. 20. Cape Town: Project for the Study of Alternative Education in South Africa.
57. Ibid., 2004, p. 4.
58. Ibid., p. 13.
59. Alexander, Neville. 2014. 'Nation Building and Language in the New South Africa'. In Martin Pütz (ed), *Discrimination through Language in Africa? Perspectives on the Namibian Experience*. Berlin and Boston: De Gruyter Mouton, pp. 29–43. https://doi.org/10.1515/9783110906677.29. p. 38.
60. The Gariep River – named the Orange River during the colonial and apartheid eras – is the longest river in South Africa, with several major tributaries. It was renamed after 1994 to reflect the original name given to it by the indigenous people of Southern Africa: 'Gariep' is the Khoekhoe word for 'river'.
61. Alexander, N. 2001. Prospects for a Nonracial Future in South Africa. In Charles V. Hamilton, Lynn Huntley, Neville Alexander, Antonio Sérgio, Alfredo Guimarães, and Wilmot James (eds), *Beyond Racism: Race and Inequality in Brazil, South Africa, and the United States*. London: Lynne Rienner Publishers, p. 486.
62. Alexander was cognisant that the denial and distortion of African history was one of the objectives of the apartheid Bantu Education system, which had among its many negative features the promotion of a narrow Eurocentric history curriculum. With colleagues at the South African Committee for Higher Education (SACHED) Trust, where he was the director of its Cape Town centre, he developed an African history course in 1980. Over a period of 33 weeks, he was the chief author of a series of articles on Africa and the struggle against colonialism for *Learning Post*, a supplement in the *Sunday Post* newspaper. Although most issues were banned, regular feedback and readership figures demonstrated that the material was read by hundreds of thousands of people and was often used for collective learning. A compilation of the articles was republished in 2019 (Motala, E., Vally, S., and Samuel, J. (eds). 2019. 'Foreword'. In *African History and the Struggle to Decolo-*

nise Africa. Republication of the *Learning Post* African History course first published in 1980. Johannesburg: Centre for Education Rights and Transformation, University of Johannesburg).
63. Mishra, P. 2017. *Age of Anger*. London: Allen Lane.
64. Alexander, 2013, p. 45 (emphasis in original).

INTRODUCTION TO PART I

1. www.pbs.org/wgbh/pages/frontline/shows/mandela/interviews/alexander.html
2. Kathrada, A, 2012. 'Memories of the Lime Quarry and Gratitude for Lessons from the "Teacher's Teacher"'. Speech at Memorials to Alexander, Belgravia High School, 8 September 2012 and University of Johannesburg, 15 September 2012. See also Desai, A. 2014. *Reading Revolution: Shakespeare on Robben Island*, Pretoria: Unisa Press.
3. Kathrada, A. 2004. *Memoirs*. Cape Town: Zebra Press.
4. The original booklet can be viewed here: https://atom.lib.uct.ac.za/index.php/za-uct-bc1538-c-c1-c1-306

ROBBEN ISLAND DOSSIER: 1964–1974

1. Alexander, Neville. 1993. *Robben Island Dossier: 1964–1974. Report to the International Community*. Cape Town: UCT Press and Buchu Books.
2. Andrew Masondo was a lecturer at Fort Hare University College before being imprisoned between 1964 and 1976. After he was released he underwent military training in Uganda, and became the ANC political commissar in Uganda. Dennis Brutus graduated from Fort Hare University in 1947 and worked as a teacher and writer in Port Elizabeth. He was an organiser of the Malmesbury Convention of 1961, which sought unity between Coloureds and Africans. Dismissed from his teaching post and banned, Brutus continued his political activities with NUSAS before being arrested in Mozambique after leaving South Africa secretly. In 1963 he was sentenced to 18-months imprisonment on Robben Island and, on his release, was placed under house arrest. Brutus left South Africa in 1966, first re-establishing the South African Non-Racial Open Committee for Sport in London, and then accepting a professorship in English at Northwestern University in the USA.
3. Whose sinister personality is so disturbing that he is described in detail in Addendum Three of this document.
4. The Terrorism Act of 1967 was a direct response to SWAPO's initiation of armed struggle in Namibia. The Act introduced penalties ranging from a minimum of five years imprisonment to the death sentence for acts of terrorism – defined as activities ranging from armed struggle to causing feelings of hostility between whites and blacks. The Act was made retrospective to 1962, allowed for indefinite detention without trial and placed the onus of proof on the accused.

5. While in exile in Cape Town from Namibia, Toivo ja Toivo was a founding member of the Ovamboland People's Organisation (OPO). Deported to Ovamboloand, ja Toivo continued to organise for the OPO until his arrest in 1966 and imprisonment in Pretoria. After being tortured, he was tried the following year under the newly promulgated Terrorism Act, which placed the burden of proof on the accused. Despite international condemnation of the trial, Ja Toivo was sentenced to 20 years imprisonment and transferred to Robben Island in 1968. Released in 1984, he was appointed General Secretary of SWAPO in 1986.

6. Jafta Masemola was a founder member of the PAC. Masemola worked for the PAC Youth League in Atteridgeville (near Pretoria) before launching the PAC's military operations in South Africa. Jailed for more than 26 years, he was South Africa's longest serving political prisoner after Nelson Mandela. Masemola died in a car accident shortly after his release in 1989. Chiloane, a student and PAC member, was imprisoned on Robben Island for 15 years. He subsequently left the country and now resides in England.

7. See Addendum Four of this document on the case of Don Mantangela.

8. Louis Mtshizana studied as a lawyer and joined the Unity Movement. He was banned from practicing law and later imprisoned on Robben Island for ten years. He later became a prosecutor for the Matanzima Government in the Transkei.

9. Staff were trained at the Prison College for six weeks to two months if they had completed military service or had been in the police force. School leavers were trained for six months.

10. 'Bandiete', 'kaffers', 'Hotnots', and 'Koellies' are terms of racial abuse, polar opposites to polite forms of address.

11. 'Meneer' is a respectful form of address, while 'baas' is a term reflecting complete subservience on the part of the speaker. 'Inkosi' (literally, 'Chief') has also become a form of subservient address of Blacks towards whites.

12. The National Party was elected to power in 1948, and introduced major legislation that systematically entrenched racial discrimination as the basis for the organisation and functioning of the South African state.

13. In 1964, the Delegate General of the International Red Cross was invited to visit Robben Island. The publication of the Red Cross report in 1966 led the South African government to claim that it was exonerated from serious criticism, and that it had nothing to hide. In contrast, the International Defence and Aid Fund pointed out that the report did, in fact, reveal major abuses. Mr Senn was the first IRC representative to visit Robben Island.

14. See Addendum Six of this document.

15. In 1967, the South African Parliament passed the Terrorism Act, intended to supplement the earlier Suppression of Communism Act. The Terrorism Act was made retrospective to 1962, and stipulated that a person charged with 'terroristic activities': should be found guilty unless he proved himself innocent. On the basis of these provisions, the state brought 37 men to trial in the same year, charged with terrorist activities in Namibia (then South-West Africa). The accused included executive members of the South West Africa

People's Organisation (SWAPO) and others arrested during South African Police actions in northern Namibia. Convicted and described by the judge as 'easy, misguided dupes of communist indoctrination', they were sentenced to terms of imprisonment ranging from five years to life.

16. In Addendum Six of this document it is seen what dire consequences this situation had and what sacrifices innocent, responsible prisoners were forced to make.

17. The Population Registration Act (1950) instituted a system of rigid racial classification in South Africa, defining white, Coloured, and Native (later 'Bantu') groups, and allowing for ethnological sub-categories. 'Borderline' cases could be officially investigated by Race Classification Appeal Boards.

18. See Addendum Seven of this document.

19. The Junior Certificate is generally taken by white schoolchildren at the age of 15, and they do not leave school before this. The Matriculation Certificate is taken two years later and qualifies children for higher education. The inequalities of apartheid education have ensured that few Africans reach Junior Certificate level, with the result that the basic educational standard for whites is a goal for achievement by Africans.

20. Nelson Mandela.

21. Gordon Hendricks.

22. UNISA (University of South Africa), based in Pretoria, is South Africa's correspondence university. Rapid Results College, based in Cape Town, offers a high school education through correspondence. Transafrika provides high school courses through correspondence. Volks Correspondence College not only offers high school courses, but also caters for post-secondary learning, offering language, technical, business, and agricultural courses.

23. The National Union of South African Students (NUSAS) was formed in 1924. By 1945, the organisation had developed a broadly liberal political position which, after the election of the National Party to power in 1948, brought it into increasing conflict with the government. By the mid-1960s NUSAS had become the most outspokenly radical of the legally existing opposition organisations inside South Africa. In the 1970s, NUSAS was further radicalised, a process accelerated by increasing state action against the organisation and its leadership. In 1974, NUSAS was declared an 'affected organisation' and external funding was outlawed. However, political activities continued, including a campaign to free political prisoners.

24. The Front for the Liberation of Mozambique (FRELIMO) was founded in 1962 and, two years later, embarked on extended guerrilla warfare. The overthrow of Portugal's right-wing regime in 1974 led to a cease-fire and formal independence in 1975.

25. In 1973 Kader Hassim and Devikie Venkatrathnam brought separate actions in the Supreme Court against the Officer Commanding Robben Island. Hassim and Venkatrathnam argued that recreational activities and permission to study were rights, rather than privileges, and therefore could not be withdrawn by the Officer Commanding in terms of the Prisons Act. They also argued that their isolation in solidarity confinement was illegal. The

court found that study and recreational activities were privileges that could be withdrawn by the Officer Commanding, but that it was unlawful to hold a prisoner in solitary confinement without a hearing.

26. The prison had a safe in which they kept the prisoners' belongings, although these were not necessarily returned on release.

27. Croce, B. 1914. *Historical Materialism and the Economics of Karl Marx.* London: Howard Latimer Ltd; Majeke, N., 1950. *The Role of the Missionaries in Conquest.* Johannesburg: Society of Young Africa.

28. In February 1968, the United Nations Commission on Human Rights reported to the General Assembly of the United Nations, condemning the torture and ill-treatment of prisoners in South African prisons. The Commission called on South Africa to abide by the minimum rules set for the treatment of convicts, and to release all political prisoners. The Standard Minimum Rules for the Treatment of Prisoners had been adopted by the UN in 1955.

29. Ahmed Mohammed Kathrada's political career began as a full-time organiser for the Transvaal Passive Resistance Council. After almost a year working for the World Federation of Democratic Youth in Budapest, Kathrada returned to South Africa to help organise the Defiance Campaign. He was arrested for treason in 1956 and was a defendant in the Treason Trial until 1961, Between 1962 and 1963, Kathrade worked underground as a leader of *Umkonto We Sizwe* until he was arrested at Rivonia. In 1964 he was sentenced to life imprisonment and was moved to Robben Island.

ONE AZANIA ONE NATION

1. Alexander, N. 1979. *One Azania One Nation.* (Introduction). London: Zed Press.

2. See, for instance, Carr, E. H. 1950. *The Bolshevik Revolution:1917-1923 Volume One.* London: The Macmillan Company, pp. 415-422. Also Wolfe, B. 1966. *Three Who Made A Revolution.* Harmondsworth: Penguin, pp. 637-638.

3. One is reminded of Marx's acid comments on his son-in-law, Lafargue's ridiculing of nationalities as 'nonsense'. See Carr, 1950, pp. 42-42.

4. 'Grey, dear friend is all theory. And green the golden tree of life'. Mephistopheles in Goethe's *Faust, Part 1.*

'THE MOVEMENT FOR NATIONAL LIBERATION'

1. Alexander. N. 1979. *One Azania One Nation.* (Chapter 5: The Movement for National Liberation). London: Zed Press.

2. The CPSA disbanded after it was declared an unlawful organisation in 1950.

3. Printed in Karis T., Carter G.M. 1972. *From Protest to Challenge: A Documentary History of African Politics in South Africa 1882-1964,* Vol. 3. *Challenge and Violence, 1953-1964.* Stanford, California: Hoover Institute Press, p. 205.

4. Potekhin, I.I. 'Extract from "'The Formation of the South African Bantu into a National Community'", Chapter 12 (mimeo, n.d.).
5. Ibid., p. 15.
6. Ibid. Compare Potekhin's dubbing of the Defiance Campaign and the evolving Congress Alliance as an example of 'proletarian internationalism'!
7. See Lerumo, A. 1971. *Fifty Fighting Years: The Communist Party of South Africa 1921–1971*. London: Inkululeko Publications, pp. 191–192.
8. Potekhin, n.d., p. 16 (my emphasis).
9. See Potekhin, p. 100ff.
10. Yengwa, M. B. 1971. 'The Bantustans: South Africa's "Bantu Homelands" Policy'. In A. la Guma (ed), *Apartheid: A Collection of Writings on South African Racism by South Africans*. New York: International Publishers, pp. 111–112.
11. See ibid., p. 113.
12. 'Strategy and Tactics of the South African Revolution'. In ibid., pp. 197 (my emphasis).
13. 'The Freedom Charter', ibid., pp. 231–232.
14. Ibid.
15. Turok, B. 'Class Structure and National Ideology in South Africa' (unpublished mimeo, n.d.), p. 5.
16. Ibid., p. 6 (my emphasis).
17. Maatla Ke A Rona. 1976. 'Letter on: The National Question'. *African Communist*, First Quarter, p. 115.
18. Ibid.
19. See ibid., pp. 112–113.
20. Ngwenya, J. 1976. 'A Further Contribution on the National Question', *African Communist*, Fourth Quarter, p. 52.
21. Ibid.
22. Ibid., p. 51.
23. Ibid., p. 54.
24. See ibid., p. 56.
25. Ibid., p. 49.
26. Ibid., p. 55.
27. Ibid., p. 84.
28. Molapo, B. 1977. *African Communist* (my emphasis throughout).
29. Ngwenya, J. 1976, p. 49.
30. Quoted in Michael Harmel, 'The Communist Party of South Africa'. In A. La Guma (ed), *Apartheid: A Collection of Writings on South African Racism by South Africans*. New York: International Publishers, p. 223.
31. Quoted in Wolpe, H. 1973. 'Pluralism, Forced Labour and Internal Colonialism in South Africa'. Discussion Paper, Conference on 'The Southern African Economy and the Future of Apartheid, University of York: Centre for Southern African Studies, pp. 14–15.
32. Ibid., p. 13.
33. Ibid., p. 15.
34. Wolpe, 1973, p. 22.

35. Molteno, F. 1977. 'The Historical Significance of the Bantustan Strategy'. Paper delivered at the Eighth Annual Congress of the Association for Sociology in Southern Africa held at the University College of Swaziland, 30 June–5 July 1977 (unpublished mimeop), p. 14.
36. Ibid., pp. 14–15.
37. See *Sunday Times*, 18 April 1976.
38. Slovo, J. 1976. 'South Africa – No Middle Road'. In Basil Davidson et al., *Southern Africa: The New Politics of Revolution*. Harmondsworth: Penguin, pp. 134–135.
39. Ibid., pp. 137–138.
40. Ibid., p. 135.
41. However, he had no use for the concept of 'Internal colonialism' though he uses the colonial analogy in a way that is extremely fertile: 'The South African possessions of Great Britain form a Dominion only *from the point of view* of the White minority. From *the point of view* of the Black majority, South Africa is a *slave colony*' (Trotsky, L.D. 'Remarks on the Draft Thesis of the Workers' Party of South Africa' 20 April 1933. *International Socialist Review*, 27(4), Fall 1966, pp. 157–160) (my emphasis).
42. Ibid.

'STEVE BIKO'S LAST ATTEMPT AT UNITING THE LIBERATION FORCES'

1. Alexander, N. 2007. 'Tribute to Steve Biko', Rhodes University, unpublished text.
2. See Alexander, N. 1991. Black Consciousness. A Reactionary Tendency? In B. Pityana, M. Ramphele, M. Mpumlwana, and L. Wilson (eds), *Bounds of Possibility. The Legacy of Steve Biko and Black Consciousness*. Cape Town, London, and New Jersey: David Philip and Zed Press, pp. 238–252: Alexander, N. 2008. 'An Illuminating Moment: Background to the Azanian Manifesto'. In A. Alexander, N. Gibson, and A. Mngxitana (eds), *Biko Lives*. New York: Palgrave Macmillan.
3. Biko, S. 1987. *I Write What I Like*. Oxford: Heinemann, p. 147.
4. Ibid., p. 148.
5. Ibid., p. 149.

'NATION AND ETHNICITY IN SOUTH AFRICA'

1. Alexander. N. 1985. *Sow The Wind: Contemporary Speeches*. Braamfontein: Skotaville Publishers. (This address was delivered at the first National Forum meeting on 11 June 1983 at St Peter's Conference Centre in Hammanskraal).
2. Yacoob, Z., speech presented at the first general meeting of the Transvaal Indian Congress on 1 May 1983. Unpublished speech.
3. Ibid.
4. 'South Africa Destabilised … Machel Responds'. In *Work in Progress*, 26th April, 1983, No. 26. Southern African Research Service, pp 26–28.

5. Saul, J. 1978. 'The Dialectic of Class and Tribe'. *Race and Class*, 20(4), pp. 347–372.

'TEN YEARS OF EDUCATION CRISIS: THE RESONANCE OF 1976'

1. Alexander, N. 1990. *Education and the Struggle for National Liberation in South Africa*. Braamfontein: Skotaville Publishers. (Address delivered at the National Consultation on Education for Affirmation 27 August 1986 – Wilgespruit Fellowship Centre, Johannesburg.)
2. For a schematic and general account of the resistance to separate and inferior schooling, see Christie, P. 1985. *The Right to Learn..* Braamfontein: Ravan, pp. 219–249.
3. Cited Philcox, S. 1980. 'Understanding the School Boycotts of 1980' (unpublished seminar paper), p. 3.
4. Ibid., p. 7.
5. Ibid., p. 4.
6. See Gibbs, G. 1980. 'A Community In Crisis: The Need for Overall Involvement in Planning'. In *Educational Crisis in the Western Cape*. University of Cape Town: Centre for Extra-Mural Studies, p. 25.
7. See Colin Bundy's brilliant 1986 vignette entitled 'Street Sociology and Pavement Politics: Some Aspects of Student/Youth Consciousness During the 1985 Schools Crisis in Greater Cape Town' (unpublished mimeo), p. 10.
8. Cited by Bot. M. 1985. *School boycotts 1984: The Crisis in African education*. Durban: Indicator Project/Centre for Applied Social Sciences, University of Natal, p. 5.
9. See his article: van den Berg, O. 1981. 'Education Equality: Central Issue in the Education Debate?' In *The Education Debate*. University of Cape Town: Centre for Extra-Mural Studies.
10. *Cape Times*, 27 January 1986.
11. See Alexander, N. 1986. 'Approaches to the National Question in South Africa'. *Transformation*, 1: 98.
12. Hunter, A. P. 'The Present Situation in Education: Constraints And Opportunities' (unpublished mimeo, n.d.).

'AN ILLUMINATING MOMENT: BACKGROUND TO THE AZANIAN MANIFESTO'

1. Alexander, N. 2008. 'An Illuminating Moment: Background to the Azanian Manifesto'. In A. Mngxitama and A. Alexander (eds), *Biko Lives: Contemporary Black History*. London: Palgrave Macmillan.
2. See for example Lodge, T. and Nasson, B. 1991. *All Here and Now: Black Politics in South Africa in the 1980s*. New York: Ford Foundation.
3. See Alexander, N. 1991. 'Black Consciousness. A Reactionary Tendency'? In B. Pityana, M. Ramphele, M. Mpumlwana, and L. Wilson (eds), *Bounds of Possibility. The Legacy of Steve Biko and Black Consciousness*. Cape Town, London and New Jersey: David Phillip and Zed Press, pp. 238–252; Also see

Motlinabi, M. 1985. *The Theory and Practice of Black Resistance to Apartheid: A Social-Ethical Analysis*. Braamfontein: Skotaville Publishers, especially Chapter 4.

4. Readers will have to accept my word for it that this is an unaltered quote from an authentic minute of the executive meeting of the BPC, referred to in the text. I have taken it from a letter I wrote from Germany to comrades in South Africa in 1970, which is in my personal archives.

5. See Villa-Vicencio, C. 1993. *The Spirit of Hope: Conversations on Religion, Politics and Values*. Braamfontein: Skotaville Publishers, pp 3–4.

6. See Alexander, N. 1985. *Sow the Wind: Contemporary Speeches*. Braamfontein: Skotaville Publishers.

7. In an acerbic altercation with Mac Maharaj in the London home of a mutual friend toward the end of 1978, he accused people such as Biko and myself of trying to establish a 'third force' and of being either the dupes of, or willing collaborators with 'American imperialism'. Also see McKinley D. 1997. *The ANC and the Liberation Struggle. A Critical Political Biography*. London and Chicago: Pluto Press, p. 59.

8. Alexander, 1985, pp. 16–17.

9. Some of the papers delivered at the Forum as well as the reports of the Commission (large breakaway groups), the resolutions and the Manifesto itself were published in NF Committee, 1983. *National Forum*. Johannesburg: National Forum Committee.

10. Rev. Boesak was actually in Scandinavia at the time of the conference but sent a telegram to convey warm greetings and full support.

11. Tutu, D. 1983. 'Unity and Liberation'. In *National Forum*. Johannesburg: National Forum Committee, pp. 10–11.

12. See, for example, Mzala, N. 1984. *Latest Opportunism and the Theory of the South African Revolution: A Critique of an Ideological Trend against the Freedom Charter*. Lusaka (publishers unknown). To my regret, I met Comrade Mzala only briefly at Yale University in 1990 or 1991 and found him to be a very different person from the apparatchnik that peers from underneath the cloak of scholarship he presents in this forgettable pamphlet.

13. Alexander, 1985, p. 175.

14. Ibid., p. 9. pp. 178–179.

INTRODUCTION TO PART III

1. Biko, S. 2004. *I Write What I Like*. Craighall: Picador Africa, p. 51.

2. Alexander, N. 2010. 'Schooling in and for the New South Africa'. *Focus*, 56: 8.

"'RACE" AND CLASS IN SOUTH AFRICAN HISTORIOGRAPHY: AN OVERVIEW'

1. Alexander. N. 2002. *An Ordinary Country: Issues in the Transition from Apartheid to Democracy in South Africa*. (Chapter 1: 'Race' and Class in

South African Historiography: An Overview). Pietermaritzburg: University of Natal Press.

2. There is ample evidence that the San (So-called Bushman) communities were systematically hunted down right up to the mid-nineteenth century.

3. Authoritative historical studies are numerous, but the following short list (arrange chronologically) is a good reflection of the different approaches adopted by historians who have written general histories of South Africa: Walker, E. 1928. *A History of South Africa.* London: Longmans, Green and Co.; Macmillan, W. M. 1929. *Bantu, Boer and Briton: The Making of the South African Native Problem.* London: Faber & Dwyer; de Kiewiet, C. W. 1941. *A History of South Africa: Social and Economic.* London: Oxford University Press; Wilson, M. and Thompson, L. 1969, 1971. *The Oxford History of South Africa.* Two volumes. Oxford: Oxford University Press; Muller, C. 1969. *Five Hundred Years.* Pretoria: Academica; Van Jaarsveld, F. 1975. *From Van Riebeeck to Vorster, 1652-1974.* Johannesburg: Perskor; Davenport, R. 1977. *South Africa: A Modern History.* London: Macmillan; Thompson, L. 1990. *A History of South Africa.* New Haven: Yale University Press.

4. Cory, 1910–1930, reprint 1965, is the classical example: Cory, G. 1965. *The Rise of South Africa.* Cape Town: Struik.

5. Theal, G. M. 1964 (Reprint). *History of South Africa.* London: Swan. Van Jaarsveld, in various essays, has discussed the contributions of the early historians of South Africa. Also see Saunders, C. 1988. *The Making of the South African Past: Major Historians on Race and Class.* Cape Town: David Phillip.

6. See Wilson, M and Thompson, L. 1969. *The Oxford History of South Africa.* Oxford: Oxford University Press, p. viii.

7. Gie, S. F. N. 1924. *Geskiedenis van Suid-Afrika of Ons Verlede.* Stellenbosch: Universiteitsuitgewers, a Stellenbosch-based historian of some repute in Afrikaner circles, was still putting forward as a serious proposition that Jan van Riebeeck, that is, the Dutch East India Company, had every right to appropriate the land of the Khoi and the San people at the Cape of Good Hope, because the latter did not know how to use it productively.

8. Even such an enlightened analyst and social commentator as Olive Schreiner doubted the capacity of the San ('Bushmen') to become 'civilised' (see Schreiner, O. 1923. *Thoughts on South Africa.* London: T. Fisher Unwin Ltd, pp. 96–97).

9. There is an abundance of evidence for the view that, initially, religion rather than 'race' was the decisive criterion for acceptance of the individual as an equal in the milieu of the colonists (see, for example, Jordaan, K. 1979. 'Iberian and Anglo-Saxon Racism: A Study of Portuguese Angola and South Africa'. *Race and Class,* 20(4): 391–412. p. 397).

10. Thom, H. 1936. *Die Geskiedenis van die Skaapboerdery in Suid-Afrika.* Amsterdam: Swets en Zeitlinger; Van der Merwe, P. J. 1938. *Die Trekboer in die Geskiedenis van die Kaapkolonie.* Cape Town: Nationale Pers Ltd; Muller, C. 1969. *Five Hundred Years.* Pretoria: Academica, among others.

11. Walker, 1928.

12. Macmillan, 1929.

13. de Kiewiet, 1941.
14. van den Berghe, P. 1967. *Race and Racism: A Comparative Perspective*. New York: John Wiley and Sons, p. 18.
15. Macmillan, W. M. 1963 (Reprint). *Bantu, Boer and Briton: The Making of the South African Native Problem*. Oxford: Clarendon Press, pp. 19–20, 74–75.
16. van den Berghe, 1967, p. 267.
17. See Saunders, C. 1988; Worden, 1994; O'Meara, D. 1996. *Forty Lost Years: The Apartheid State and the Politics of the National Party, 1948-1994*. Johannesburg: Ravan Press.
18. The political publicists and writers on the left made no concessions in this regard. They attacked these intellectuals as people who prostituted themselves in the service of a neocolonial and racist state that was no more than the instrument of 'gold and maize', that is, the white ruling class of imperial investors in the mines and large-scale, mostly Afrikaner, farmers. See, among others, Mnguni, (pseudonym). 1952. *Three Hundred Years*. Cape Town: New Era Fellowship; Majeke, N. 1952. *The Role of the Missionaries in Conquest*. Johannesburg: Society of Young Africa.
19. Posel, D. 1983. 'Rethinking the Race-Class Debate in South African Historiography'. *Social Dynamics*, 9(1): 50–66. p. 60.
20. The most sophisticated and detailed research studies in this regard are those undertaken by Giliomee, H. 1983. 'Constructing Afrikaner Nationalism'. *Journal of Asian and African Studies*, 18: 83–98; Giliomee, H. 1986. *The History of Our Politics*. Cape Town: University of Cape Town Press; Du Toit, A. 1983. 'No Chosen People: The Myth of the Calvinist Origins of Afrikaner Nationalism and Racial Ideology'. *American Historical Review*, 88: 920–952. However, none of the earlier liberal writings on the ideological origins of racism reached the sophistication of the kind of analysis undertaken by a scholar such as George Mosse, 1978. *Towards the Final Solution: A History of European Racism*. London: Dent, which traces the modern origins of racial ideology to the absolutist and universalist pretensions of the Enlightenment. In a crude way, the liberals agreed more with the radical views of Oliver Cromwell Cox, 1948. *Caste, Class and Race: A Study in Social Dynamics*. New York: Modern Reader Paperbacks, who traced the origins of racism as the systemic subordination and exploitation of blacks by whites to the institution of trans-Atlantic slavery.
21. Worden, 1994, pp. 72–73.
22. For this reason, some analysts refer to this school as the 'Liberal Africanists' (see Saunders, 1988).
23. Macmillan, 1929.
24. de Kiewiet, 1941.
25. Wilson and Thompson, 1969.
26. Saunders, 1988, p. 159.
27. In the earlier, pre-1960, versions of the liberal manifestoes, citizenship would be granted equally to everyone but it was qualified by property and literacy criteria.

28. In an allusion to the polemic she conducted against the 'revisionist' historians on the relevance of 'agency' in social analysis, Posel comments wryly that 'there comes a point at which an explanation of the transition to apartheid devolves on the simple fact that the National Party had a surprise and slim election victory in 1948' (Posel, 1983, p. 59).

29. O'Meara, 1996.

30. Mnguni, 1952.

31. Majeke, 1952.

32. The only work of some historical pretension that came out of the Communist Party milieu in this period was that written by the ex-Communist Edward Roux, 1948. *Time Longer Than Rope*. London: Victor Gollancz. It was a peculiar mixture of liberal and radical analysis, firmly empiricist and materialist but without much theoretical sophistication.

33. Majeke, 1952, p. vi.

34. Saunders, 1988, p. 138.

35. Muller, C. 1963. 'Die Groot Trek'. In F. van Jaarsveld, T. van Wijk, C. Muller, and G. Scholtz, *Die Hervertolking van Ons Geskiedenis*. Pretoria: Universiteit van Suid Afrika, pp. 69–71.

36. see Saunders, 1988, pp. 135–139.

37. Roux, 1948.

38. Although our initiative could not be sustained, I ought at this point to refer to the fact that at about the same time, some of us incarcerated on Robben Island established what we called the Society for the Rewriting of South African History and began posing similar questions to those that were exercising the minds of the revisionist historians in exile.

39. Saunders, 1988, p. 172.

40. Ibid., pp. 174–175. Legassick's original article is reprinted in Marks and Atmore (eds). 1980. *Economy and Society in Pre-Industrial South Africa*. London: Longmans.

41. Moore, B. 1966. *Social Origins of Dictatorship and Democracy: Lord and Peasant in the Making of the Modern World*. Boston: Beacon Press.

42. Saunders, 1988, p. 175.

43. See Worden, 1994, pp. 75–76.

44. One of the implications of this position was that in South Africa a 'non-racial capitalism' could never develop, a position which I myself held and, indeed still adhere to with some modification. The palpable failure of 'Black Economic Empowerment', understood as the creation of a layer of black bourgeois individuals in post-apartheid South Africa underlines this statement.

45. For a succinct summary of the revisionist theses, see Davies, R., O'Meara, D., and Dlamini, S. (eds). 1984. *The Struggle for South Africa: A Reference Guide to Movements, Organizations and Institutions*. Volume 1. London: Zed Press, pp. 3–20.

46. It is pertinent to point out that as early as 1983 already, scholars such as Deborah Posel had identified these reductionist tendencies of the revisionist historiography. She excoriated the rigorous but myopic class reductionism

of Wolpe as well as of the 'Sussex School' and in effect aligned herself closely with the position which subsequently came to be identified with the school of social history associated with the names of Charles van Onselen, Phil Bonner, Belinda Bozzoli, Peter Delius and others. An excellent summary of the polemic is provided by Bozzoli and Delius in their Introduction to *Radical History Review,* 46/47 (1990).

47. Fukuyama, F. 1992. *The End of History and the Last Man.* New York: Free Press.

48. Wolpe, H. 1988. *Race, Class and the Apartheid State.* London: James Currey.

49. Ibid., p. 8.

50. van den Berghe, 1967, p. 267.

51. Saunders, 1988.

52. Worden, 1994.

53. In a lecture delivered in 1979, Johnstone said, among other things, that 'The historical role and sociological significance of Afrikaaner nationalism cannot be entirely grasped in these new and important terms of its class instrumentality ... we are faced with a situation in which the salient role of ethnic factors, while not understandable without class analysis, is not fully understandable through class analysis alone' (cited in Saunders, 1988, p. 188).

54. Saunders, 1988, p. 188.

55. O'Meara, 1996, has performed a Herculean task in the 'Theoretical Appendix' to his work on the apartheid state. It is a work that should be studied carefully by all future South Africanists, even though it is, like Wolpe's work almost ten years earlier, essentially an attempt to salvage the analytical relevance of the work of the revisionist historiographers. In a sentence, O'Meara acknowledges the functionalist understandings of racist policies and practices as well the reductionism which inform most of that work, and insists on the centrality of agency and the autonomy of 'the political'. The corollary to this position is that the theory of the state has to be liberated from the stranglehold of instrumentalist notions. As stimulating as this essay is, I am left with the impression at the end of it that, except for his materialist point of departure, O'Meara has left open the question of the relevance of Marxism as a method of social analysis.

'THE PECULIARITIES OF THE TRANSITION TO DEMOCRACY IN SOUTH AFRICA'

1. Alexander. N. 2002. *An Ordinary Country: issues in the Transition from Apartheid to Democracy in South Africa.* (Chapter 3: The Peculiarities of the Transition to Democracy in South Africa). Pietermaritzburg: University of Natal Press.

2. Giliomee, H. and Schlemmer, L. (eds). 1998. *Negotiating South Africa's Future.* Johannesburg: Southern Book Publishers.

3. Horowits, D. 1991. *A Democratic South Africa? Constitutional Engineering in a Divided Society.* Cape Town: Oxford University Press.

4. Lee, R. and Schlemmer, L. 1991.*Transition to Democracy: Policy Perspectives 1991*. Cape Town: Oxford University Press.
5. Adam, H. and Moodley, K. 1993. *The Negotiated Revolution*. Johannesburg: Jonathan Ball.
6. Friedman, S. (ed). 1993. *The Long Journey: South Africa's Quest for a Negotiated Settlement*. Johannesburg: Ravan.
7. Friedman, S. and Atkinson, D. 1994. *The Small Miracle: South Africa's Negotiated Settlement: South African Review 7*. Johannesburg: Ravan.
8. Murray, M. 1994. *The Revolution Deferred: The Painful Birth of Post-Apartheid South Africa*. London: Verso.
9. Sparks, A. 1994. *Tomorrow is Another Country: The Inside Story of South Africa's Negotiated Revolution*. Johannesburg: Struik.
10. O'Meara, D. 1996. *Forty Lost Years: The Apartheid State and the Politics of the National Party, 1948–1994*. Johannesburg: Ravan.
11. McKinley, D. 1997. *The ANC and the Liberation Struggle: A Critical Political Biography*. London: Pluto Press.
12. Adam, H., Moodley, K., and Slabbert, V. 1997. *Comrades in Business: Post-Liberation Politics in South Africa*. Cape Town: Tafelberg.
13. Marais, H. 1998. *South Africa: Limits to Change: The Political Economy of Transformation*. London: Zed Books.
14. Bond, P. 2000. *Elite Transition: From Apartheid to Neoliberalism in South Africa*. London and Pietermaritzburg: Pluto Press and University of Natal Press.
15. From El Salvador and Nicaragua to Mozambique, Angola and Vietnam, among many others, revolutionary movements and regimes learned the bitter lesson of revolutionary politics, namely, that you should never let your strategy be dependent on the support of a foreign state, since any change in the fortunes or the foreign policy of that state will inevitably affect the capacity of the revolutionary movement.
16. See especially McKinley, 1997; Marais, 1998.
17. McKinley, 1997, p. 78. In one of the first political discussions, we (of the 'National Liberation Front') had with the ANC leadership in prison Nelson Mandela told us in 1964 that they had never believed, and did not believe, that it was possible to overthrow the apartheid regime by military means. He had been advised by President Boumedienne of the Algerian FLN government not to set the overthrow of the regime as their military objective, since this could not be accomplished without a catastrophic bloodbath. Their strategy was to force the regime to negotiate on terms that would be acceptable, that is, not humiliating to the government.
18. Note from editors: Alexander discusses this point in greater detail in the final chapter titled, 'South Africa: Example or Illusion'? of his book: Alexander, N. 2002. *An Ordinary Country: Issues in the Transition from Apartheid to Democracy in South Africa*. Scottsville: University of Natal Press, pp. 137–173.
19. Marais, 1998, p. 74.
20. Ibid., p. 81, n. 83.

21. Huntington, S. 1991. *The Third Wave: Democratization in the Late Twentieth Century*. Oklahoma: University of Oklahoma Press, pp. 112–115.

22. As recently as January 2000, the Secretary-General of the SACP, Blade Nzimande, is quoted as saying: 'I have to admit it, the party is battling for its soul … How do we fight the market and at the same time participate in the very marketplace we are opposing? This is the most vexing question facing the party' (Gumede, W. 'SA Communist Party. Left, Right: Time Marches On'. *Financial Mail*, 5 January 2000, p. 16). And Gumede adds, somewhat facetiously: 'The SACP faithful have characteristically coined the phrase for it: "fighting with and against capital"' (ibid.).

23. Bond, P. 2001. *Against Global Apartheid: South Africa Meets the World Bank, IMF and International Finance*. Cape Town: University of Cape Town Press, pp. 119–121, 144, discusses the vacillation and dilemmas faced by the ANC leadership in this connection. Sampson, A. 1999. *Mandela: The Authorised Biography*. London: Jonathan Ball, pp. 433–435 traces Mandela's personal road to Damascus with regard to the economic policy of the ANC.

24. Of course, the actual process of arriving at the Rubicon and, the even more agonising moment of deciding to make the crossing (from apartheid to something unknown in South African history) was one involving dramatic conflict, inter-personal rivalries, inner party struggles, breakaway movements, and all the other events that accompany such historic ruptures. Some of the detailed personal, and even private, aspects of this process have been described and analysed by, among others, O'Meara, 1996; Rosenthal, 1998. *Mission Improbable: A Piece of the South African Story*. Cape Town: David Phillip; Giliomee, H., 2000. 'Critical Afrikaner Intellectuals and Apartheid, 1943–1958'. *South African Journal of Philosophy*, 19(4), pp. 321–339, as well as by many Afrikaans authors, including some of the dramatis personae such as P.W. Botha and F.W. de Klerk.

25. Sparks, 1994, pp. 197–235.

26. Adam et al., 1997, p. 55.

27. I agree, thus, with another position put forward by Adam et al. to the effect that: 'faced with a racial war, South African whites opted for negotiations precisely because there existed no other way out of an existential predicament. Settlers who had become indigenous finally realised that they had to co-exist on equal terms with the disenfranchised, even if this meant losing political power, but falling short of a destructive war that neither side could win' (Ibid., p. 52).

28. Ibid., p. 51.

29. In modern theoretical terms, the issue is discussed in voluminous and sometimes casuistic detail by sociologists and other social scientists under the rubric of the relationship between 'structure' and 'agency'. This is undeniably an exceptionally important debate. However, it is also without any doubt the result of monistic approaches to the understanding of human societies. It is the inevitable outcome of the futile search for monocausal explanations of complex social phenomena and, as such, the recent debates in this regard among South Africanists constitute a healthy corrective to the reductionist

orthodoxies of the 1970s and 1980s. For a useful introduction to the issues (see O'Meara, 1996). Earlier, sometimes overtly aggressive polemics on the question can be read up in Posel, 1983; Wolpe, 1988; Bozzoli, B. and Delius, P. (eds.). 1990. *History from South Africa: Radical History Review*, 46(7).

30. Section 212[2] [a] and [b].

31. In the person of Mandela, incidentally, the Weberian categories of traditional, charismatic, and representative leadership converge in a most intriguing manner. Indeed, a perceptive South African theorist, Andrew Nash, 1999. 'Mandela's Democracy'. *Monthly Review*, April 1999: 18–28, was inspired by this intersection of the Weberian triad to erect a unique model of democracy around the peculiarities of Mandela's vision of a post-apartheid South Africa. In my view, Nash's 'tribal model of democracy' is no more than an attempt to account for the peculiar circumstances under which the populist politics of the Mandela generation of ANC leaders persuaded the vast majority of their compatriots to accept the logic of the negotiations and of the subsequent settlement. The inarticulate premise of Nash's argument is the fact that a very large section of South Africa's population accepts the pre-industrial structures and ideology of chiefs and traditional leaders. This entire set of practices and beliefs continues to resonate strongly even among second and third generation workers in urban areas. Without that backdrop, Mandela would have been whistling in the wind.

32. Mandela, N. 1994. *Long Walk to Freedom: The Autobiography of Nelson Mandela*. London: Little Brown, p. 627.

33. See Note 30 of this chapter.

34. As unpalatable as it is, we shall have to leave the 'final' word on this matter to future generations. Of course, the successful realisation of what all progressive South African people refer to as a non-racial South Africa will make any consociational deviation based on 'race' that much more difficult.

35. Adam et al.,1997.

36. Sparks, 1994.

37. Rosenthal, 1998.

38. Cited in McKinley, 1997, p. 93.

39. Adam et al., 1997, p. 61.

40. McKinley, 1997.

41. Marais, 1998.

42. Bond, 2000, 2001.

43. Marais, 1998, p. 96.

AFRICA AND THE NEW WORLD ORDER

1. Alexander, N. 1993. *Some Are More Equal Than Others: Essays on the transition in South Africa*. Cape Town: Buchu Books. Africa and the New World Order was first presented as the keynote address at the Humboldt Colloquium held in Cotonou, Benin, 17–19 July 1992.

2. Brand, J. 1991. 'The New World Order: Regional Trading Blocks'. *Vital Speeches of the Day*. Alexandria, Virginia: City Publishing Company.

3. Chomsky, N. 1991. *The New World Order*. (Pamphlet No. 6 in the Open Magazine Pamphlet Series). Westfield, New Jersey, p. 23.
4. Brand, 1991, p. 158.
5. Brzezinski, Z. 1991, 'Selective Global Commitment'. *Foreign Affairs*, 7(1), p 20.
6. See ibid., p. 67.
7. Ibid., p. 3. Also see Amin, S. 1991. 'The Democratic Question in the Third World'. *Africa World Review*. April 1991, pp. 6–9. p. 6.
8. See Kühne, W. 1992. *Demokratisierung in Vielvolkerstaaten unter schlechten wirtschafilichen Bedingungen – ein Diskussionsbeitrag am Beispiel Afrikas*. Benhausen: Stiftung Wissenschaft und Politik; Yeebo, Z. 1992. 'The Way to Africa's Second Liberation'. *Africa World Review*, October 1991–March 1992, p. 44.
9. Joseph, R. 1991. 'Africa Feels the Winds of Change. Nations are Restless to Achieve Democracy'. *The Atlanta Journal/The Atlanta Constitution*, March 31, 1991.
10. Kühne, 1992, p. 14.
11. Ibid., p. 13 (*Alexander's translation*).
12. Campbell, H. 1992. 'Pan-Africanism and African Liberation'. *Africa World Review*, April 1991, pp. 25–30, 26.
13. Nyong'o, P. 1992. 'Africa – The Failure of One Party Rule'. *Journal of Democracy*, 3(1).
14. Ibid., p. 1.
15. Brand, 1991, p. 158.
16. Ibid., p. 157.
17. *The Economist*, 'The IMF and the World Bank'. *Survey*, 12 October 1991, p. 3.
18. Permanent Peoples' Tribunal. 1990. 'Tribunal on the Policies of the International Monetary Fund and the World Bank, West Berlin, September 26–29, 1988: Verdict'. *International Journal of Health Services*, 20(2), pp. 320–347, 334.
19. See ibid., p. 331.
20. Charnley, S. 1992. 'Africa's Freedom on a Shoestring'. *South*, 14 May, Reprinted from Index on Censorship.
21. Permanent Peoples' Tribunal, 1990, p. 331. Also see *The Economist*, 12 October 1991, p. 32.
22. *The Economist*, 12 October 1991, p. 35.
23. See, e.g. the informative article by Erdmann, G. 1991. *Demoktatisierung in Africa und Menschenrechter- Konditionalitat der Entwicklungshilfe; Neue alte Aufgaben fur NRO*. Bonn: Weltwirtschaft, Okologie, und Entwicklung e.V.
24. Council of Economic Advisors (CEA), 1992.
25. Council of Economic Advisors (CEA), 1992. Excerpt from Chapter 6 of the Annual Report, 1992.
26. Permanent Peoples' Tribunal, 1990, p. 310.
27. Ibid., p. 311.
28. Amin, 1991, p. 6.
29. Bangemann, M. 1992. 'Regional Cooperation: A New Perspective for Africa'. Speech delivered on the inauguration of the office of Friedrich-Naumann-Stiftung on February 21, 1992 in Cape Town (Unpublished, p. 31).

FOREWORD TO THE ISIZULU TRANSLATION OF THE COMMUNIST MANIFESTO

1. Alexander's Foreword to the first isiZulu translation of the Communist Manifesto by Lwazi Brian Ramadiro, 2002. Johannesburg: Workers' Organisation for Socialist Action (WOSA).

FOREWORD TO *RACISM EXPLAINED TO MY DAUGHTER*

1. Alexander's foreword to Ben Jelloun, T. 2003. *Racism Explained to my Daughter*. Cape Town: New Africa Books in cooperation with PRAESA.

FOREWORD TO *TAKING SOUTH AFRICAN EDUCATION OUT OF THE GHETTO*

1. Neville Alexander's foreword to Smit, W. and Hennessey, K. 1998. *Taking South African Education Out of the Ghetto: An Urban Planning Perspective.* Cape Town: UCT Press.
2. See Mather, C., Paterson, A., and Sebego, M. 1994. 'Mapping Village Schools – Beyond Apartheid'. *Matlhasedi*, April 1994.

'SOUTH AFRICA: AN UNFINISHED REVOLUTION?'

1. Alexander's address at the fourth Strini Moodley Annual Memorial Lecture, held at the University of KwaZulu-Natal on 13 May 2010. Reprinted in *Enough Is A Feast – A Tribute to Dr Neville Alexander 22 October 1936-27 August 2012*. Vally, H and Isaacson, M (eds). Braamfontein: Foundation for Human Rights.
2. In the language of Marxist theory, revolutions become inevitable when the relations of production are outstripped by the development of the productive forces in a given social formation.
3. My book, *One Azania, One Nation. The National Question in South Africa*, published pseudonymously in 1979, was one of the first attempts to deal with this period comprehensively.
4. This is the real meaning of Mandela's biographical reference to how he came to his crucial decision to steer the ANC towards accepting the need to negotiate. (See Mandela, N. 1994. *Long Walk to Freedom: The Autobiography of Nelson Mandela*. London: Little Brown, pp. 513–515.)
5. Ibid., p. 605.
6. In the cut-and-thrust of politics, this language is taken for granted but when one sets out to explain a historical phenomenon, a different discourse is essential.
7. Cited in McKinley, D. 1997. *The ANC and the Liberation Struggle: A Critical Political Biography*. London: Pluto Press, p. 122.
8. Terreblanche, S. 2002. *A History of Inequality in South Africa 1652–2002*. Pietermaritzburg: University of Natal Press, pp. 95–96.

9. Luxemburg, R. *Reform or Revolution*. New York: Pathfinder Press, pp. 49–50 (non-italics in the original).

10. See Bensaid, D. *Revolutionary Strategy Today*. Amsterdam: International Institute for Research and Education, p. 30.

11. COSATU/SACP. 1999. *Building Socialism Now: Preparing for the New Millennium*. Braamfontein: COSATU (unpublished paper, p. 68).

12. I cannot take up the question of the so-called developmental state here but my critique of that fashionable concept would proceed along similar lines.

13. Occasional references to this scenario do appear in the literature and, I am sure, in the speeches, of COSATU and SACP activists. They are, however, negated by the anti-revolutionary practices of most of the leadership of those formations.

14. We have to bear in mind, of course, that today abundance is no longer a utopian vision.

15. It should be noted, of course, that all of the mentioned formations, except for ALBA, are based on a vision of reforming the international institutions that keep guard over the international division of labour.

16. Colin Leys, cited in Saul, J. 2006. *The Next Liberation Struggle. Capitalism, Socialism and Democracy in Southern Africa*. Scottsville: University of Kwa-Zulu-Natal Press, p. 284.

17. Monga, C., cited in ibid., p. 49.

SOUTH AFRICA TODAY – THE MORAL RESPONSIBILITY OF INTELLECTUALS

1. Lecture delivered at the tenth anniversary celebration of the Foundation for Human Rights in Pretoria, 29 November 2006.

2. Said, E. 1995. 'On Nelson Mandela and Others'. *The Politics of Dispossession. The Struggle for Palestinian Self-Determination 1969–1994*. London: Vintage, p. 371.

3. Privatisierung bringt keine Freiheit. 2006. *Die Neoliberale Politik beschaedigt das Gemeinwesen*. Frankfurter Rundschau, 23 September 2006.

4. Said, E. 1994. *Culture and Imperialism*. London: Vintage, p. 225.

5. Adam, H. 1995. 'The Politics of Ethnic Identity: Tentative Theoretical and Comparative Conclusions From the South African Case'. Paper presented at the World Congress of Sociology RC 05. Bielefeld, Germany, 18–24 July 1994 (unpublished mimeo).

6. It is one of the most hopeful signs of the intellectual renaissance that is beginning to stir on the margins of our society that besides those of us who are intent on and serious about finding a new language for and a new approach to adapting the fundamental insights of historical materialism to the changes in the world capitalist system, there are many initiatives from within the system itself that are beginning to ask the right questions about alternatives to the barbarism of real capitalism as it becomes manifest in neoliberal practice, structured in line with the requirements of the primacy of finance capital. Searching analyses of the consumerist model and its manip-

ulation and exploitation of desire as opposed to the determining effects of the principle of sufficiency – along the lines of the French economists and philosophers, Andre Gorz and Bernard Stiegler, such as those by Johann Roussouw in recent issues of *Die Vrye Afrikaan* as well as the numerous stimulating articles by Margaret Legum and other exponents of the South African New Economics (SANE) Network in which the possibility of creating model enclaves based on production and exchange for use rather than for maximising profit, point the way towards re-establishing the credibility and the viability of economic and systemic alternatives that transcend the existing system. For, unless we are able to do this, it will be virtually impossible to find the Archimedean leverage that will ultimately remove the mental blockages by which the system maintains itself.

'LET US RETURN TO THE SOURCE! IN QUEST OF A HUMANISM OF THE 21ST CENTURY'

1. Address delivered at the annual Sipho Maseko Memorial Lecture, University of the Western Cape, 8 October 2009. A version of this address was published as the chapter 'Enough is as Good as a Feast' in Alexander's posthumous book: Alexander, N. 2013. *Thoughts on the New South Africa*. Braamfontein: Jacana Media.
2. Biko, S. 1987. *I Write What I Like*. Oxford: Heinemann, p. 147.
3. See Mngxitama, A., Alexander, A., and Gibson N.C. (eds). 2008. *Biko Lives: Contesting the Legacy of Steve Biko*. New York: Palgrave, Macmillan.
4. A fusion of the words 'comrade' and 'tsotsi' referring to criminals operating under the cloak of activism in townships.
5. See, for example, Gorz, A. 1987. *Ecology as Politics*. London: Pluto Press; Gorz, A. 1989. *Critique of Economic Reason*. London and New York: Verso.
6. This is not an arbitrary act on my part; Gorz in fact derives the principle from the same pre-industrial period in which this aphorism originated.

'"RACE" IS SKIN DEEP, HUMANITY IS NOT'

1. Alexander, N. 2011. '"Race" is Skin Deep, Humanity is Not'. *Cape Times*, 15 April 2011.
· 2. Jimmy Manyi, now Mzwanele Manyi, and the spokesperson for the Jacob Zuma Foundation, referred to the 'oversupply' of 'coloured' people in the Western Cape. He was formerly a spokesperson for former President Zuma's cabinet.

'THE ELEPHANT IN THE ROOM'

1. Alexander, N. 2013. *Thoughts on the New South Africa*. (Chapter 4: The Elephant in the Room). Braamfontein: Jacana Media.

2. Proverbs 29, Verse 18.
3. Terreblanche, S. 2002. *A History of Inequality in South Africa 1652–2002.* Pietermaritzburg: University of Natal Press, pp. 95–96.
4. Adam, H., Moodley, K., and Slabbert, V. 1997. *Comrades in Business: Post-Liberation Politics in South Africa.* Cape Town: Tafelberg; Seeking, J., Nattrass, N., and Leibbrandt, M. 2004. 'Income Inequality After Apartheid'. CSSR/SALDRU Working Paper, No. 75; Simkins, C., and Patterson, A. 2005. *Learner Performance in South Africa: Social and Economic Determinants of Success in Language and Mathematics.* Cape Town: HSRC Press.
5. Seekings et al., 2004.
6. For a more detailed treatment of the subject, see Alexander, N. 2004. *Implications of Brown vs Board of Education: A Post-Apartheid South African Perspective.* PRAESA Occasional Papers, No. 20. Cape Town: Project for the Study of Alternative Education in South Africa.
7. Schlemmer, L. 2005. 'Black Advancement: Hype Outstrips Reality'. *Focus,* 39, Third Quarter, pp. 2–5.
8. Recent examples abound. See, for example, S. Graham, 2005; M. Le Roux, 2005; T. Mabanga, 2005.
9. Schlemmer, 2004, p. 4.
10. Alexander, 2004.
11. Terreblanche, 2002.
12. This terminology is obviously at variance with that of many other analysts, including myself. Most of his 'black bourgeoisie' would fit into Schlemmer's category of 'middle and upper middle classes' or into Seekings and colleagues' 'upper class'.
13. Afrikaans slang for cheap fermented wine.
14. Alexander, N. 2002 *An Ordinary Country. Issues in the Transition from Apartheid to Democracy in South Africa.* Pietermaritzburg: University of Natal Press.
15. Terreblanche, 2002.

'THE LANGUAGE QUESTION AND SOCIAL INEQUALITY'

1. Alexander, N. 1989. *Language Policy and National Unity in South Africa/Azania.* (Chapter 1: The Language Question and Social Inequality). Cape Town: Buchu Books.
2. Most people think they know ('by intuition') where one 'language' ends and another begins. However, 'languages' become such not simply because sounds produced by human beings are understood by others. They get definition in the course of class struggles in the history of peoples. 'A language', in other words, is usually the result of political and economic developments in an area and not simply of particular rules of grammar and syntax.
3. In the companion study referred to in the Preface, I have tried to look at some of the more uncertain aspects of the subject against the test of various theories.

Index

Black Critique

Series editors: Anthony Bogues and Bedour Alagraa

Throughout the twentieth century and until today, anti-racist, radical decolonization struggles attempted to create new forms of thought. Figures from
Ida B. Wells to W.E.B. Du Bois and Steve Biko, from Claudia Jones to Walter
Rodney and Amílcar Cabral produced work which drew from the historical
experiences of Africa and the African diaspora. They drew inspiration from
the Haitian revolution, radical Black abolitionist thought and practice, and
other currents that marked the contours of a Black radical intellectual and
political tradition.

The Black Critique series operates squarely within this tradition of ideas
and political struggles. It includes books which foreground this rich and
complex history. At a time when there is a deep desire for change, Black
radicalism is one of the most underexplored traditions that can drive emanci-
patory change today. This series highlights these critical ideas from anywhere
in the Black world, creating a new history of radical thought for our times.

Also available:

*Moving Against the System: The 1968
Congress of Black Writers and the
Making of Global Consciousness*
Edited and with an Introduction
by David Austin

*Anarchism and the Black Revolution:
The Definitive Edition*
Lorenzo Kom'boa Ervin

*After the Postcolonial Caribbean:
Memory, Imagination, Hope*
Brian Meeks

*A Certain Amount of Madness:
The Life, Politics and Legacies of
Thomas Sankara*
Edited by Amber Murrey

Of Black Study
Joshua Myers

*On Racial Capitalism, Black
Internationalism, and Cultures of
Resistance*
Cedric J. Robinson
Edited by H.L.T. Quan

*Black Minded: The Political
Philosophy of Malcolm X*
Michael Sawyer

*Red International and Black
Caribbean Communists in New York
City, Mexico and the West Indies,
1919–1939*
Margaret Stevens

*The Point is to Change the World:
Selected Writings of Andaiye*
Edited by Alissa Trotz